Read For Your Life

LITERATURE AS A
LIFE SUPPORT SYSTEM

JOSEPH GOLD

Fitzhenry & Whiteside

Read for Your Life: Literature as a life support system
Copyright © 2001
First published by Fitzhenry & Whiteside 1990

For Brenda: My Story Sharer

In the United States:
121 Harvard Avenue, Suite 2
Allston, Massachusetts 02134

ISBN 1-55041-625-1

Fitzhenry & Whiteside acknowledges with thanks the Canada Council for the Arts, the Government of Canada through its Book Publishing Industry Development Program, and the Ontario Arts Council for their support in our publishing program.

10 9 8 7 6 5 4 3 2 1

National Library of Canada Cataloguing in Publication Data
Gold, Joseph, 1933-
   Read for your life : literature as a life support system
Includes bibliographical references and index.
ISBN 1-55041-625-1
1. Books and reading. 2. Bibliotherapy. I. Title.
Z1003.G65 2001   028'.8   C2001-930687-3

Publisher Cataloging-in-Publication Data
Gold, Joseph, 1933-
   Read for your life : literature as a life support system /
Joseph Gold. – 2nd ed.
[400] p. : cm. Includes index.
Summary: Self-help through reading with suggestions for support through specific problems.
ISBN 1-55041-625-1 (pbk.)
1. Bibliotherapy. 2. Bibliotherapy – Psychotherapy. 3. Reading, Psychology of. I. Title.
615.8516 21   CIP   RC489.B48.G65 2001

Cover: George Reid (Canadian 1860-1947) *Forbidden Fruit 1889*, oil on canvas
Art Gallery of Hamilton, Gift of the Women's Committee, 1960

Cover design: Wycliffe Smith

Book design & layout: Darrell McCalla

Printed and bound in Canada

C O N

Part Six — The End of the Beginning

Appendices

Credits

Index

Acknowledgements

I am grateful to the University of Waterloo, to its Dean of Arts, Robin Banks, to the Teaching Resource Officer, Chris Knapper, and to my department chairman, Gordon Slethaug, all of whom have given me support, both financial and moral, and who have been flexible and understanding as I ploughed my way through times often turbulent and full of change in the last six years.

This book would not have been possible without my training as a marriage and family therapist, most of which took place at the Interfaith Pastoral Counselling Centre in Kitchener, Ontario. I am grateful to all the teaching staff there, but particularly to Arthur Waters, the Executive Director, whose trust in me made my internship possible. Among the many gifts the IPCC gave me (including the opportunity to work toward clinical membership in the American Association for Marriage and Family Therapy), perhaps the greatest was my association and friendship with Peter Van Katwyck. Peter is not only a brilliant therapist and an outstanding teacher, but a wise and warm mentor whose friendship has been more to me than I can express. Speaking of friends, I want to thank my colleague Roman Dubinski, who has been a ready listener, a loyal supporter and an intelligent and valuable critic. His integrity and fairness have been a staff to lean on.

Closer to home, I want to thank all my children, Deborah, Anna, Joel, Naomi and Sarah, who somehow have managed never to waver in their belief in my work. They have given me enthusiastic support at every stage and have been understanding even when that work has taken up time they needed with me. They have a part in any merit this book may have. My wife, Brenda, to whom this book is gratefully dedicated, has never stinted of herself in discussion and encouragement of my ideas. From her I have learned more than I can rightly sift out. She has been my most uncompromising and intelligent critic. I really believe that without her this book would not have been written.

There are many people who helped directly in the production of the book. First, I want to thank Helen Heller, formerly of Fitzhenry and Whiteside, who believed in this work and was willing to urge its publication when she had seen only a fraction of it and most was still to be written. And I am grateful to Rex Williams who drew the fledgling manuscript to Helen's attention. Theresa Griffin has been a painstaking and supportive editor, and only another author can know what a source of strength such careful editing can be. Since she was the first person to read the completed manuscript, I waited with some anxiety for her judgement. Tessie's warm approval was one of the high moments of this whole project. I am grateful to Wendy Stocker, who did the typing of my original manuscript and even managed to read most of my handwriting. I have valued her advice and good sense at various stages. I am also lucky to have found Wendy Wiese, who expertly did my revisions on the computer, under considerable pressure but without ever losing her good humour or her cooperative spirit. And at the final stretch, Sandra Whittaker appeared like a miracle to help me with the hundreds of detailed changes and corrections that had to come before publication, often sacrificing her own study time to the demands of my timetable.

I want to thank the librarians at the University of Waterloo for their unfailing assistance in digging up all sorts of information and for phoning me back when they promised to do so. I am also grateful to Fred Gloade of Wilfrid Laurier University, who in the course of working with me on other research projects, introduced me to the work of Seligman and first pointed out to me its relevance to my own.

I am infinitely indebted to the work of Carolyn Schrodes, who had some links with the Bateson-Watzlawick group and who was a pioneer in bibliotherapy. She showed me the way. Finally, I want to acknowledge the work of Louise Rosenblatt, who among many educators urging more attention to readers, seems to me to have made the most sense for the longest time.

Finally, I am more grateful than they will ever know to my students, who have patiently borne with my experimental ramblings, have generously participated in my experimental classes and exams, and have often had the courage to come along with me and trust me on journeys that were not always clearly mapped or provisioned and that were often scary. My students and my clients have provided much of the insight and information that I have relied on in this project. Their courageous stories have no small part in this book, as readers will quickly see. Except where specifically indicated, all names and some details have been altered to protect their privacy.

I feel compelled to say one more word of thanks before moving on. I am obviously acknowledging my biggest debt when I try to express here my appreciation to all those writers of prose and poetry who have enriched my life. Often against overwhelming odds, political, financial, social, these women and men have persisted in telling the truth as they see it, in the most entertaining way possible. I believe that whatever is good about human history is owing in large part to the imagination and courage of our writers. There is no more valuable talent, no higher calling.

For the scholarly background to this book, and further acknowledgements, those interested may turn to the Afterword.

Preface

Many years before this book first appeared in 1990, I gave an interview to Peter Gzowski on CBC radio. I told him I believed that literacy, full range literacy which embraced the reading of literature, was threatened. Literacy is power, and we faced the possibility that this power was likely to fall under the exclusive control of what I had called the *Literate Elite*, a phrase that captured the attention of the press and led to the interview. Around that time there was much talk of writing and reading somehow being replaced by some form of vaguely imagined magical electronic communication. Film, television and computers would somehow render reading and writing irrelevant and passé. Such thinking was greatly advanced by Marshall McLuhan's medium advocacy, and his theory that something more instant and powerful was displacing the linear slowness of language discourse. This became a popular myth, and I sensed that the energy for literacy was dissipating. I believed then and of course I believe now that language is fundamental to being human. Language is stored in usable and reusable models called stories, poems and essays. I had no doubt that some educated people would never stop reading and writing and that those that continued to do so would have the political power and control of thought, ideas, and persuasion conferred by reading. Were this to happen, democracy would *be doomed.*

Some time later, I undertook the training to become a therapist, and in my subsequent work with families, couples and individuals, learned that people *are* their stories. Naturally I came to this view from and with the bias that a lifetime of reading and teaching literature had produced. I knew that language formed reality for individuals, that people wrote their biographies every minute of their lives, even in their dreams. I learned couples wrote their stories together and families created their own histories as they grew, and they passed on, indeed, shaped the identities of their offspring with these stories. And it seemed to me that literature could, and did, supplement and assist the process of story formation that people needed to organize, control and manage their lives. In other words, literature played a role for those who could read it. In fact, literature was therapeutic. I came to believe that it could be more effective and more therapeutic if the reader was made aware of this process, and could deliberately and self-consciously pay attention to this process of relevance to the self while reading. This new understanding would naturally lead to a deliberate seeking of literature that might assist the self-healing and development process. Every response to the first edition of this book has confirmed that such is indeed the case and that literature is indeed a powerful species aid in human life adaptation and problem solving.

In the more than ten years since this book was first published, much has happened that is relevant to its application in mental, spiritual, social and political life. The 90s is now called the Decade of the Brain. Research has shown much more detailed mappings of the brain's activities. We understand better how it does many of its tasks and some of the chemical processes that help it do astounding things. We see a bit more clearly how the parts work together and how emotion is part of the thinking process. We begin to understand how trauma and shock alter the patterns of memory and speech. We can now theorize about how language and identity coalesce. But as with all complexity, the more we know, the more we stand in an appropriate awe about what we don't know. Our respect for the brain's power to think and create and feel, to integrate the workings of its trillions of connective pathways, has also grown. This sense of wonder is itself of immense value, and indeed may be what finally saves us. Self-awareness and self-respect for our long evolution and our own humanity may be what is required to save us from the self-destructive folly and the contempt for our habitat that is the glaring characteristic of human behaviour at this, the beginning of a new millennium.

The last decade brought us alarming changes in our economic and political practices. In our Western world we face stresses and confusion that threaten to overwhelm us. Once again I have a sense that reading and literacy are threatened. We are raising a generation of children who are bombarded at home and at school and through the media with pressure to serve the computer and its own forms of thinking. Between television and computer games and surfing the Internet their time is consumed and divided into fragments of bits and bites of disconnected information. Such discontinuity interferes with the formation of identity. Community is breaking down as cities and towns grow ever more populated and the natural world recedes into fantasy and the mists of forgotten times. Species disappear daily along with our forests. The world is shrinking and graying into homogeneity. And most alarming of all, our sense of control, order and power to alter any of this is eroding with the Global Economy, the threats to Democracy represented by the concentration of economic power and information power into a few hands and into Councils of unelected managers whose motive is profit and whose constituencies are investors.

While the electronic media made promises to save us and help us talk to others around the world, there is the risk that this is illusory and that in fact we are caught up in a brain disabling frenzy of activity that reduces our humanity, distracts us into despair, and gobbles up our time. While we are being distracted, the world's new, invisible managers are making our connections to power and decision making more and more remote. So both human brains and human organization are being changed at a rate that seems to preclude thoughtful and influential input from most of the world's people.

More than ever we need to read literature. The act of reading, and especially of reading narrative fiction, does two things for the reader which are crucial to personal development. The first is the activation of the pre-frontal cortex of the brain and the temporal lobes where some of the major language control centres are located. These sites are connected to many others to form a web activity that creates thought. The second important function of reading literature is to assist in building personal identity in narrative form.

Now both of these consequences of reading narrative have the effect of freeing us from a barrage of disconnected sensory input and slowing down to manageable levels the data processing of brain function. Most of the distracting input from a barrage of entertainment and advertising is in visual form, allowing no time for thought responses to organize the visual-cortex brain responses, which register without thought or integration, into the whole of our complex identity formation. The result of such virtually continuous input of ever more visual images into human brains is a growing sense of personal lostness, despair and passivity. Educational psychologist Jane Healy calls this "Sensory Hucksterism." Reading literature, reading narrative frees us from sensory input because it requires us to process already stored sensory messages. This becomes a purely internal activity of reassembling memory, thought and feeling to make sense of the text. The result of this is an increased sense of personal control, more self-knowledge, strengthened identity and clarification of feelings, values, beliefs and ideas.

William Greider, in his recent book, *One World Ready Or Not*, describes the Global Economy in this way: "Imagine a wondrous new machine, strong and supple, a machine that reaps as it destroys.... Now imagine that there are skillful hands on board, but no one is at the wheel. In fact, this machine has no wheel nor any internal governor to control the speed and direction." The world of commerce, consumerism and greed in which we find ourselves requires us to pay renewed attention to our own biological survival, indeed to invent or revisit with new awareness older forms of self defense. The best of such defenses is reading literature. The global economy, the faceless impersonal monster that Greider tries to describe, seeks to control the lives of all populations and seems to represent no other value but economic profit. There is certainly no evidence that our leaders, business or political, are concerned with the well-being of human brains.

Unless we can maintain or regain the feeling of control and individual effectiveness, we will have no way to influence the political, economic and social course of events that will shape our lives. We will become separated from our humanity. We will become more and more like robots — organic robots, the most perfect kind of slave — and I fully believe that without our vigilance and our READING, this can happen.

Reading seems such a puny weapon against such forces as we seem to have unleashed. Yet if we can slow down long enough to take a look, we will see that writing and story are part of our evolution and part of our brain equipment. The big challenge we face is to protect our humanity, our biology, and we must take action to do this both individually and as communities. We are rushing somewhere on the well-greased wheels of unexamined assumptions. The time has come to take stock and catch our breath and ask what kind of life and world we want. I believe that if we do this we will conclude that such a life must include reading, story, essay and poetry. Literature is a biological tool that we have evolved to produce and nurture thought and feeling. It helps us to grow our own minds. And at this point in human history we need minds of our own. We can start this process by becoming self-conscious about our reading. We can deliberately relate it to our selves. We can use our reading to enhance our language and the story control of our lives and relationships. In a very real sense our freedom lies in reading. To speak of knowledge is not to refer to countless bits and bites of information. Not till the data is woven into a narrative account of our lives can we be confident that we know who we are and how we choose to live.

When individuals, couples or families encounter problems that seem insuperable we must think of them as having reached a point in the composition of a life story that makes continuity of composition difficult or impossible. This story is a kind of self-life-narrative that *is* the person writing it. How is the narrative assembled? What material provides the content for this process of chronological collecting and arranging? The processor is the human brain. It creates this story by using a combination of memory, language and emotion. All three are neural agencies in the body for examining and selecting sensory data for coded storage in brain cells that communicate with each other. The I of the life story continually regulates, modulates, readjusts and confirms a baseline self of which the I is aware and on which it counts for environmental stability. In other words, we rely on a sense of knowing who we are and all new data from experience must be accommodated into this knowing. Such knowing for human beings is inherently formed as story. Our own story is a biological representation of accumulated sensory data and it depends on continuous interaction with the stories of others. We weave a story on the loom of our minds and a necessary part of the warp and the woof, the pattern we create, is other people's stories.

Often however, and inevitably, we meet obstacles to the writing of our story and seem unable to go on. A metaphor may help to make this imaginable, since little stories like the one I'm going to invent are what the brain visualizes and so apprehends most naturally. Imagine that you have a favourite walk through the woods, a familiar and well worn path that you know well and take daily for healthy and pleasant exercise.* This is a preferred and well known route, mapped in the brain. Things change on the path and keep it interesting: weather changes it, birds appear, leaves and branches alter and sometimes people are met, greeted or avoided. But one day an obstacle appears that prevents the walk from continuing: a log falls across the path, or an accident happens which makes the path seem unavailable, or a housing development destroys large necessary stretches of the path.

The life story is like this path, and when it is blocked by grief or loss, unforeseen events such as war, job loss, earthquake, or divorce, it may feel to the sufferer that the path or story cannot be continued or recovered. Among the various healing strategies that can help recovery, literature is primary for those able to access it. Locked into the logos, or prison of personal experience, the isolating perspective of the private store of events and people, it may seem as though no one can understand, that there is no way to see out of or around the trap of defeat or helplessness. Literature can be used as a story to get you free of your own truncated narrative. It can add to or modify your own story. It can model the power and control of storied events. It can model character and attributes you need to continue. It is inexpensive and inexhaustible. Sometimes the reconstruction of story requires a therapist, who can act as an editor to your creativity, but

*The image of the path or road is a persistent and powerful metaphor in human discourse. The path is obviously ancient, as old as mammal mobility itself. The path precedes all other channels of communication and provided the route to hunting and therefore food, to novelty seeking and to mate seeking, as well as representing an escape route. Hardly surprising that the path or road taken, or not, should come so easily to the mind of humans as a metaphor for life itself. And like time and life itself, reading is linear and the linear is mentally inescapable.

often, without assistance, the reading combines and extends your own story making power and so helps to free you from paralysis, the freezing or writer's block of painful experience.

The more we learn about how brains work the less surprising this should be. We are made up of the stuff of stories and stories all interact and combine, joining our brains to others and expanding, growing if you like, the range and secondary experience of our own knowing.

This book makes no attempt to be definitive or even comprehensive in its listing of resources, or how to use them. Rather it models and explains some of the principles and examples of the use of fiction to empower readers to manage their lives. You can read this as a guide to practice, a how-to-do-it for yourself.

It is amazing to me how people in need find the books they require to help themselves. And it is equally and continually surprising, though of course it should not be after my long advocacy for the process, that readers can change perceptions and feelings radically when they read what seems pertinent and relevant to their situations. Nor are these readings always predictable or obvious. It is not always the book about divorce or grief that speaks to the person separating or grieving. People find what they need in the most unlikely places.

One sure thing is that reading produces brain activity like no other behaviour, and the second is that the more reading done the better. One useful and engaging text is more than an enormous but pleasantly and easily acquired body of information. It is a brain exercise and a training course for writing life narrative. Reading is healing. Its effectiveness as a healing activity is greatly enhanced by the reader's awareness that this is self-healing behaviour. And strange as it may seem, one can beneficially affect and alter one's own brain. The brain consumes, stores and uses information, and this information can be good or bad for our bodies and our lives. The good news is that we can make choices, we can decide what information we offer and invite our brains to process. We need to become active for our own well-being.

Before he died, Moses offered the people a choice between life and death and urged them to choose life. I think we have pretty well come to that place again. The way of passivity, the way of unexamined assumptions, the way of submission to monopolies of information and the limitations of electronic machines, the mindless dedication to consumerism and the pursuit of money: these are the paths to death. Respect for our own identities, our brain power, our bodies and health, our relationships and communities, our future through our descendants—these are the ways to life.

We cannot wait until our story path is blocked to turn to reading. It is much harder work to find our remedies and recover our brain power in adult life when we have not been practicing the reading of literature all our lives, though of course such recovery is possible. We must start with our children and make sure they read widely and frequently. Reading creates coping skills and joins us to community over time and space. It makes us stronger as individuals and collectives. This book is meant to guide you to models that demonstrate the ways in which fiction works to assist in the management of life under stress. But it does assume a literate and a thinking audience, and it does seek to validate a reading behaviour that may appear to some people in your life to be a frivolous and non-productive activity. I will never apologize for reading, any more than I would for eating, and I urge you to be proud of your own reading activity. I recognize the biological necessity of reading and I am asking you to do the same. Sooner or later we will restore reading to its rightful place in our evolutionary growth. Let's hope, no, *let's make sure* we do so before we have done more damage to ourselves and our world than we can ever repair.

Preface — To the Original Edition

I see that I have written a kind of testimonial to reading, a eulogy, a celebration. I have revealed my addiction. Books, of all kinds but especially novels, are one of the central, unwearying pleasures of my life. Indeed, as I get older, my love of reading grows.

So this is an appreciation of literature. But I hope it is more than that, because I have tried to take up Plato's challenge. I want to explain how literature is useful to human life. Being a justification for literature, this book grows from a long tradition of enthusiastic "defenses" of fiction and poetry, some by very famous people like Philip Sidney and Percy Shelley. We know that literature is entertaining, gives delight, as Plato admits. We know it is often "cultural," artsy as well as artful. What has not been so obvious, I think, is that literature is healthful and maybe necessary as part of our overall response to the demands of life-living, working, forming families and dealing with problems. What readers need now is not another defense, but some offense.

As I looked back over all the readings I remember best, I was astounded to see that the reading I did as a child was more real, more memorable, more informative to me than the rest of my life. I read a lot. As an asthma sufferer, I missed a lot of school. There was, fortunately, no television. There was radio—BBC—with its wonderful dramas for which I will always be grateful. Mostly, though, there were books, books my mother brought me from the library, books I bought at Casey's, the local tobacconist and news-agent, where volumes in shiny new dust jackets could be had for a few shillings.

Grey Owl showed me another world, a wild world of beauty and air, innocence and space, where I dreamed of breathing freely and where air raid sirens were unknown. William Johns' Biggles, in his various roles, helped me to defeat the Nazis in my mind and made me stronger and braver. Percy F. Westerman showed me what growing up could mean and the challenges that had to be overcome. Rider Haggard and W. H. Hudson showed me romance, bigger, broader worlds to free me from the rubble of war-torn London and endless row-houses. H. E. Bates showed me glimpses of sex and passion and forbidden feelings and fantasies. I devoured Hugh Lofting's Dr. Dolittle, who amused and transported me from my sick bed. I hooted and howled at William's escapades in the Richmal Crompton books and learned to be "bad" from some of them—a very good thing for me, who threatened to aspire to sainthood and martyrdom. No doubt William was Crompton's way of being naughty, also, for this clergyman's daughter was stricken by polio and unable to run around like William and his sidekick, Violet Elizabeth Bott. I blame William for inspiring me to dismantle my brother's bed, with the help of an industrious friend, because we wanted some small but crucial springs for a reason I cannot recall. When my big brother retired for the night, the bed collapsed, and the roof, so to speak, fell in on me. Literature and life came together, as they often do.

Then there was the fat and frightening volume, *Great Tales of Terror and the Supernatural*, that my sister gave me in December, 1947, and that I still have, with its inscription, "To Joe, Pleasant Dreams," a book to scare the daylights out of me with works by the masters, Edgar Allan Poe, Saki, W. W. Jacobs and fifty others. This, without my knowing it, was my first engagement with the great storytellers I now teach in courses on the short story. Without my being aware or being a "critic," the shape and structure of fiction, the experience of being held in suspense and of being released and resolved, gave me by practice an ordering skill, a way to manage data, a way to "write" what was happening to me by a mental shaping process. I learned language. I was explained to myself. I found fellow spirits, what May Sarton calls "kin," whom I may not have found in real life.

I am under no illusion. I know that what I suggest in this book has radical, subversive and dangerous implications. Reading has always been a political act, and the authorities have always known it, since writing was invented. The Bible tells us that King Ahasuerus, mighty emperor of the Near Eastern world, when he could not sleep was wont to read the royal records—a kind of White House logbook. This, in fact, led to an ancient Watergate, a sort of Esthergate, that eventually unravelled the plot of wicked Haman and so changed the history of the world. It is only a story, but the moral of the story has been taken to heart by every dictator in history: Reading is dangerous to the status quo. To give reading power to the people is to undermine the power of reading authorities, to lose control of classrooms, to expose thoughts, feelings and attitudes to close examination, to challenge authority generally—in other words, to change the world.

Plato knew the danger of literature and its power to undermine political control. The power of technocracy, megacorporate wealth, military might and ideological thought-control by church and state are all threatened by fiction. The war between the imagination and the stone heart is as old as communities. Blake knew the power of fiction and talked about it to Tom Paine, who used the word to spur on the American Revolution. Dickens knew it, Disraeli knew it, the opponents of the vernacular Bible knew it, John Bunyan knew it and censorship everywhere knows it.

In short, a well-developed, fully responsive, free readership is the most powerful force for personal and social change. Those who say fiction is over and reading is dead would only like to think so. Fiction is not a fad. It is a human survival strategy. What follows is a mixture of memoir, theory and instruction, an attempt to give some insight into how the strategy works. Literacy demands action and reading is action. In the beginning was the word. We must not stop beginning.

PART ONE

Enjoying Fiction without Guilt

CHAPTER ONE

Introduction: Reading for Your Self

This book is for everyone who likes to read and everyone who wants to like to read. It is a book about the value of reading fiction, about the importance of story to your personal life, your coping skills, your mental health and your relations with other people. Reading is too important to toss away and lose through indifference or taking it for granted. There is, I believe, some risk today of increasing illiteracy. I want to rescue the power and pleasure of fiction from the control of professors, from the contempt of the market place, from the competition of television, and from the assault of censorship, in all its forms.

Put very simply, fiction therapy, or bibliotherapy as it is sometimes called, works like this. When you read fiction or poetry you experience feelings, emotions, as well as thoughts and images. You see pictures in your mind and you have feelings associated with the pictures. Now most people are not in the habit of identifying these feelings or even of being aware of them. When you learn to do this, you can use your feelings about what you read to explore yourself, your relations, your attitudes to job, home, sex, children and parents, aging, death and religion, for example. There is a direct link between what you feel about stories and what you feel about everything else, *especially about yourself.*

With the help of fiction you can learn and understand your own feelings, identify the sources of your anxieties, angers, likes and dislikes. Fiction can reflect for you, like a magic mirror, the veiled parts of your self and your life. The other wonderful function of story in human cognition is its power to alter the reader's way of thinking and perceiving. Fiction can help you to reorganize thinking, resolve problems, remember the past when you need to review it and see it differently. In other words, fiction can be a powerful agent for creative and healthy change. Not only does it show you material you recognize, it shows you slightly altered versions of what you recognize and so produces an incredibly complex set of relational possibilities. Fiction helps you to restory yourself. Oliver Sacks tells us, in his compassionate recent book on brain dysfunction:

> We have, each of us, a life-story, an inner narrative whose continuity, whose sense, *is* our lives. It might be said that each of us constructs and lives a "narrative," and that this narrative *is* us, our identities.
>
> If we wish to know about a man, we ask "what is his story, his real, inmost story?" for each of us *is* a biography, a story. Each of us *is* a singular narrative, which is constructed, continually, unconsciously, by, through, and in us, through our perceptions, our feelings, our thoughts, our actions; and, not least, our discourse, our spoken narrations. Biologically, physiologically, we are not so different from each other; historically, as narratives, we are each of us unique.[1]

Fiction helps us to rewrite our stories, helps us to revise, review and add on stories, so that we can continue living our narrative in a creative way.

How have we lost the knowledge of the power, the almost primal power, of story? There is a whole professional industry dedicated to what is called "literary criticism," which is based in universities. There is a publishing industry busily trying to figure out and publish what will sell. Yet there is no book that tells readers in clear language, using up-to-date information, how to read for the greatest personal pleasure and growth, or how to select books that will help them to read their way to mental health, or how the reading process works to produce the results that fiction readers everywhere recognize, or how fiction relates to and illuminates the life of the reader. This book attempts to begin the story of story. It is about the fictive *process*, about how the pleasures of reading can also be important aids in coping with stress, life crises and growing up.

There are two extreme attitudes towards fiction and poetry. On the one hand, reading "literature" has been regarded as reserved for experts, professors and other students; it has become a "discipline," a very serious business. On the other hand, from a sort of hardnosed business person's point of view, it is thought to be a frivolous entertainment not much connected to "real life." Reading fiction doesn't change the bottom line, the GNP, the boardroom. Reading stories is what you do for children, or when the important chores—cleaning the car, washing the dishes, cutting the grass—are over for the day and you want to "kill time." You can also "kill time" (as though there were more than enough of it to spare, like mosquitoes or pollution) by reading in airports, on buses, or in physicians' waiting rooms, and the reading for these places is in magazines that provide passing, trivial, unimportant distraction. There are millions of guilty readers, even millions of secret readers, who feel secretive or guilty because they have been taught the myths that reading is for specialists or that it is a waste of time. Many people say they were "no good at English" in school which means that they could not play the literary games that their teachers learned in their turn from university professors. Put in another way, these myths say that what experts approve as literature is worthwhile and that the rest is trash for those who want to fool around. But readers of fiction know from their own experience how important their reading is to them; they know that fiction that is not "classical" can still be important to their lives; they are in conflict with what they have been taught, so they keep their reading habits to themselves.

Escape seems to be a bad word. We have become infected with the notion that reading is an avoidance of reality, a running away from the tough daily challenges of paying the bills, doing the chores, going to parent-teacher meetings and keeping fit. This suspicion of fiction reading as an activity divorced from the practical life comes from a cultural devaluing of feeling, imagination, mental pleasure, and language. We are obsessed with being physically busy. If we sit and think, sit and feel, or read for pleasure we are in danger of being seen as doing nothing. Wordsworth warned of this:

> Getting and spending we lay waste our powers;
> Little we see in Nature that is ours.[2]

In reality, escaping into literature, into someone else's story, is an exercising of our imagination, feeling and language. Reading restores us by providing a necessary relief from the struggle of moment-by-moment ad hoc reacting. The story we read is a relief from chaos. The degree of control we can exercise over life events is limited. The weather, the economy, our relatives and friends require continuous, spontaneous responses. This is tiring. We regenerate by reading a story that takes care of us, leads us sure-footedly through complex paths of experience and language and lets us imagine an alternative life. So we can come back from reading refreshed, renewed and with more energy to shape our own ends. We have escaped the trap of our own struggle by glimpsing other, ordered experience; we have enlarged our world. Literature is an aid to mental and spiritual health.

Our educational system has taught that reading has to be done a certain way. Millions of adults remember spending months on *Macbeth* or *Oliver Twist* and becoming thoroughly bored with it. Students and children have been forced to pore over images, symbols and characters, hunting for clues, forcing together interpretations and meanings, playing guessing games to "psych out" the teacher, that is, to find out what the teacher wants. It's the rare student who gets lucky enough to be allowed his own feelings about the text, or to have his thoughts or opinions truly respected or taken seriously. Most often, whatever the pretense, the student has to finish up having it the teacher's way. What is good for you is what "they" choose, and what it means is what "they" say it means. People who like to read, or who liked to read before the schools finished pounding "the truth" into them, know differently. They know the truth of their reactions, the strength of their feelings and what really "grabbed" them in books. It is for all readers, present, potential and not yet born, that this book is written.

My message is, *respect your own reading power* because fiction is one of the most important resources of your life. Having taught in universities in Canada and the U.S. for the last thirty-four years, I am well aware how many readers are turned off by their education, how many are forced to play games they don't believe in to get grades. Both as a teacher of literature and as a marriage and family therapist, I know the power of reading fiction in the personal lives and relations of readers.

The reading process itself, which I am about to discuss, is immensely complex and, indeed, most of it is little understood in terms of human brain function. I have tried to explain what I know as simply as possible. In order to be fair to my subject, however, I have used some words that are possibly unfamiliar and a little obscure. They may not be well defined in your dictionary, or I may have coined them or be using them in a special way. To make things easier, therefore, here is a short glossary or list of words and their meanings as used in the text:

Affect: a term from psychology meaning the feeling experienced as a result of being emotionally involved or stimulated, like angry, sad, excited. Also affective, affectional and so on.

Analogue: a model or substitute for the thing itself, by which the reader can learn more about the thing itself. For instance, Robinson Crusoe's loneliness and isolation could be an analogue for the loneliness and isolation of an immigrant from Asia arriving to take a job in North Bay, Ontario. Also analogous, analogic and so on.

Cognition/Cognitive: The term describes that power of the human being to know, understand, figure out, change thinking and so on. Distinct from reflex and learned behaviour. In this book, reading is treated as an affective/cognitive act, the power of the reader to change or modify perception and thinking, with the aid of emotional response.

Constraint: a boundary imposed by the environment or by the nature of the individual's mind or body. The term is usually used in economics ("spending constraints"), but space, time, temperature and not having wings are also constraints. Control is active, constraint is passive. Control is part of design. In reading, the novel assists the reader in generating control by "framing" experience. I will explain "framing" in the book.

Feedback: the information I receive and interpret in response to what I have said or done. Feedback tells me if I've been heard and how or whether my actions have produced results I like or don't like, and it tells me how to modify my signals to produce a desired feedback. If I want to be loved and my messages produce hostile feedback, I will have to alter my messages or find another receiver.

Process: This word appears to be obvious and most of us use it frequently. I mention it here because I attach great importance to it as an idea. Process is a state of becoming, as against static states, which we think exist but which don't. For instance, we are used to thinking of good/bad, right/wrong, sick/well and so on. "Things" are not fixed and final and do not have absolute characteristics. Everything is always in process, which leads us to...

System, subsystem and supersystem: These terms are from a very recent branch of modern thought called General Systems Theory. Everything, from subatomic particles to human families and solar systems, is part of a system and is itself a system. Things do not exist in isolation. Each system is the subsystem of a larger supersystem that consists of many subsystems. The human body is a supersystem consisting of subsystems—blood, nerves, tissues, skeleton and so on—but is also part of a social and environmental supersystem consisting of homes, parks, church, school, traffic, government and so on. *Reading* is a systemic activity made up of the book (word-story) in process with the reader in a particular setting at a particular time.

Transference: a term from psychotherapy that means the client has come to see the therapist as a powerful attraction, love object, hate object, father figure and so on. The client's powerful emotions become focused on the therapist-agent-for-change. In the fictive process the novel can act as a deflector/dissipator of disabling emotions in the reader's personal relations. That is, it does not do what therapists sometimes do, project their own hang-ups onto their clients. The reader, using the mirror quality of fiction, can become her own therapist.

Transformation: When the exchange of energy is such that the system is altered in its nature or form, it is transformed. When human beings as a result of some experience (which could be reading a novel) think differently or perceive in a quite new way, they are said to be transformed. Transformation is called "second order change" and is quite different from the kind of change that occurs when we merely add a new idea or meet some new people. The mindset has to change. Transformation can also be described as the "Eureka!" or "Aha!" principle.

These are the most crucial terms. The rest should be quite familiar.

Before we get going, I want to say one word on my use of gender pronouns, "he" and "she," "his" and "her." I have used these randomly and I hope more or less equally throughout the book. This seems to me the fairest and most natural way. I confess, however, I haven't counted these up to guarantee absolute equality. If someone does do that, please write and let me know the result.

1   Oliver Sacks, *The Man Who Mistook His Wife for a Hat, and Other Clinical Tales* (New York: Summit, 1985), p.105.

2   William Wordsworth, "The World Is Too Much with Us," in *The Norton Anthology of English Literature*, Third Edition, Vol. 2, ed. M. H. Abrams, et al. (New York: Norton, 1974).

CHAPTER TWO

Fear of Feeling: The Conspiracy Against Reading

W hen I was an undergraduate in the 50s at university in Britain, I studied "English," which consisted mostly of reading a lot and participating in what was called a tutorial. Education in English universities has traditionally taken place through the tutorial, though things may have changed by now. This means that once a week for about twenty weeks a year a professor, known over there as a lecturer or reader or fellow, gathers together in his office three or four quailing, green, hungover, tweedy students assigned to him for a one-hour discussion of some book or other they're all supposed to have been reading. This professor, while never growing rich, did seem to have an extraordinary amount of leisure time, during which he was able to do any number of other things, like writing plays for the BBC (much more lucrative) or simply going fishing (much more fun). Perhaps the frequent absence of professors was connected to the scarcity of students—hardly anybody could get into a university.

In any case there I was in my tutorial, even more naive about academic life than I am now. We had been reading *Tom Jones* by Henry Fielding with a view to having our tutorial on it, and one of us had prepared an essay on *Tom Jones* for delivery on this particular occasion. My tutor, who was fairly young, prematurely aged,

11

extremely bad-tempered, crusty and pretentious, bustled in, full of pomp, circumstance and impatience, to supervise the weekly ritual. I don't remember what the essay of my peer was all about, but when he finished reading it, I do remember wondering what lay behind it and what we were all doing there in the first place. The whole thing was a mystery to me. What did the exciting blood-and-guts vitality of *Tom Jones* have to do with this flat, lifeless, incomprehensible essay being monotonously read aloud by a self-conscious teenager?

I had gone through a reading lifetime up to that point, beginning to read when I was about five and becoming a voracious and avid reader through early schooling and high school, where I had done very well as a student of literature. So not unnaturally I had decided to major in English at university. During all of that time— the fifteen years or so of my formal schooling—I had read books for fun, for life, for information, for excitement, just enjoyed them and enjoyed talking about them. I had learned about writers and how they influenced each other, and I had learned how to write essays that made reasonable sense to me about how books seemed to be put together and what characters were doing to each other and how plots worked out and so on. I enjoyed language.

My first real attachment to literature as an independent reader came from reading English comic books, the kind full of stories rather than strip cartoons. These comic books will be immediately recognizable to people of my generation—*Wizard* was one, *Hotspur* was another. What these did was to take famous stories, either short stories or novels, and rewrite or adapt them in a serial form that we read from week to week, almost like a kind of adventure soap opera. I lived a lot of my preadolescent years waiting for the arrival of these comic books so that I could get on with the real life they contained. I was lucky; I was not discouraged from doing this, because I had parents who loved to read. They had no high school education at all.

And my teachers had not been through the academic rigours of professional "English" training. They just loved books.

Now I had always assumed that I was doing all this because I loved literature, stories, and because it felt good for me. It seemed to be important—humanly, socially, politically—to have literature in the world. It had never occurred to me to wonder or to ask anyone else or myself *what all this was for*, or how books came to be written, or how they related to other human activities, or whether there was anything special about novels as opposed to poems or essays or other kinds of human production, until I got to university. Wouldn't you think it the most natural thing in the world for professors to explore these questions? What else could studying "English" mean? It's very much part of English life to grow up believing that other people know what's best for you. This trust in grownups is a very deep-rooted respect for authority and goes far beyond the belief that big people know what is good to eat and how you should dress in November and how to cross the road. It continues into how you should think and what you should read and whom you should go out with and when you should speak and what questions you should ask.

So there I was, having heard this paper, which I can't remember a word of, on *Tom Jones*. My tutor began a polite discussion of issues raised by the paper: characterization, motivation, plots—all that sort of thing that we're all familiar with from school discussions. At no point in any of this talk would you have known that there were four sentient human beings in the room. We had for the purposes of this academic enterprise taken on the roles of soulless robots, programmed to talk in the shallowest way about a lively work of art, and make it sterile and dead if we could. A visitor from Mars would have been hard put to it, listening to our discussion, to know that the people in the room had private, personal lives or feelings, lives that were filled with emotion, complicated relationships and a turmoil of hopes, ambitions, fears and unresolved passions.

There were three young men in the room, all struggling to realize their sexual identity, preoccupied with acquiring life experience—which in the 50s was an agonizingly tortured and thwarting process. One of them was probably a homosexual, which must have been a perfect, private hell for him in our social circumstances. There was our youngly aged teacher there. I was told he was a widower who had remarried. Perhaps he was tormented by unresolved grief and anger, some of which he displaced onto us. In any case, he seemed always irritated. In the backgrounds of his tutees there was social class conflict, there was economic stress and anxiety, there was family tension, there was pride and guilt at being in university, and there were undoubtedly a thousand other pieces of floating dynamite that could have been used and called into play to blow open our understanding of the passion, force and feeling, not to mention the social issues, evocable by the writing of Henry Fielding. Had this happened, had we been permitted, or, further still, encouraged, to explore our personal responses to the text, or to discuss its relation to ourselves, to acknowledge our *feelings* in reading it, then surely we would have learned something, about each other, about the text, about literature, about ourselves. That would have been a joy. That would have been a real education.

And yet, amazing though it may seem when looked at now in this way, these potentialities for expression and exploration of personal emotion and life, for creativity, were never realized or brought to the fore. Now I realize that they rarely are in English classes, and this is confirmed year after year by the testimony of my students. *Tom Jones* describes and raises problems and conflicts, pain and resolution around the search for personal identity, in relation to natural and adoptive families. It could raise questions about incest, about romantic love and about the quest for marriage, happiness, status and sexual union. The novel looks at issues of social justice and class conflict, snobbery, hypocrisy, pretension, seduction and lust, leaving home, and the contrast between cities and city dangers and the stability, peace and insularity of country life. Above all, *Tom Jones* invites thought about the storymaking process. All literature, I believe, is connected to life.

Readers, students want to talk about this connection. I wanted to talk about these things because so many of them related to my own situation. I had left home to be the only person in my family to go to university. I was alone for the first time. I was living very poorly, mostly on beans and beer, and was aware of my family's economic hardship. I felt guilt at being in a university reading novels while my mother, brother, sister and father were working long, hard, tedious hours at thankless occupations. I had not figured out how to describe my vocation in such a way that I could overcome my misgivings that what I was doing was idleness and self-indulgence. I needed to talk about these things, and there was no one to talk to. There was no such thing as a counselling service. So I made the extraordinarily naive error of trying to initiate discussion in this tutorial about basics, about life and its relation to literature. I began by asking, full of trust, a question something on the lines of "what is a novel?" and was proceeding to elucidate my interest in how novels involve us, in what Fielding's view of the world was. I wanted to know how we could begin the process of understanding and writing about the real forces and power somehow unleashed when fiction interacts with the reader's life.

Of course the language I am using here, and the clarity of my understanding about the issues as I express them here, were not available to me then, so my inquiry may have been somewhat faltering, confused and garbled. This does not mean, however, that I could not be understood. A good teacher is one who is listening very carefully, who makes a space in himself to hear not only what is being said or asked, but what lies behind what is being said. Sad to say, many teachers hide themselves behind a rigid mask they learn to put on in university. They talk set pieces at students, whom they see only as receivers, not as whole human beings who need to be heard. Only a secure, humane, caring teacher can commit his sympathies and empathies to an understanding of the person who is groping for words.

What I got was a totally unexpected cold blast of contempt from my tutor. To my shock and humiliation he ranted at me for five minutes, about how "we" don't ask absurd questions like that and "we" stick to the subject, and about how I was not discussing the paper that had just been read and so on and so on. He told me that if I did not know what a novel was I should not be in a university. (Well, I'm still in a university and I still don't know what a novel is only now it's become fashionable not to know.)

In other words, I had broken some rule I didn't understand and didn't know was there, a rule from a class and a profession that was new to me. *I understand it now.* It's one of a set that goes something like this: Students must believe their professors unquestioningly; the works the professors select for study and enlightenment are always the best works; students must all pretend to know why they are there, and they are not to discuss this or disagree with professors or doubt the claims of great literature; students must not introduce personal concerns or curiosities into discussions of great works; they should have resolved all their personal issues for themselves before coming to university, but if they haven't they're not supposed to work them out during the precious hour devoted by the tutor, who has deigned to interrupt his busy private life to come in and spend time with these inferior beings. If you don't know something, don't admit it. Professors know everything; students know nothing. Most important rule of all: Don't mention these rules.

These rules are very much the same ones as apply in the kingdom where the little boy stood up in the crowd and shouted out that the emperor's new clothes were not really there, that in reality he was stark naked. I can see now the power of my question and the panic it generated in my tutor. He did not know the answer. If we broke silence and the ranks by asking questions about the validity of the activity we were engaged in, the whole enterprise of "literary criticism" would be called into question. In truth, the selection of books for study is a completely arbitrary process, simply agreed upon (and often disagreed upon) by professors. But the claim of divine sanction for arbitrariness is so entrenched that it's instinctive for teachers to say that everybody knows that Milton and Fielding and Shakespeare and George Eliot are the obvious and unquestionably right and proper materials of study and concern, and that only an ignoramus would doubt this. The game is to intimidate the nonacademic unwashed. What is chosen for study depends of course on what we study it *for*. Particular political, national, or social goals might dictate the study of other works.

Anyway, some good comes of everything. My innocent and abortive line of inquiry in my tutorial had certain beneficial results for me. I have been asking these same questions ever since. In that no one to this day is quite clear about what a novel is, and in that these questions are not stupid but difficult, I have had to try to provide the answers for myself. Incidentally, that day's experience is the only classroom experience that I remember from my undergraduate years. The real value of my going to university, in addition to having an excuse for years of reading wonderful books, was in the discussions and interactions I had with other students over coffee or a beer, and in the social life I learned to lead outside of classroom and books.

But to get back to the main point that comes out of all of this, fiction engages the minds and feelings and experiences of readers. Until very recently formal education has gone to extreme lengths to avoid this powerful and personal encounter between books and readers, and instead has created for itself a massive industry of depersonalized, intellectualized "literary criticism." Like the atomic bomb, carbon monoxide and thalidomide, literary criticism is a product of Western civilization and sophistication. Universities have produced and hired experts in literature who tell everybody else what is great and what is important, and the proper way to read what is great and important. A fear of feeling firmly underlies the intellectual games played around literature, games that are characteristic of our educational system, which seems to have persuaded itself that if feelings are acknowledged, permitted, or owned by students or teachers (or by teachers on behalf of students), then all hell will break loose. Professionalism has on balance worked against pleasure and enthusiasm in reading literature.

For one thing, acknowledging feeling or admitting feeling compels an encounter with the individual doing the feeling. Individuality in the educational system is inefficient and expensive. If emotions are valid and accepted as appropriate responses, then all feelings are equal. This undermines power, discipline, authority, teacher control—so it is thought. It is also thought that feeling responses, if they're valid responses, cannot be taught, because they're part of who the reader is at any given time, and that acknowledging them might therefore put teachers out of a job; if teachers are not the possessors of the "right" answers, not the transmitters of these right answers to the empty vessels in front of them, then what is there left for them to do? For the most part, children in the school system are okay until they run into teachers who have degrees and who have been significantly influenced by the university system in which they

trained. Until that time, children learn to read more or less efficiently, even though they do so according to a timetable that may
not be very individualized; on the whole, they are pretty well protected from having their reading academically programmed.
Elementary and junior schools are working hard to create a love of
reading in children, with varying degrees of success.

In universities things are very different. There, something
called "children's literature" is regarded by some as a simple-minded
playworld of fantasy and imagination that has very little to do with
the real, hard, tough issues of life itself—"Oh, that, that's just kiddy
lit." Others regard such writing as full of hidden psychological meaning discernible only to academics. In actual fact, of course, this desig-
nating of some literature as "children's," like all the rest of the theoretical and mythological bits of the system, is pure nonsense. There
are no absolute, fixed states of innocence-childhood and experience-
adulthood. Indeed, nothing is fixed, and such conditions as are
described in terms of stupid/clever, good/bad, lazy/diligent,
child/adult to label students and readers exist only in the minds of
those who insist on them. We are all more or less stupid, lazy, clever,
or talented, and we are all part child all our lives. The cup is always
part empty and part full. There are certainly other ways of looking at
human development and human relations to language, literature,
art and society, ways that make more sense, are more creative and fit
more with the data of our common sense, than those that presently
slice up literature in universities. Not all education need aim for the
emotional engagement of students or focus on the personal relevance of the material studied. It's just that literature provides the
natural opportunity for such education.

The defining characteristic of fiction and poetry, the power of
literature to influence, entertain, help and illuminate, resides in its
ability to call forth feeling along with thought in the reader. To

ignore or deny this emotional response component in the reader is to ignore the reality of the process. To refuse to bring emotional information into a discussion of literature itself is to diminish both the literature—to devalue it by reducing its usefulness—and the reader's full understanding of it. It is disrespectful to the text and to the reader to discount the affective experience of the reading act.

Anyway, once children start to encounter the teachers who are products of a university system, they fall foul of the "serious business" that is the academic baggage brought by graduate teachers. At this point, students will begin to drift into two streams—those who do well at English and who might think of it as a possible course of study, and those who are not good at English and drift away from reading altogether. To practice what they were taught to do, English teachers need an audience pretending they don't feel anything when they read fiction or poetry. Now the cycle starts. The teachers in the universities who taught the teachers in the schools had to work very hard to be teachers in universities, and they learned to keep feelings out of it. Most of them exhausted and brainwashed themselves getting that highest of all degrees, that crown of academic achievement, the PhD or Doctor of Philosophy degree. The doctorate is usually a third degree, after the Bachelor's degree and the Master's degree, so you can see that by the end of this process, which might take normally anywhere from eight to twelve or more years, those who went this route have a pretty substantial investment in keeping others' noses to the grindstone and in making those others do what they once had to do, that is, suffer. No joy here. After such effort, these doctors are often incapable of any other activity, so specialized and narrow was their training. I have worked with and met many hundreds of teachers with PhDs who have followed this pattern, sometimes teaching what they learned in graduate school, barely altered, for the next forty years, and giving little evidence of any excitement at the literature in their custody. I am sure their exhaustion and frustration are increased by the long struggle to keep feeling and personal relevance out of the critical process.

University departments of English have a lot of power, more power than departments of History or Philosophy or Religious Studies, because everybody reads. They set standards and they teach teachers how to carry on with the exercise of power. University English departments determine what is good literature by selecting what they will teach, neglecting what they have not approved. They can partially control what gets published because the publishing industry is so competitive and so tough that those books that do not sell in large numbers (to students) simply go out of print and are not available any more. Novels that might be extremely valuable from the point of view of certain readers, like popular novels focusing on the family and marriage, divorce, sex, growing up and adolescence and so on; those books, since they don't find their way onto English courses, can't be kept in print. Prescribing books for courses in universities in North America has become one way to keep titles in print and so help publishers make a living. English departments also determine who gets in and out of their programs—in other words, they determine who can read and who can't read. This sort of Good Housekeeping Seal of Approval on readers is part of the power structure our educational system has encouraged by prescribing what people must read and how they must read it.

So academics control *what* is read and also *how* students must read the texts that are chosen for them. We don't permit students to read just any old way they feel like, when they come into courses. We teach people that the proper way to read is, for instance, to look for hidden messages, mistakenly believing that hidden and deep are the same thing.

The primary strategy for avoiding feeling in reading while creating a professional expertise is control of the technical aspects, the craft of literature. Looking for "symbols" has long been an approved way of reading. People who are trained to do this in universities graduate "in English" and then go into teaching—or mostly into teaching, because, as I've said, the people who graduate with degrees in English are usually not able to do anything else but teach other people to do the same thing they have learned to do. But symbol hunting, along with other methods of analyzing writing that have come to seem the normal professional way of reading, is really only one very special kind of reading; it's also a special kind of knack, like flipping pancakes. Not everyone can do it or wants to do it, *but if you can't do it you're not approved of as an official reader.* Now normally it doesn't matter one iota whether readers can find symbols or hidden signs in a book that gives them pleasure. What really matters to readers is how much fun they have reading when a book relates to their own lives, and this is not always easy to explain. It is often hard for individual readers to say why a book became most important for them or registered very strongly with them at a particular time in their lives. It may have been a book that does not lend itself to symbolic reading. But merely enjoying a book and seeing its connections to your own life has not been enough to win academic approval. There is something terrible in the recognition that the "English" academy has stood by like an overseer while huge percentages of our school population have grown disenchanted with reading. Professors of English ought to interest themselves in giving the gift of literature to everyone who can read.

I have just finished a novel by James Carroll called *Family Trade.* I thought it was a gripping, a very brilliant piece of storytelling, but it doesn't seem to me to lend itself to the kind of reading techniques that are insisted upon in professional programs of English that practice what is called literary criticism. For that reason *Family Trade* is a novel that will probably go out of print along with millions of others that won't find a place on a university course, even though it has a lot to say about father-son relations and contains a marvellous description of the fall of Berlin in the Second World War. We do not teach literature in order to assist family relations.

People can learn to read perfectly well without learning the professional method usually favoured. Let me show you a sample of the conventional techniques. Here is an excerpt from D. H. Lawrence's *The Fox*, followed by an official reading:

> The young man—or youth, for he would not be more than twenty—now advanced and stood in the inner doorway. March, already under the influence of his strange, soft, modulated voice, stared at him spellbound. He had a ruddy, roundish face, with fairish hair, rather long, flattened to his forehead with sweat. His eyes were blue, and very bright and sharp. On his cheeks, on the fresh ruddy skin were fine, fair hairs, like a down, but sharper. It gave him a slightly glistening look. Having his heavy sack on his shoulders, he stooped, thrusting his head forward. His hat was loose in one hand. He stared brightly, very keenly from girl to girl, particularly at March, who stood pale, with great dilated eyes, in her belted coat and puttees, her hair knotted in a big crisp knot behind. She still had the gun in her hand. Behind her, Banford, clinging to the sofa arm, was shrinking away, with half-averted head.[1]

This story tells of two progressive young women who take up farming and try to make a go of it without a man. There is a simmering homosexual relationship between the two women, whose farming activities are plagued by a predatory fox against whose assaults they are helpless. Here is a student commentary that I think most English professors would like:

> The young man who intrudes on this not quite
> perfect scene symbolizes the fox itself. Like the fox he
> is "ruddy" and alert, quickly sizing up the situation
> for his own advantage. Here the girls, like the hens in the
> henhouse, are the hunted, powerless and fascinated at
> the authority of the male presence. The contest for domi-
> nance, in a series of triangles, ends as all Lawrence's sexual
> encounters end, in a struggle for power, between phallic
> cruelty and action, and power by submission, the repro-
> ductive passivity of the receptive female.

And so on. I wrote this because I know how to do it. I have had a good many articles on these lines published in academic magazines that approve of this stuff. I don't think it adds any meaning, pleasure, or relevance that the text itself will not convey to the average interested reader, who will soak up the connections, the dynamism and the atmosphere without being able to write like this, as I was trained to do.

D. H. Lawrence is very good for this kind of reading and is therefore one of the writers popular among academics, though to me that's not the most interesting thing about his writing. There are other "great" writers who do not have wide audiences but are popular with English professors because they are good for reading in a professional way. Henry James is one good example. James Joyce is another. Charles Dickens, who was immensely popular with millions of lay, that is, nonprofessional, readers, had to wait a hundred years to achieve any status with the academics, who had decided that since he was very popular and anyone could read him, he could not have been a serious writer. He seemed to the PhD factories to be too self-evident. There is some validity to the academic fear that if readers don't need professional help in deciphering an author, professors will be out of work, or at least out of the kind of work they are trained to do at present. There are changes coming, but very slowly, and against enormous resistance. I believe teachers have always wanted to share their joy in literature with students. Their love of reading must have been what took them into English in the first place. We can't afford to wait much longer. Now is the time to teach literature as a life resource, before English goes the way of Latin and Greek, and we are left with only commercialese.

This elitist attitude, which we inherited from those great colonizers the Victorians, is regarded as inevitable. In fact, it's merely a fashion and a style. What is regarded as great literature is what the authorities have decided will last. Even saying this here and now in print will be treated as blasphemy by those who are incapable of seeing they have made the choices in these matters rather than seeing that there is something inherently compelling or demanding or cosmic in the study-object itself, in the book, in the text.

Look at other writers who because of their popularity have not made it into the academic basket of good books—for instance, Mazo de la Roche. I taught a Mazo de la Roche novel to graduate students once. As I was carrying a copy under my arm along the corridor toward the class, a colleague asked condescendingly, "What have you got there?" When I replied, "A novel by Mazo de la Roche," he said, "You're not teaching that, are you? Nobody teaches Mazo de la Roche." And that was the end of that conversation. He was joking, and not joking. The disapproval was only just short of official. The fact that Mazo de la Roche was a best-selling writer, one of the most popular writers in the world at the peak of her career, was almost a sure guarantee that she would not be acceptable to the academic value makers. In my opinion, Mazo de la Roche is a wonderful writer who gives extraordinarily colourful pictures of early Ontario and some of its settlers. She has created a kind of saga for this part of the world in the same way Willa Cather, William Faulkner, Ellen Glasgow and John Steinbeck have done for areas of the United States. I think Mazo de la Roche is certainly every bit as accomplished and interesting a writer as John Steinbeck, even though she didn't win a Nobel Prize. But these are matters of taste.

Take the case of *Anne of Green Gables*. This is what a Canadian critic says about the failure of poor little *Anne* to make it into the approved lists of professors' choices:

> Surely Montgomery's accomplishment ought to earn her a secure place in any study of the development of English-Canadian letters. Yet it remains a fact that most critics outside the children's literature fraternity have felt uncomfortable when dealing with her work. The plain truth is that Montgomery's book has committed what comes close to being the unpardonable literary sin—*Anne of Green Gables* has attained a vulgar commercial success without first securing academic approval as "serious" art.[2]

Indeed, the whole field of Canadian literature was until recently an illustration of the point he makes and I am making.

When I came to Canada in 1960, Canadian literature was virtually not studied at all in Canadian universities. It was considered not up to snuff, second-rate, provincial, not accomplished—even though impressive writing had been going on here for a hundred years—and my colleagues said so with loud conviction. Colonial mentality seeped through everything, and English departments studied English literature, with some reluctant condescension to American. This was only one step removed from my own undergraduate years in England, where American literature was not studied at all, and Canadian literature or any other upstart writing from the "colonies" was unknown. Among my first experiences of Canadian literature were the animal stories of Charles G. D. Roberts, and I wrote about them. These animal stories, which in their own day had attained immense popularity sufficient to make Roberts famous around the English-speaking world, were virtually unknown and out of print in Canada. This wonderful, detailed, naturalistic writing about the wilderness, Canadian wildlife and Canadian consciousness, this brilliant exploration, was almost totally ignored.[3]

The point is that professors in Canada, who had been trained for the most part in Britain or the U.S. (or at the University of Toronto, which for a long time aimed to be more English than the English), were trained to see greatness in the texts they were forced to read. Naturally they could not see greatness in literature not available to them. Now students read Canadian literature and see greatness there because it is offered to them and comes with the approved label. We could certainly do the same thing for a whole group of writers of contemporary popular social fiction, like Judy Blume, James Carroll, Stephen King, Judith Guest and so on and so on, if we studied novels that concerned themselves with popular contemporary issues. If "experts" labelled these great and taught them in schools and universities, everyone else would say they were great too. The grounds for making such a judgement would have to be different from the ones that apply now. Perhaps the route to Henry James lies through Judy Blume. If academics don't see this soon, we may be left with neither.

The message is, I hope, clear: You don't need the professors' approval of what you read to justify reading. Reading fiction is good for you, and important and necessary to you. Go ahead and do it. It is not a fringe activity or "merely" entertaining; it is profoundly useful as part of normal development in a civilized, literate community. To test this, just imagine what it would be like to live without being able to read. Some teachers today make judgements about the appropriateness of certain types of books for their pupils without regard to what those children need at a particular time. This kind of judgement is usually based on some vague and abstract morality to which the teacher subscribes. For instance, I know of an actual case—having talked to the mother involved—of a child who wanted to read a Judy Blume book about divorce because her parents had recently been divorced. She tried to get it from the school library, but was told it was not good for her, she was too young to read some of the stuff in it—presumably basic facts about menstruation or developing sexuality or other such matters, matters of immediate concern to an eleven-year-old girl but repugnant to the teacher. What we have here is a teacher with the gall to tell a girl she should not get the information she needs from a well-written work of fiction. The mother, thank the Lord, had the sense to express her indignation, and promptly went out and bought the book. I think her action was the preferable route to take anyway—it gave Judy Blume another royalty, and it approved of the child's good sense by adding the book to her own personal library. We have to fight the new so-called moral Philistinism, just as we have to fight the narrow-minded elitism of academic power. What I'm saying is that in this climate don't be surprised when some immensely useful book by someone like Margaret Atwood, Margaret Laurence, Mordecai Richler, Ernest Hemingway, J. D. Salinger (*The Catcher in the Rye*), or Hugh MacLennan (*Barometer Rising*) is banned, or there are screams for its banning or its burning or its withdrawal or whatever from time to time. What is more horrifying is to find teachers or school boards not only yielding to this kind of totalitarian intimidation, this pedagogic ignorance peddling, but actually proposing it, as in the case I've just reported. There is no reason for you to accept this situation for yourself or your children. You have the right to read, the need to read. Read on.

1   D. H. Lawrence, *Three Novellas: The Fox, The Ladybird, The Captain's Doll* (Harmondsworth: Penguin, 1960), pp. 92-93.

2   T. D. MacLulich, "*Anne of Green Gables* and the Regional Idyll," *Dalhousie Review* 63: 3 (Autumn, 1983), 489.

3   My attention was captured by a brave, thin little volume of his stories published by McClelland & Stewart and edited by F. L. Lucas, who led the way in restoring Roberts to his rightful place as one of the major writers in the history of Canadian literature.

CHAPTER THREE

How to Read for Your Life

If you read a story that really involves you, your body will tell you that you are living through the experience. You will recognize feelings that have physical signs—increased heart rate, sweaty palms, or calm, relaxed breathing and so on, depending on your mood. These affects are the same as you would feel in similar real-life experiences—fear, anger, interest, joy, shame, or sadness. Amazingly, you can actually "live" experience without moving anything but your eyes across a page. Imagine an ideal reading situation. You pick your favourite chair or your bed, a place that's familiar and comfortable. The book you have chosen is a gripping one for you. You have been wanting to get back to it all day. How strange that is, that the most mentally real experience may be the least action-based, least time-oriented part of your schedule. Sometimes, when we are well into a book that really engages us, our own world seems to be less real than the world of our novel, and we stop reading to go to work or dinner very reluctantly. This is because our reading has engaged our *real* feelings, safely. It's as though we had another life, another magical place we could go to as soon as we had time. As a matter of fact, there are many stories that gain appeal from describing just such magic places and how to get there, stories that describe states of imagination as though they were geographical. C. S. Lewis's *The Lion, The Witch, and The Wardrobe*, Ursula K. Le Gum's *The Beginning Place*, Mary Norton's *Bedknob and Broomstick* and all such fantasy trips describe the power of the imagination to alter time and place by story.

Because reading is like this, fiction has often been called a magic carpet, an escape, a mental journey. In later chapters I will look at why someone chooses a particular novel, why it seems so real and gripping for one person when it might not be so for someone else, and how you can get the maximum personal benefit from reading experiences.

A novel, *The Neverending Story* by Michael Ende, gives the best account of the reading process (metastory) I have come across. The hero is a boy who loves to read, and here is a wonderful description of what the passion for reading feels like to Bastian. You will recognize it, if you are one of the lucky ones.

Bastian Balthazar Bux's passion was books.

If you have never spent whole afternoons with burning ears and rumpled hair, forgetting the world around you over a book, forgetting cold and hunger—

If you have never read secretly under the bedclothes with a flashlight, because your father or mother or some other well-meaning person has switched off the lamp on the plausible ground that it was time to sleep because you had to get up so early—

If you have never wept bitter tears because a wonderful story has come to an end and you must take your leave of the characters with whom you have shared so many adventures, whom you have loved and admired, for whom you have hoped and feared, and without whose company life seems empty and meaningless—

If such things have not been part of your own experience, you probably won't understand what Bastian did next.

> Staring at the title of the book, he turned hot and cold, cold and hot. Here was just what he had dreamed of, what he had longed for ever since the passion for books had taken hold of him: A story that never ended! The book of books! [1]

The story that never ends is the story of life. We story our worlds, our selves, our friends and family. When we settle down to read a novel, we agree to put on the mind of the creator, to try on for size another world view, another way of looking at things. Sometimes we like this and make it part of our own. Sometimes we reject it and are glad it's not our story. Whatever our reaction, this borrowing of other minds gives us the excitement of being able to extend our own experience and learn without limit.

STORY AND PSYCHOTHERAPY: HELPING YOURSELF

It is well known that imagery is a powerful force in the lives of human beings.[2] People have images, more or less, waking or sleeping, on a fairly continuous basis. Imaging is widely used as a helping device in psychotherapy, and its effectiveness can be attributed to two main things: it helps the patient become aware of how he thinks and sees his world and his relation to it, and it gives him the power to change this thinking. Yet fiction, the richest and most complex source of imagery, of models of human experience, remains largely unexplored as a healing power in affective problems and disorders, in depression, life crises, family dysfunction and so on. If you like to read, you can use your reading as a resource for coping by increasing your awareness, your consciousness of the relevance of what you are reading to yourself.

What is an ideal reading situation like for you? Is it a struggle for you to read? Do other family members resent your reading? The act of reading is essentially private, but the consequence of reading is a shared experience, first with the writer, often with some other reader of the same book. Where one spouse resents any separateness or independence in the other, he may very well resent her reading, or discount its importance. This kind of attitude produces furtive or guilty reading, or rations the activity, or spoils it in other ways. The best solution here is assertiveness or explanation. Figure out how reading matters to you personally. You may use Questionnaire 1 at the back of this book to help you to decide what you want to read. Think of some of your favourite books and make a list of what appealed to you most in them and what they offered you. Estimate the contribution of fiction reading to your life, what it adds or what your life would be like without it. Then, if you need to, insist on some talking time, and explain to spouse, children, parents, whoever needs to be educated about you, what you have discovered about reading's importance to you. You may need to specify a daily time for your reading; you may need to contract for a private period for reading when other noise or demands are stilled to respect your reading. Such arrangements are part of good, functioning family life. The benefits you receive from your reading will pay back your family in other, indirect, ways. Share pieces of your reading with your family. Reading aloud something you have enjoyed is a powerful means of sharing and creating family intimacy, as well as an important way to model reading for others. You may want to keep a reading journal. If reading is an important part of your life, then what happens to you when you read is worth recording, and you will learn a lot about yourself from keeping track of your responses.

Imagine that there are no distractions and settle yourself to read, to go inside yourself to your imagination. You are sitting in a small, friendly pool of light. The light is important; if you care about reading, a good adjustable reading lamp is something you will want to indulge in. A good lamp is one you can raise and lower and swivel-direct easily; its look pleases you, and you value it. The pool of light it casts on your hands and book increases the sense of privacy. You have created your own world. Outside you and your circle of light the room is dim and distant. You choose a physical position that creates the least distraction for your body, because you don't want discomfort or interference with the inward journey you are now beginning. You will also want a seating situation where you can frequently change body position—*the* problem with reading in school or airports is the fact that comfortable seating, with appropriate back and head support, is impossible to find.

For Westerners this reading process may be akin to meditation, a cognitive meditation. In typical Western fashion it is much more active, more result-oriented than the Oriental kind of search for mind—stillness. Even so, when you activate the story, the word system, you do still the chatter and confusion of your own mind's busyness and disorder. The most famous form of meditation is called Dhyana, and here is what one famous practitioner says about it:

What is dhyana, then? Dhyana literally means, in Sanskrit, pacification, equilibration, or tranquilization, but as religious discipline it is rather self-examination or introspection. It is not necessarily to cogitate on the deep subjects of metaphysics, nor is it to contemplate on the virtues of a deity, or on the transitoriness of mundane life. To define its import in Buddhism, roughly and practically, *it is the habit of withdrawing occasionally from the turbulence of worldliness and of devoting some time to a quiet inspection of one's own consciousness.* When this habit is thoroughly established, a man can keep serenity of mind and cheerfulness of disposition even in the midst of his whirlwind-like course of daily life.

> Buddhists through dhyana endeavor to reach the bottom of things and there to grasp with their own hands the very life of the universe, which makes the sun rise in the morning, makes the bird cheerfully sing in the balmy spring breeze, and also makes the biped called man hunger for love, righteousness, liberty, truth, and goodness. In dhyana, therefore, there is nothing abstract, nothing dry as a bone and cold as a corpse, but all animation, all activity, and eternal revelation.[3] [my italics]

This sounds to me like having a good read. Reading stories is an effective method of "withdrawing from the turbulence of worldliness" and getting at the reality of "one's own consciousness," though we don't usually think of it like that.

When we practice reading as an art and a discipline we are not wasting time and being frivolous and irresponsible. On the contrary, reading fiction that involves us is a responsible and important way to grow mentally and spiritually. When we still the outside world and turn to our inner minds we are exercising our imagination, and getting in touch with our feelings, increasing our information, coping with the world through simulated situations. We come back from reading refreshed, restored, recharged. We are *more* in touch with the world, not less, because we left its unorganized, mad randomness and entered a world of managed, involved, carefully coded information that we were able to decode and understand.

It is important at this stage of our discussion to say something about the power of fiction as compared to nonfiction, though I say more about this later on. It is precisely the "lived-through" quality of fiction that gives it the power to alter the way we feel and think about our world and our relation to it. Nonfiction gives us information and instruction, but usually without emotion, without evoking feeling. It may change our *cognition* but it does not produce *affect*. Fiction's combination of *affect* plus *cognition* is what makes the material more fully retained, more related to the rest of our experience (which has also been *affective*), and helps us to reorganize and rethink our ways of seeing and thinking about things. *The understanding we get from reading fiction is earned by psychic, mental, imaginative experience.* We live through what we need even as we sit still in our chair. My experience with clients in therapy shows that readers take what is personally applicable from what they read—what they select is what they most relate to and remember, and this is another advantage of fiction as a rich resource. Because fiction uses image, metaphor, character, situation and temporal sequence, there is a layered, complex network of meaning and information. The reader is able to select and reorganize this to make it relevant, even to make it understandable, to her own experience, which is stored in the form of story in her mind. Readers *make meaning* in what they read. Any class of students, asked to respond to what they see, value, notice, like, or remember in the same piece of fiction, comes up with a variety of answers.

Read the following excerpt without judging or thinking about it, just be there and let it happen, noting only your body reactions as you are aware of them. Joe is the owner of a huge dog called Cujo. Joe's wife, Charity, and his son are away on a trip to relatives, and Joe has planned a trip to the big city with his friend Gary.

Joe hurried down to the shape, his heart hammering in his ears. He knelt by it, and a sound like a squeak escaped his throat. Suddenly the air in the hall seemed too hot and close. It seemed to be strangling him. He turned away from

Gary, one hand cupped over his mouth. Someone had murdered Gary. Someone had—

He forced himself to look back. Gary lay in a pool of his own blood. His eyes glared sightlessly up at the hallway ceiling. His throat had been opened. Not just opened, dear God, it looked as if it had been *chewed* open.

This time there was no struggle with his gorge. This time he simply let everything come up in a series of hopeless choking sounds. Crazily, the back of his mind had turned to Charity with childish resentment. Charity had gotten *her* trip, but he wasn't going to get his. He wasn't going to get his because some crazy bastard had done a Jack the Ripper act on poor old Gary Pervier and—

—and he had to call the police. Never mind all the rest of it. Never mind the way the ole Pervert's eyes were glaring up at the ceiling in the shadows, the way the sheared-copper smell of his blood mingled with the sickish-sweet aroma of the honeysuckle.

He got to his feet and staggered down toward the kitchen. He was moaning deep in his throat but was hardly aware of it. The phone was on the wall in the kitchen. He had to call the State Police, Sheriff Bannerman, someone—

He stopped in the doorway. His eyes widened until they actually seemed to be bulging from his head. There was a pile of dog droppings in the doorway to the kitchen... and he knew from the size of the pile whose dog had been here.

"Cujo," he whispered. "Oh my God, Cujo's gone rabid!"[4]

I have read the whole of Stephen King's *Cujo* (which I found compelling and scary), so when I read this part I can supply all the other bits I have stored in my mind to frame this passage. Perhaps you won't find this so gripping if you don't know the whole story. But did you feel anything? Do you feel surprise? Do you feel interest, revulsion, fear, anxiety, resentment, curiosity, admiration? Can you picture anything?

The sensations you can experience in reading a passage like this are very subtle, very fleeting. If you are not paying attention to them they will be over and gone before you know it. Do you feel any repulsion or distaste at the description of the man's vomiting? Do you catch yourself trying *not* to visualize the torn throat of the dead man? Do you feel any fear, any pulse of anxiety at any point in the reading? Where in your body do you feel it? How do you know what the feeling means? If there is any suspense here for you, what is the suspense, what are you waiting for? Do you want to read more? What are the things you fear in your own life? Were you ever scared by a dog? A dog is "man's best friend," so there is something especially awful about one going mad and becoming your worst enemy. How do you feel about trust and stability? Are you ever afraid of finding something horrible, especially at home?

All these issues and many others are raised by King's novel, which explores the trust issue in marital fidelity, in childhood fears, in the role of coincidence and chance in human affairs. Take a pencil and paper and jot down some answers to these questions. Answering will help you focus on your feelings and your involvement. You will learn more about your own fears and your own ways of reading.

Stephen King has been enormously successful as a writer by understanding that the ordinary and familiar are terrifying, the most terrifying, when they turn monstrous and harmful. The things we trust most can hurt us most—which is why we are so cautious about trust. This is the gamble, the risk-taking of a courageous life. The idea of our friendly, cuddly pet, or our house, or our car, or a friend, spouse, or child suddenly becoming evil and dangerous is a source of fear we normally repress. Keeping such anxiety hidden—which is normal but not necessarily helpful—does not mean it is not there. Stephen King exploits this and shows us our fear. He is a master at creating a mood, a place, an event about to happen. He does not describe so much as put us there, inside the skin of the frightened person. Maybe our skin goes goose-pimply, our hair moves or feels as though it does (and as it probably did on our ancestors millions of years ago), our hands go sweaty, or we just become generally uncomfortable. Perhaps we feel the faint edge of nausea or at least disgust. We try to avoid seeing and smelling the dog droppings, but to do this we have to see them. We can use this discovery, as we read, to become stronger, more aware and more in control of our lives. This is typical of how fiction can work, and does work if we let it, to inform our lives.

There is considerable value in horror fiction, which has had a big twentieth-century following and fashion. At those times in history when "niceness" and appearances, respectability and purity, seem dominant, when law and order and control are the watchwords of the majority, along comes fiction to show us that we have a dark underside, an irrational and monstrous side. We live in the New Age of reason, science and artificial light. The hype is that there will be a cure for everything. Wealth, growth and progress are our gods, and technology is our path to happiness. The primal fears of darkness, savagery and the unknown are being swept away with the rain forests. Not so, says the horror writer. Look inside yourself, look at how little it takes to scare you, look at your own anger, greed, frustration and sadism, and having looked, respect the power and beware.

I once had a student who was supposed to be doing a PhD in literature. I sent him away to read William Faulkner's *Sanctuary*, which contains a fairly gruesome event involving a sexual assault on the heroine by a psychotic gangster wielding a corn cob. My student returned and I asked him what he thought of the book. "I didn't read it," he said. "Too busy, or did you have the flu?" I naively inquired. "I couldn't read it—I can't read stuff like that." This seemed to me about as professional as an ambulance driver being unable to stand the sight of blood. For most readers, who are not professional, there is an infinite freedom of choice about what to read, but what repels you can be as informative, though not as pleasurable, as what attracts you.

The Power to Reframe

"Reframing" is a common term in counselling and psychiatry for describing what happens when someone learns to think about some person, situation, or problem differently. A typical example from my own clinical experience will illustrate. A mother was convinced that her sixteen-year-old adopted daughter disliked her and had no respect for her authority. For instance, when the mother, driving with the daughter, had a little accident, and the man in the other car came around and started yelling at the mother, the daughter fired back at the man a torrent of verbal abuse and foul language. The mother was shocked and reported to me that she would like her daughter to be more controlled and polite. My version of this, to her, was that the daughter, far from being disrespectful of the mother, was taking care of her; since the daughter knew her mother was not assertive and was likely to be intimidated, she had to fight on her mother's behalf and model verbal karate for her. I was helping the woman to engage in reframing, and when she could begin to see her daughter's behaviour as protective, caring and not hostile, their relationship could change. The daughter was doing the parenting. I invited the mother to take care of herself and in the process free the daughter to grow up and attend to her own needs.

I have found nothing more effective for reframing, reordering, reorganizing perception than fiction, or perhaps poetry. Indeed, if our own teachers had discussed literature in terms of its function for the reader, we would long ago have seen that this is essentially a major charm and power of story—to help us see things, things related to us, differently.

How can literature be so powerful in changing our moods, our feelings, our thinking? Because, let's face it, this is what it does. When we read a story it can actually direct our brain processes so that the same signals are sent to our nervous system as would occur in the same situation in a life experience. This is how erotic writing works for some people. This is how suspense works. Fantasy is the power to create a felt experience-situation from within. True, the particular events, places, persons, experiences that produce these results will vary from reader to reader. We all possess unique happenings that we have lived through and remembered. But we can all be reached, moved, by *some* story. We have the capacity to feel the fear, lust, laughter, anger programmed into our genes as we developed in the womb and thereafter. The frightening, funny, or desire-making stimuli, the events or things outside of us, are what give us memories, psychic scars, *experiences*. It is our feelings-in-response-to-experiences that teach us how to be scared or angry, how to avoid danger and how to seek pleasure or solve problems.

Each person is a unique combination of her own neurology and her own experiences. Even if people have had similar experiences, as in the case of twins raised together, they will have undergone or realized, *known* these experiences somewhat differently, because they have different equipment for processing what their senses encountered, and because no two sets of experience are identical. Imagine a company trying to make identical computers, but with no luck: no matter how hard they try, every computer that comes off the assembly line finishes up slightly different. Each one looks slightly different, alters every program to fit itself and produces slightly different output unique to itself. This would be bad, because we the users want computers to produce identical results so that we can transfer programs and results identically; *we the users want the control.*

On the other hand, individuality is good for humans, because being different is what makes us so interesting to each other and enables us to learn from each other in a growth system. Difference and control always work against each other. Totalitarian governments abhor differences and try to minimize variety in their populations, partly by controlling what people read. So do certain churches. So do all organizations that value control more than creativity. But for survival, pleasure and creativity, variety and difference are much to be preferred. We know that crossbreeding makes bigger and stronger cattle—hybrid vigour, it is called. But we don't want to be so different that we can't communicate or interact. We are also like each other enough to be able to share experiences. *We do this by using the results of one experience to understand another experience.* These results are recorded in our brains. Writers count on this sharing power in the reader. They know what is likely to produce a feeling, and they know readers want to have these feelings. People read to stimulate thought and feeling in order to stay alive. Just as most people don't want to die and so try to avoid fatal situations, so they don't want to die emotionally, imaginatively. Part of the drive to live is the quest for new information, new experience. And we all want to pass on our experience, tell our stories and so add to the general store of life knowledge. Those who are especially talented in language and driven to this passing on of experience become writers.

IDENTIFICATION

This is the first of many reading responses we will be considering.

Here is a passage from Sue Kaufman's *Diary of a Mad Housewife*. Tina is writing in a diary about the routines, chores and expectations that can drive you crazy; the writing it down is her way of staying sane. Later we shall see how this process of telling a story can indeed help to make sense of life. Jonathan is Tina's husband.

> IT CAME. The cold weather. Three days after the last entry in here, too soon, too abruptly, from Indian Summer to bitter cold. Luckily I'd gotten Jonathan's things out of storage in the nick of time, but on Monday, the second day of the changed weather, he took one look at the girls setting off for school in thin cotton dresses covered with sweaters and raincoats for warmth, and Thundered, "Why the hell didn't you get their warm stuff up from the basement yesterday afternoon?" Why indeed: "yesterday" had been a Sunday, and though I could easily have gone down there while he was out with the girls, I'd been too damned frightened to go alone. Even on weekdays our basement is a spooky place with endless dark crannies—storerooms, a laundry room with defunct machines, and a furnace room that looks like a set for *The Hairy Ape*. No one's ever around, not even the super or a handyman. And ever since that gory murder this summer, where some poor Bronx woman was raped and stabbed in the basement of her building, and stuffed in the cold furnace with her feet dangling out ("The badly decomposed nude body was discovered by Mr. Otto Grunzenhauser, the superintendent, who told this reporter ..."), wild horses couldn't drag me down to our basement alone.
>
> This being something I couldn't exactly tell Jonathan, I said as authoritatively as I could, "I'm going to bring up

all their warm clothes today. Since there's too much to carry, I had it *scheduled* for today, when Lottie could help me. And since everything else is scheduled to get done this week and next, I'll thank you to drop that critical tone and leave me alone, Jonathan."

Once committed, I was as good as my word. Two weeks have passed since I last wrote in here. The drapes have been hung, the rugs relaid, the floors waxed, the walls washed down, the closets cleaned and filled with everybody's winter clothes. And I managed all sorts of extras besides. I attended a meeting at the Bartlett School to help plan the annual Christmas Fair. I took the girls shopping for winter coats. Because there was a case of hepatitis at their school, I took the girls to Doctor Miller for shots of gamma globulin, and to make up for that, took them and two friends to lunch and the movies the next day, a Saturday. I wrote a letter to my parents, enclosing snaps of me and the girls taken in one of those machines at Woolworth's. I even went to the dentist, but that didn't go off as smoothly as everything else. I made the mistake of taking two Equanils (leaving me two), and when he injected the Novocain it occurred to me that Equanil and Novocain might be incompatible, that the combination might produce a lethal toxicity that would stop my heart. Luckily that didn't happen, but I sat there with a rubberized cheek while he pried off the old inlay and began to drill, entertaining a new possibility: the supersonic drill would hit the nerve, I'd scream and jump and the drill would rip my whole mouth apart. I finally left with a temporary filling and an appointment for the following week (yesterday), wrung out, but damned proud of myself—like everything else, I was getting it *done*. 5

Think about yourself. Try to imagine your typical day. A good robot could do a lot of what you do. By the time you get to work or the kids have left for school, you might have done several things, most of them unthinkingly. If you could get to read a newspaper, let alone a novel, you might start to get your mind in gear, be aware that you are conscious. Most of us do not have this privilege. If you think about all you can do without being aware that *you are conscious*, you can just imagine all the mindpower you have that you don't use. Many readers will recognize from this last quotation the feeling of frantic, dutiful activity that seems to go on and on and be inescapable, that seems to ignore the inner life and leave untapped some really important part of the self. If you recognize yourself in a book, if this portrait of a housewife, for instance, seems like you in some respect, the process is called *identification*. You are putting yourself in that part in the book, acting the role because it feels right, it fits. "Wow," you say, "right on, that's exactly how it is, boy, do I know that scene!" Sometimes reacting against what you read can be valuable in showing you who you are and how you feel. For now, however, I want to concentrate on "you" being in the novel. I have been saying that writers are just like you. They are human, they have human experiences and human emotions. What novelists do is to order and organize these experiences and thoughts so that they can get control over them. They do this by, and while, writing them into a story, a novel. Then other people can join the experience of their reading the novel to the experience of their lives. Why does it feel good when this happens? Well, for one thing, *it makes you feel less alone and more "normal."* When you see that someone else can have known about how you feel, you are being recognized, understood and known.

ABREACTION

A few years ago I ran a self-help group for children of separated or divorced parents. All of these children, locked into their pain, anger and insecurity, and not feeling free or able to talk to others at home or school about how they felt, came to the group feeling isolated, victimized and a bit freakish. Just at the time when they needed to talk and be heard, to be connected, they met silence—people in their home and school worlds were embarrassed to talk to them about the divorce or afraid of upsetting them. The group itself helped to dispel the feeling of unreality and isolation by providing a fellowship of sufferers to "normalize" their situation. They were all in the same boat, even though it felt pretty leaky and unstable. I asked them all to read Judy Blume's *It's Not the End of the World*, and this helped a lot too. What this skillful writer does is to show that quite ordinary and normal children may have to go through an experience such as divorce. She portrays how it feels, and how it is possible to survive the changes. If she, the writer, could write a story about it, then maybe it's just part of life today, and we're okay. So the kids in my group got some relief from this discovery, from being *recognized by the book!* Someone had told their story. But I also gave them another book, *The Pinballs* by Betsy Byars, about foster children, and in this case they reacted against, said it wasn't them and those kids were worse off than they, the readers. This response is called abreaction. They felt less hopeless and confused by comparing themselves favourably to those they read about.

Abreaction may be felt in response to a character or a place or a situation. If the reader feels negatively towards a character, the result can be a discovery of the kinds of people he does not like and the kinds of people he wants to know. I am extremely attracted to a character named Joe in Bobbie Ann Mason's story "Graveyard Day." In discussing this story with students, I came to realize how many repulsive male figures there are in fiction. Joe is kind, patient, fun and generous. Through attraction and abreaction the reader can make comparisons that help move him towards his own character formation. He can be encouraged to strive for those behaviours that help improve relationships. The same mental process applies to place, work and so on. The kind of place we read about that repels us can help us to plan for an environment that we want to create and occupy. May Sarton's *As We Are Now*, with its grim and ugly portrait of a nursing home, led a group to discuss the arrangements and accommodation they wanted in old age. Some participants were led to make specific plans for their future.

FEEDBACK

Recognizing some part of yourself on your situation in fiction is called "identification." Dissociating yourself from what you read about other people is "abreaction." Both are examples of feedback. Sometimes you can be brought to an emotional relief that Aristotle, thousands of years ago, called "catharsis." By recognizing and experiencing yourself "outside yourself," you can sometimes get relief, clarity, perspective—a kind of shedding of confusion through intense feeling. This is in part a relief at recognizing that you are not alone.

We all know how we feel safety in numbers, how relieved we are not to be alone in dangerous situations. Solitary confinement is one of the most cruel punishments known to humankind. Probably some basic herding or tribal instinct is built into our genes from millions of years ago. We prefer not to hunt alone. But more than that, for human beings it is necessary *to communicate in order to find out what we think.* We need *feedback* to know if we are being heard. Novels do this in a very special way, by allowing us to try on stories, like clothes, to see if they are "us," if they "feel right." This is a feedback experience that we can then incorporate into our own perception.

I have known several clients who got pregnant at fifteen or sixteen or even earlier, who married the fathers of their children out of obligation, shame, or pressure, and who spent the next ten years resenting the guys who got them pregnant and feeling trapped in a web of confusion. And the husbands were angry also. The blame is an endless and often unspoken cycle—poor stuff for making happy marriages. Novels tell us about situations like this, novels like Linda Lauren's *Honesty*, in which Lizzie, the heroine, gets married, moves into a house, has a baby and two miscarriages, puts on all the grown-up behaviour society has modelled for her, and then at twenty-one suddenly discovers in a panic that she's in the wrong place. Literature speaks for us, says back to us truths too painful for us to utter in our own words. It shows us that getting into such traps is human and forgivable and can be remedied. Making mistakes is part of living—we need them, we learn from them. It's a profound relief to discover we are like other people. When we find this out we can accept ourselves, stop blaming and get on with some new, realistic life response.

MAPPING

So we see that identification and recognition are profoundly important parts of learning to accept ourselves, of coming to terms with the reality of life situations, and that reading can be a basic aid to this growing-up process. Beyond this process of feeling part of a larger world of similar fellow sufferers, there is a very important cognitive result of the process of identification in reading. I like to call this the "Bicycle Kit Effect." Imagine it's Christmas morning. Let's say you are fifteen. You have been given a bicycle in kit form. You open the box, start pulling out the parts. You are excited and nervous as you see the familiar shiny painted sections emerge, the chrome handle-bars, the wrapped black chain, the 12-speed sprockets and gears and the glossy red frame. Great, just great! But as all the parts become spread around you on the floor, the frustration begins. There are cables and plastic packages full of screws and bolts and clamps. Your heart begins to sink. You know what a bike looks like, but how can all these pieces fit together in the right order, how can you make sense of it? You look in the box and now you have everything out and excitement and anticipation begin to turn into anger and despair. Dad comes in to see how you're doing and sees the disappointment on your face. "What's up?" he asks. You tell him you are confused, lost in your lake of parts like a piece of driftwood. "There must be instructions," he says. He takes the box and opens up the whole thing, and there, stuck under the bottom flaps, is a set of instruction sheets. Hope dawns, so you begin to put parts A and B together and to sort out 2-inch bolts from hex screws. Finally, by dinner time, your shiny new bike is standing there gleaming and ready to carry you around, to take you away from home to new adventures and differ-ent places. The instructions are a map to the experience of the bike, which can be seen, touched, even smelled, but which comes togeth-er only through the organizing power of the code, language.

Like the bike only infinitely more complex, personal growth and successful moving on to new developmental stages require sort-ing out, ordering and putting together from separate pieces of expe-rience. We need a map! We live through events and happenings, pleasures and disappointments, that confuse and bewilder us like the streets of a great foreign city, full of sights and sounds, where we drift lost, without charts, or with maps written in a language we can't read. It is very probable that solving jigsaw puzzles or playing card games or board games gives us a special and peculiar satisfac-tion because they are models for organizing results out of confusion, and they take us through the paradigm of gaining control. They introduce *control* into the chaos of chance and randomness by inviting us in to exercise our problem-solving power. Through them we practice operating within the comfort of rules and constraints. I believe that this problem-solving pleasure is what makes detective fiction pleasing to many people, especially people who long for control they don't think they have or who want to think of themselves as masterminds.

It is well known that children are extremely uncomfortable trying to live in families without rules. Some fundamentalist religious sects and cults are attractive to people who feel confused, insecure, or unable to put the pieces together. The cult provides a rigid framework and frees its members from continuous thought, sifting, judging and decision making. The price is a heavy one, however, or we would all join. The trade-off is that the individual member of a group that accepts obedience in exchange for the stress of personal decision making, sacrifices individuality and freedom of thought and growth—the one great decision eliminates hundreds of other decisions. The individual surrenders his personal will, and trust in himself is yielded for trust in the group. Uniforms have always signalled this sacrifice of individual identity. But under the uniforms, human beings are unique instances of general principles. Each person must fulfill certain developmental goals within limits, safety limits, that provide the stable structure. Each individual also lives in a context of family, culture, environment, economy and so on. The maximum allowable freedom and growth are never without limits. Too many rules, on the one hand, are like a suit of armour that in trying to protect restricts growth and movement. Too few constraints and guidelines, on the other hand, cause us to have to work too hard, to flounder and to drift. I suspect that children who run away from home and join cults come from families that are either chaotic or too rigidly controlled to foster independence.

Here again fiction comes in. Stories can be enormously helpful to our sorting out of experience. So far, the bicycle kit manual is a good model. Fiction, however, goes much, much further in simulating and coding our lives. All how-to books simplify; sometimes they are helpful. But where how-to books give instruction, novels "story" behaviour by evoking emotion in the reader as well as providing information. This is very effective since we memorize best through the emotional responses associated with people and events. Most of us live in stories we spend a lifetime trying to organize. Our bicycle manual shows us step-by-step how to assemble the bicycle. But when we use it we still finish up with only a bike. The bicycle was designed by somebody who was able to write the manual because he knew every piece of the bike. Your life experience is part of a much more complex system, and only you can figure it out. Novels help you to do this because they are the figuring out of other life experiences by other people who are human like you. Only a novel that simulates experience, with its emotional content, can parallel the process of your own experience, *because your own experience is too complex to be reduced to a set of how-to descriptions.*

ANALOGY

When a system is so complicated that it is not explicable, graspable by a series of step-by-step explanations, we come to know it, feel comfortable with it, by *analogue*. Novels are analogues of life experiences. We relate these back to our own life experiences to help us to sort out what happened, how we work in our systems and how to deal with the future. The power of story to help us in this way lies in our ability to go through the story experience *without getting lost in it.* Since we can live life by analogy we can *at the same time* stay detached in our real-life selves, stay distanced even while entering the novel, and can then bring it back and apply it to our own lives. When we read a story, we lead a borrowed life, one we need to help us to possess our own.

Imagine that our family system had broken down and we were having problems we just couldn't figure out. We knew that nearby was a town where the families all worked well and were happy and harmonious. So we left our spouses and children, whom we loved very much, and went to live there for a while. Now the way these other people live is too hard to describe—you have to live there for a while. Without getting wholly involved or being bigamous or buying another house there, we experienced what it was like, and then we came back to our everyday life, bringing with us the experience. The similarities and differences we saw while away now help us to see more clearly how we are living at home. The distance has helped us to see more clearly now that we're back because while we were away we lived another experience without getting lost in it. If we had got lost in it things would get worse at home, of course. If people read novels and become *wholly* involved in them, so that they can't tell their ordinary life experience and memories from their fictive experience, they are seriously disturbed and need psychotherapeutic help. Such people are usually called schizophrenic, and they don't get this way from reading. They just bring their confusion to reading as they bring it to other experiences. For most readers, however, the value of reading fiction for personal growth is that the fiction-analogy is an experiential tool for re-seeing and reordering their own confusing experience. Avid novel readers do not do this just once or rarely, of course. They go back and forth continually and forage for psychic or spiritual supplies like squirrels getting ready for the winter. In this way they use fiction as a continuous resource, a supply base for life on the front lines. Movies serve a similar function, but not nearly as usefully or powerfully unless used in conjunction with reading.

GETTING OUTSIDE OF EXPERIENCE

Life experiences are often confusing and make us feel trapped and overwhelmed. We are lost in content, like the boy inundated with bicycle parts and lacking the key to their relations. What we need to do in such cases is to get outside of *content* and into *process*, that level of perception that is like a distancing view that shows us more of the whole picture, the bigger picture. When we learn to manage something well we learn the process of it, and we can learn to manage our lives better than we often do. Fiction has a great power to assist us in seeing process, in seeing order and relation, and when we have done so we can apply it to ourselves. Of course the characters in the fiction are often confused and lost in content. That is how they help us, for they take on our confusion, bear our burdens and leave us to see the larger picture they cannot see, being too close to it.

We are all storymakers. We use story to organize and control. Without the management and order of story, the chaos and confusion of disturbing experience *controls* us by confusing us. Human beings strive for order, control and peace, but we can never be static. We must change, age, learn more, grow and adapt. So we are always in a cycle of creative struggle, changing and striving to manage our changing and to integrate what we learn into our own story. If during our growing up, for instance, we have suffered trauma—grief over a lost parent, or accident, divorce, or disease—we can get locked into the guilt, anger, rejection and so on, that we felt at that time. To escape the feeling of helplessness and confusion that we carry with us we need to organize, package, index our experience, do what we mean when we say "get a handle on it," so that we can carry the baggage of our experience comfortably and not have bits and pieces falling all over the place. This is what we do when we "story" it.

Imagine a movie cartoon of a deep-sea diver getting tangled up by a monstrous super-octopus with 229 tentacles all wrapping around the diver's limbs and mask and neck; then imagine him carefully unwrapping the beast from himself tentacle by tentacle, tying it up in a neat package, putting it under his arm and, all calm and confident, taking it back to the zoo. Very satisfying, don't you feel? That's what it's like when you "story" the confusion of powerful experience and go from being coiled inside to being in control of the tentacles of life.

I once had a soldier for a client who was having real problems coping with his divorce—his wife had left him, saying she was tired of his closed-off, cold, unemotional way of relating to her. Eric had, like his older brother, joined the military at the first opportunity. I wondered why they had both been so keen to join the army. Eric seemed to me to be a gentle, sensitive man, as well as a physically very powerful one. There was no doubt about his control, but his control was over his feelings rather than over his experiences. He was unable to confront his experience. He was armoured against himself. He kept a stiff upper lip all through his sessions, rarely expressed or showed any feeling and condemned himself for needing help. Eventually, when I got him to describe his childhood home in detail, we came to talking about his father's death. Before this Eric had insisted he couldn't remember much of his childhood and had said nothing had happened worth mentioning. Now I learned that Eric had watched his father die instantly of a heart attack while he was helping Eric, then age ten, to build a dog house in the basement. Eric screamed and his brother ran down to help, but Dad died right there. The consequence, to make a long story short, was that Mom withdrew more and more (eventually she remarried), and Eric, aside from tagging after his brother whenever possible and without being welcome, virtually raised himself. His loneliness was extreme, his fear very great and his grief and anger at being suddenly and inexplicably de-parented at ten had never been properly owned or expressed.

I gave this man S. E. Hinton's novel *Tex* to read. Eric had worked so hard to control all his feelings that he had needed the army to help him to do it. The army worked for him like a cult. The cost had been a loss of the ability to relate to people, especially women, because intimacy and sex are a real challenge to remoteness. You really have to work at removing yourself emotionally while in a naked embrace, and obviously you can't do it without your partner noticing. Eric had practically turned himself into a machine. Now *Tex* is not exactly the story of Eric. But it is the story of two brothers, of whom the younger is Tex, who live parentless, as mother is dead and father is away riding the rodeos and not thinking much about the boys. It took a lot to get Eric to cry, but he cried at parts of this book. I was going on a hunch. I wanted Eric to be able to get at his own pain, his "blocks," and I had to go around them, since he'd put them in place for the very purpose of preventing himself or anyone else going through them. What he saw in the story were enough of the *feelings* he recognized, the anger, love, frustration, sibling depend-ence and rivalry, *that he was able to get in touch with his own story.* This made it possible for him and for me to go back to his weakened defenses and see that he had survived those experiences, that he could have the pain and still be a man, and that he would be stronger not weaker by having feelings. He found his own story by *analogy.* He was surprised to find that some writer could be aware of a child's suf-fering like that, a discovery that helped to normalize his experience. He was able to share with me his responses to the book when he was-n't able to talk easily about himself. By coming to grips with his own past feelings, Eric was able to "rewrite" his story so it made sense to him. Getting himself organized like this meant he could go on and grow into new experiences.

Over the past few years I have done a number of interviews with readers to find out some of the benefits they have found in fiction. Here is a small sample of transcripts of what one group of students said during a taped discussion about their reading experience:

Jeanne: I've read a lot ever since I learned to read. My mother reads constantly. She's either reading or sleeping. My father hardly ever reads—only when the weather's too bad to do anything else. So there's always been a conflict in our house—if you got caught by the wrong person reading, you were told you should be out in the sun instead. At different times, reading has been very important, but at other stages, less so. But I think when I was growing up, I learned about what the world might be like, or about what it might be like to be adult, or what I hoped it might be like.

Eileen: [My reading life was] often a form of constructive fantasy— [my reading] led and directed me. That phase passed after a while—I got sick of reading things that were too far removed from what I could anticipate finding. Then I started looking for people just like me.

Jeanne: Escape is getting to a place where you have some power— especially since you feel like you don't have any power in your life as a kid.

Megan: If you learn a lesson from a heroine, or a book, you apply it to your life.

Carol: I've always had this secret ambition to be an actress, so when I was actually reading I'd be acting out the parts. Even today I do it a little bit.

Eileen: I think that's something you judge the quality of fiction by. At least I do—it's how much it brings you into it. If the book caused a "suspension of disbelief," that's a hallmark of something excellent.

Carol: There can also be some very believable things in books—like characters. You can go out on the street and say that someone reminds you of a character in a book.

Jeanne: You do build visual images of characters, even when they aren't described.

Eileen: I think I'm looking for both—sometimes I just want entertainment, and sometimes I want to know how to cope with life on a day-to-day basis. Sometimes fiction is a "comforting" way to find out how to cope. It's doing two things really—telling me what I need to know, but also letting me get away from something that might be too difficult to deal with at a certain time.

Jeanne: I think the process for me is often much more internal—I'm understanding what's going on inside me by reading, not understanding what's going on out there. It gives me a new way to look at my own experiences. The way I use books is more internal.

Carol: I think it's much more of an emotional thing—you're actually feeling something when you read, but you can't explain it in so many words. If I'm reading a book where something emotional or tragic happens, the reaction is physical for me.

Jeanne: Reading is much more active than watching television because you have to create the visual stuff. Some writers make that easier than others do. I feel more in some books than others, but it's a more demanding activity than watching a film or TV—sometimes reading isn't at all relaxing because it asks for too much.

Eileen: If I come home at the end of the day, I opt for television if I'm really tired, but if I'm less tired, then I'll read a book. It's much more rewarding for me to read a book, and much higher in my value system. I would assume that I have a higher level of participation with a book—I put more in and get more out.

This discussion leads to a comparison with television, which is a major, perhaps the most widespread and pervasive, transmitter of stories today. Do we need to read in the television age? I try to answer this question in the next chapter.

1   Michael Ende, *The Neverending Story*, tr. Ralph Manheim (Harmondsworth: Penguin, 1984), p. 10.

2   Donald Meichenbaum, "Why Does Using Imagery in Psychotherapy Lead to Change," in *The Power of Human Imagination: New Methods in Psychotherapy*, ed. Jerome L. Singer and Kenneth S. Pope (New York and London: Plenum Press, 1978).

3   Rev. Soyen Shaku, "the practice of dhyana," in *Anthology of Zen*, ed. William Briggs (New York: Grove Press, 1961), pp. 268, 272.

4   Stephen King, *Cujo* (New York: New American Library, 1981), p.126.

5.   Sue Kaufman, *Diary of a Mad Housewife* (New York: Bantam,1968), pp. 107-8.

CHAPTER FOUR

Reading Against the Tube

I am part of the radio generation, about the same vintage as Woody Allen. Radio is what came between reading and television. Oddly enough, radio, in its golden era, enhanced reading. Radio talk, drama, story reading, newscasts gave listeners more language; it modelled the sound of words, the expression of dramatic reading, the rhythms of the spoken syntax, so that we were helped to hear the sound of what we read to ourselves. Radio was an extension of the story process. In one way, radio did recall an earlier, pre-literate stage of human development, when the oral tradition made most people listeners to a few storytellers. But since only a tiny portion of radio programming was story, we were encouraged to read for ourselves if we wanted more story entertainment. With the advent of pictures, however, we took a giant step backwards towards pre-historic humanity. Language was devalued, pictures took over and sound gave way to images. Since sound is the root of language, the TV generations are much less experienced in language than the radio generation. Not only is language a minor accompaniment to TV images, but the thousands of hours spent in silent viewing are hours stolen from other forms of language practice—reading, conversation, story listening or telling.

Whenever I do workshops or lectures on reading and its benefits, I can be sure that one question will be asked before the session is over. Here is the question in its various forms: What about TV? Have television and film replaced reading? Can't we get the same things from watching TV? The answer is fairly complicated. The short version is "No," but explaining that "No" takes a bit longer. Let's look at some of the differences between watching moving images on TV and reading.

The Real TV

Let's face it, real TV, the actual programming available to us, is a very different kettle of fish from what television might be. Remember, I am not speaking here of the idea of TV—the concept—but the reality. As we shall see, though, even TV as an ideal cannot replace reading. TV as we know it in North America is owned and operated by commercial interests, with very few exceptions, maybe one network in Canada and some local programs in the U.S. All public broadcasting is struggling for survival in North America. The people who want to sell things to TV viewers also control most of the programming. They do this because they want to maximize the size of the audience for their product and control the kind of audience their program/product reaches. The more control the seller has over the consumer, the happier he is.

Now the key to successful production and merchandising is *standardization*. The goal is to *reduce variety* as much as possible. Difference is encouraged only in cosmetics and trim, in packaging, not in fundamental design or function. The idea is to make production costs small per item, while increasing the volume of sale. *The more sameness in the product, the less the risk in selling. The more sameness in consumers the more they buy the same thing.* TV is the seller's dream come true. First, you put one or more sets in every home. It is antisocial, subversive, not to own a TV set. (I believe the single most radical act of civil protest possible today is to get rid of your television set. Millions of American homes now have four or five of them. People can now take them almost anywhere.) Next, you put on programs that appeal to the greatest number of people. Such programs must be easy to watch, not provocative, not offensive, not challenging, not thought-provoking, not uncomfortable. In fact, if you are a seller you want to *reinforce sameness*, not create diversity, thought, or disturbing feelings. *People who think the same, buy the same.* Having devised programs to achieve sameness to the point of automation, sameness built on brief, simple stories, knee-jerk sentiments, truisms and stereotypes, you must interrupt the program frequently with the most colourful and attention-grabbing advertising possible. Here is where the creativity comes in. Serials and episodic programs are particularly effective for creating addicted audiences who can vicariously live the lives offered on TV, lives more glamorous than their own, and situations in which problems are in the hands of others and do not have to be solved or confronted by the viewer.

Most television fare is of this simple, soap opera kind. In the case of the "giveaway" shows, the greed and fantasy of the viewer is nurtured by the use of advertised products as the prizes in some very simple game of chance. Contestants model greed for things and the hope of acquiring them without spending hard-earned money. In these games, contestant skill is kept to a minimum so that viewers need not feel distanced from the desired objects by being unworthy. The contestant must be enthusiastic, even joyous, however, at winning money or things. Since only luck gets the contestant the product for "free," the viewer can share in the ecstasy of having material lust fulfilled by going out (or picking up the phone, or typing on the computer) and buying the same. The prize is never one of a kind. It is never handmade, beautiful, or rare. It must be something everyone can buy who can afford it. The goal of modern commercial production is not only to eliminate the unique, the individual, the artful, but also to eliminate the desire for the different, by modelling the craving for the same. The people who create television sitcoms, dramas and soaps are not individuals but teams of technicians writing to formula, editing and correcting according to the marketing requirements of sponsors. And please note that such programming does nothing to promote personal growth and awareness, increase sensitivity to social values and the needs of others, or deepen our understanding of the complexity of life, family and human development. So pervasive is the recognition that programs come from an anonymous team, that my students, brought up on film and TV, often refer to the author of a book or poem not as he or she, but as "they."

Now I ask you, what could be more different from literature? Every novel, story and poem that is published is "handmade," by which I mean that it is the unique, individual product of someone's mind. Even stories that are similar remain very different, because the language that makes one person's reality is interestingly special to that person's way of seeing the world. It is true that different novels from the mind of one writer are more alike than they are like those of other writers. Readers who specialize in one author can often spot the style without even knowing a title. Even so, any one novel is so complex, contains so many sentences, ideas and images, that it must be unique.

LIES THAT TELL TRUTH

Fiction is not interrupted by advertising. The writer of the story has to present whatever she has to say, up front. Motives can't be hidden when they are part of the story that is laid out in front of everyone to be read. A good example of this emerged for me just recently while I was reading a remarkable story called *The Survival of Jan Little* by John Man, Jan Little's biographer. The book rates the life and adventures of a Californian woman, married to a tyrannical "saviour" figure who looked like pictures of Jesus (strange how many men there were like that in the 60s), and their long residence in the jungles of Venezuela and Brazil, where they were ever searching for the more remote, more unspoiled, most perfect place. In some ways, what is interesting about this emotional, spiritual, ecological quest is what is not told. *But what is not told to the reader, is not told to the writer.* I mean that Jan Little cannot tell her whole story to her biographer—there are matters hidden from her, and not just matters of fact, but bits of her history that she cannot admit or name to herself. But our lives are really like that; we all have dark corners of the mind that do not get explained. The truth, then, is often the truth about what can't be told, not some sentimental Disney schlock to explain everything and make everyone feel okay. The best writing often tries to tell the impossible, convey the indescribable. Real literature, written by a real individual out of her own experiences and views of the world, invents interesting lies, narrative, to carry that authentic view of the world that is the writer's actual mind.

The Less Said the Better

Even if TV programming did the best it could, were free of commercials and provided lots of interesting viewing and information—Jacques Cousteau for hours, or endless cable movies—it would still be different from reading in basic ways—*and less valuable!* In fact, television without the irritation of commercials and the motives to be simple-minded and trivial *would be even more dangerous.* The difference between reading and reception of TV lies in the brain's passivity in the face of TV's pictures and explanation of everything. *TV supplies, the viewer receives.* When you read a story, *you supply* the pictures, the sound effects, the smells, the colours and the voices. What happens is that you run a personal movie to bring the words to life—you are the director, the cameraperson, the sound effects crew, the casting agent and the editor. Where do you get all this stuff? From your own experiences, your own memory store. This is how you can become so intimate with the story and how it can be so important to you—the story provides a framework for you to bring into play material that you need to recall, actively, in order to *make sense* of what you read. *You make sense of what you read according to your mental need.*

The excerpt that follows is from a story by C. S. Forester called "The Turn of the Tide." Slade has been embezzling money from his law firm and has been found out by a new junior colleague, whom he murders. His plan is to dispose of the body at low tide. As you read the description of his efforts, observe your own mental processes. Notice what you can see or hear. How are the men dressed? What sounds are there? How does Slade feel? What is he thinking? How is he breathing? What do you notice most clearly for yourself?

The car bumped down the last bit of lane, and Slade drew up on the edge of the sands.

It was pitch dark, and the bitter wind was howling about him, under the black sky. Despite the noise of the wind, he could hear the surf breaking far away, two miles away, across the level sands. He climbed out of the driver's seat and walked round to the other door. When he opened it the dead man fell sideways, into his arms.

With an effort, Slade held him up, while he groped into the back of the car for the plough chain and the iron weights. He crammed the weights into the dead man's pockets, and he wound the chain round and round the dead man's body, tucking in the ends to make it all secure. With that mass of iron to hold it down, the body would never be found again when dropped into the sea at the lowest ebb of spring tide.

Slade tried now to lift the body in his arms, to carry it over the sands. He reeled and strained, but he was not strong enough—Slade was a man of slight figure, and past his prime. The sweat on his forehead was icy in the icy wind.

For a second, doubt overwhelmed him, lest all his plans should fail for want of bodily strength. But he forced himself into thinking clearly; he forced his frail body into obeying the vehement commands of his brain.

He turned round, still holding the dead man upright. Stooping, he got the heavy burden on his shoulders. He drew the arms round his neck, and, with a convulsive effort, he got the legs up round his hips. The dead man now rode him pick-a-back. Bending nearly double, he was able to carry the heavy weight in that fashion, the arm tight round his neck, the legs tight round his waist.

He set off, staggering, down the imperceptible slope of the sands towards the sound of the surf. The sands were soft beneath his feet—it was because of this softness that he had not driven the car down to the water's edge. He could afford to take no chances of being embogged. [1]

Did you feel the sand giving underfoot? Did you feel the weight of the chained body? Have you ever heard the weird howl on a stormy night by the sea? What else have you read about tides? Have you ever been afraid of drowning? Is there anyone who has been "on your back," or someone who has tried to drag you down?

In television or film you would be provided with sounds and sights. The faces, clothing and scenery would be selected for you, and you would not be able to change them. The combination of all these might be very striking to watch and hear, but the images and sounds would not be your own and not nearly so intimately involving as part of your own life, your own past, would be. Feelings of fear or suspense might be called up, but since you did not provide the content, to a certain extent you would be outside of your viewing, or, more precisely, you would be more a viewer than a doer. For this reason many readers experience disappointment or resentment when they see a film of a book that has been important to them. They are watching someone else's story about a story and it does not seem "right." When you read a story that matters, appeals to you, you make it your story! Fiction offers a lot of language for you to colour in. You are given only outlines, and you have lots of room to choose the content. *The writer provides the process, the reader provides the content.* In this regard, the less said, the more room for the reader.

Some science fiction writers have predicted entertainment where not only sight and sound are provided, but also touch, "the feelies," and smell. In *Fahrenheit 451*, Ray Bradbury describes a TV room that has four walls of screen; in there, the viewer becomes an interactive participant in the program. In Bradbury's novel a TV addict loses her identity to this programming, and so loses her mind and kills herself. Some even more recent writers predict that modules will be attached to or worn on our heads so that our brains can be computed to live the entire program in all its sensory dimensions. By carrying the idea of the passive viewer to extremes we can see how a sitcom can become primary experience itself—a substitute for our own life experience and choices. In life, we choose our friends, partners, jobs and residences. On television this is done for us. Entertainment turns into primary life experience *controlled by others*. This does not help us to review, understand and rearrange *our own* life experiences. It just adds to our dependence by turning us into super-programmed puppets—the robots of which we are most afraid are *ourselves*! Do not think you cannot be robotized; you have begun to be. Your best defense is in reading.

Who's in Charge?

The great thing about reading is the control we have over the process at every stage. Novels are gifts that invite us to be ourselves and enjoy our own powers of imagination and freedom. Can you remember the pleasure you had as a child at the pure, white, unspoiled pages of a new colouring book? It's like a field of snow waiting for your angel. The outlines are there, not oppressive, rather an opportunity. Then there is the power lying in wait in a good new sharp set of crayons or pencils—all the choices, all the bright promise and all yours to control. This heady power of creativity can be an intense pleasure to children. So it is for avid readers. What can be more lovely than the invitation of a crisp, new, never-before-opened book? It promises you the pleasure of exercising the infinite store of sensory imagery and information in *your own brain!* It promises the exciting blend that comes with joining someone else's story to your own.

Fiction puts the reader in control of the entertainment process in a number of ways and for good purposes. On TV, the more information you're given, direct sensory information like sights, sounds and maybe one day even smells, the less information or interpretation you can provide. But don't run away with the idea that what you are getting from TV is "objective," a truth that exists apart from an individual's version of it. Far from it, what you are getting is precisely someone else's version of the story—even the news story. The editors and directors and producers will decide what you are to receive and so what you are to think. Is the tyranny of pictures so great that what you see on film or TV must be "true"? We now know that nothing is easier to fake than pictures or a series of pictures to produce a particular interpretation. Seeing pictures is no guarantee that something happened, any more than family group photos are proof of family harmony. Advertisements of beer and cars generating happiness and good times are not "true"—they are designed to persuade the viewer they are true. But anyone who lives with an alcoholic or spends dollars in an auto repair shop can tell you otherwise.

Control over reading has a great many other components, too. Because reading enters your own moral code and becomes part of your own language sign system, you can provide the pictures and meaning to make sense of the language. This means that you can know the material very well, so well that at any time you can think about what you have read pretty accurately. You can stop a story and carry it around in your head and then start it up again when you want. You can control your timing for absorbing the information. You can pause without losing track of what has happened and continue whenever and wherever you feel like it. You can change settings. You can read fast or slow, aloud or silently, without disturbing the clarity of the images in your mind. You can select the kind of material you want to read depending on your mood or need. You can escape, travel, learn and laugh, think deeply, or be aroused sexually. You can choose from thousands of books, at any level of difficulty and in any length. You can read in any room, town, vehicle, or position. You can read in company or privately. You can own, rent, borrow, or lend reading. You can copy out what you read exactly or memorize it precisely. All this is possible, in theory if not in practice, in every nation, and for this reason, reading is the most usable, powerful and plentiful source of information available to human beings. The more you read, the more information you get, the freer you get and the more language you get. For this reason, the restriction of print is the number one goal of totalitarian regimes. To control publication is to control thought. To control publication and television programming is to control a population very effectively. The other way to control a population is to encourage the death of reading—to let television replace literacy. That is the subject of another chapter. That is the immediate danger we are facing.

SEEING THE INVISIBLE

Last, and perhaps most important, pictures can show us only them-selves, surfaces, the one, still, spatial arrangement. Pictures are mere-ly reflections of light and so must present themselves. Let's talk about film for a minute to explain this. First, remember that film is simply a long series of individual photographs that follow a sequence. Any one of these photos carries only a tiny amount of information. As a source of information, a picture is incredibly inefficient when there is no verbal, that is, language, accompaniment. Without explanation, a picture is ambiguous, confusing. Imagine exchanging family photos without language—no names, relationships, times, events, places, except what you can guess at.

Before movies with language sound track there were silent movies. Silent films can still charm us for several reasons. For one thing, they were all action, because if there had been too much talk or screenwriting the audience would have been bored to irritation, not being able to hear a word. So we loved sitting back and watching the chase scene and hardly having to think at all. For another thing, facial expressions were extremely exaggerated, so we could amuse ourselves by projecting feelings and interpretations onto the charac-ters and their predicaments. Then again, plots had to be extremely simple. Watching silent films, we were all turned into children again. This was fun. The very complicated plots of mystery films like *Sleuth* or spy stories like *The Ipcress File* or intrigues like *The Third Man* depend wholly on language; without it, they would be totally incomprehensible. Pictures, then, require language to explain the complexities of action, event and relationship. But even with lan-guage there are many important realms of information a film cannot provide without turning into a visual novel, and film as a talking, visual novel would be a costly contradiction in terms.

The Inside Track

We can get descriptions of invisible mental processes only from reading. *The most important gift of fiction to the reader is the articulation of feeling and thought.* Novels depend heavily on showing us how it feels to be in a certain situation or relationship or place. Fiction takes us inside people and places, gives us hidden, interior information. It does not merely show us tears or laughter or anger; it describes the origins, explains the contexts, the background, the *process!* Language is much more efficient than pictures at presenting complex information. Pictures are more efficient only where they cross a language or space barrier. TV is indispensable and unparalleled where it shows the invisible or acts to magnify, as when it records surgery to the brain or heart or transmits pictures from outer space—worlds not accessible to the senses through any other medium. If you can't read French, then a picture of a train to show the way to the station is more efficient, better than nothing, if you are in France. But when trains, buses, metro trains and trucks all look alike, then the power of language is evident. Besides, pictures of objects are only language going historically backwards, to the origin of language in pictures. In the "no smoking" sign, for instance, the picture is simply shorthand for language without need for multiple translation. It is pictorial language. Language is more efficient than any other form of human communication except in one or two special cases, where a touch might be the most efficient signal. A word like "ecstasy" or "frustration" is worth a thousand pictures, for while ecstasy is not the same to everybody, anyone who knows the word can provide precise personal equivalents from experience to give it full meaning and relevance. A picture of ecstasy is not so easy to supply, because first we must determine what it is a picture of. Is it pain? Surprise? Anguish? Is the person being pleasured, or tortured? The reader can apply what is for him an accurate picture to a word, but without a word a picture can be anything, and before we can put a word to it we must somehow label it. Language is what human beings have evolved, over millions of years, for conveying meaning. Sometimes a picture can summarize thousands of words. The famous picture of the Jewish child facing the storm trooper's machine gun collects into itself reams of reports, histories, testimonies, manuscripts, novels and poems. But without all these the picture would be a puzzle. Here is the response of one poet, Ralph Gustafson, to the picture; his poem shows us the complex mix of guilt, discomfort and rationalization that brings both the picture and the invisible mind of the viewer to life. This is the power of words:

The Newspaper
That photo of the little Jew in the cap,
Back to the gun held by the Nazi
With splay feet aware of the camera,
The little boy his hands in the air,
I turn over, I don't want to see it.
As a member of the human race. I am
Civilized. I am happy. I flap the
Newspaper with the picture over
So that when it is picked up to be taken
Down cellar to be put with the trash
I won't see it. I am sensitive.
The little boy is dead. He went
Through death. The cap is his best one.
He has brown eyes. He does not
Understand. Putting your hands
Up in front of a carbine prevents
The bullet. He is with the others.
Some of them he knows, so

It is all right. I turn
The paper over, the picture face
Down.[2]

There is so much meaning, so much language in a novel, that no film could possibly convey it without taking 6, 12, or 24 hours to view and so becoming simply an illustrated novel. Reading provides us with detailed accounts of feeling, process and relationship. It also provides history, background. Without a knowledge of the past, of the time sequence that explains present contexts, it is difficult, perhaps impossible, to make sense of our observations. Here is the opening chapter of Dickens' *A Tale of Two Cities*. It consists of 1,024 words, according to eight-year-old Sarah, and takes five-and-a-half minutes to read, according to fourteen-year-old Naomi, each of whom was hired to do this research. How much information is there in it? How many pictures would it take to convey this? How would you make sense of the pictures without language?

It was the best of times, it was the worst of times, it was the age of wisdom, it was the age of foolishness, it was the epoch of belief, it was the epoch of incredulity, it was the season of Light, it was the season of Darkness, it was the spring of hope, it was the winter of despair, we had everything before us, we had nothing before us, we were all going direct to Heaven, we were all going direct the other way—in short, the period was so far like the present period, that some of its noisiest authorities insisted on its being received, for good or for evil, in the superlative degree of comparison only.

There were a king with a large jaw and a queen with a plain face, on the throne of England; there were a king with a large jaw and a queen with a fair face, on the throne of France. In both countries it was clearer than crystal to the lords of the State preserves of loaves and fishes, that things in general were settled for ever.

It was the year of Our Lord one thousand seven hundred and seventy-five. Spiritual revelations were conceded to England at that favoured period, as at this. Mrs. Southcott had recently attained her five-and-twentieth blessed birthday, of whom a prophetic private in the Life Guards had heralded the sublime appearance by announcing that arrangements were made for the swallowing up of London and Westminster. Even the Cocklane ghost had been laid only a round dozen of years, after rapping out its messages, as the spirits of this very year last past (supernaturally deficient in originality) rapped out theirs. Mere messages in the earthly order of events had lately come to the English Crown and People, from a congress of British subjects in America: which, strange to relate, have proved more important to the human race than any communications yet received through any of the chickens of the Cocklane brood.

France, less favoured on the whole as to matters spiritual than her sister of the shield and trident, rolled with exceeding smoothness down hill, making paper money and spending it. Under the guidance of her Christian pastors, she entertained herself, besides, with such humane achievements as sentencing a youth to have his hands cut off, his tongue torn out with pincers, and his body burned alive, because he had not kneeled down in the rain to do honour to a dirty procession of monks which passed within his view, at a distance of some fifty or sixty yards. It is

likely enough that, rooted in the woods of France and
Norway, there were growing trees, when that sufferer was
put to death, already marked by the Woodman, Fate, to
come down and be sawn into boards, to make a certain
movable framework with a sack and a knife in it, terrible
in history. It is likely enough that in the rough outhouses
of some tillers of the heavy lands adjacent to Paris, there
were sheltered from the weather that very day, rude carts,
bespattered with rustic mire, snuffed about by pigs, and
roosted in by poultry, which the Farmer, Death, had
already set apart to be his tumbrils of the Revolution. But
that Woodman and that Farmer, though they work unceas-
ingly, work silently, and no one heard them as they went
about with muffled tread: the rather, forasmuch as to
entertain any suspicion that they were awake, was to be
atheistical and traitorous.

In England, there was scarcely an amount of order and
protection to justify much national boasting. Daring bur-
glaries by armed men, and highway robberies, took place
in the capital itself every night; families were publicly cau-
tioned not to go out of town without removing their furniture to upholsterers' warehouses for security; the highwayman in the dark was a City tradesman in the light, and,
being recognised and challenged by his fellow-tradesman
whom he stopped in his character of "the Captain,"
gallantly shot him through the head and rode away; the
mail was waylaid by seven robbers, and the guard shot
three dead, and then got shot dead himself by the other
four, "in consequence of the failure of his ammunition":
after which the mail was robbed in peace; that magnificent potentate, the Lord Mayor of London, was made to

stand and deliver on Turnham Green, by one highwayman, who despoiled the illustrious creature in sight of all his retinue; prisoners in London gaols fought battles with their turnkeys, and the majesty of the law fired blunder-busses in among them, loaded with rounds of shot and ball; thieves snipped off diamond crosses from the necks of noble lords at Court drawing-rooms; musketeers went into St. Giles's, to search for contraband goods, and the mob fired on the musketeers, and the musketeers fired on the mob, and nobody thought any of these occurrences much out of the common way. In the midst of them, the hangman, ever busy and ever worse than useless, was in constant requisition; now, stringing up long rows of mis-cellaneous criminals; now, hanging a housebreaker on Saturday who had been taken—now, burning people in the hand at Newgate by the dozen, and now burning pam-phlets at the door of Westminster Hall; today, taking the life of an atrocious murderer, and tomorrow of a wretched pilferer who had robbed a farmer's boy of sixpence.

All these things, and a thousand like them, came to pass in and close upon the dear old year one thousand seven hundred and seventy-five. Environed by them, while the Woodman and the Farmer worked unheeded, those two of the large jaws, and those other two of the plain and the fair faces, trod with stir enough, and carried their divine rights with a high hand. Thus did the year one thousand seven hundred and seventy-five conduct their Greatnesses, and myriads of small creatures—the creatures of this chronicle among the rest—along the roads that lay before them.[3]

I have no doubt that a fourteen-year-old reader, spending about five-and-a-half minutes on this, will not have understood many of the references and sentences. But this does not detract from the wealth of information she has potentially surveyed. In such brief space, the writer has sketched the social conditions of England and France on the eve of the French Revolution; conveyed his ironic contempt for the blindness of political authorities to the forces of history; and provided a panorama of colour, smell, sight and sound in vivid images before zooming his verbal lens upon the particular individuals who will act out the story.

One technique invented for film and not used much any more is "flashback," the filling in of the background of a case story by interweaving a piece of past story. The amount of information conveyed by a few pages of language can never be approximated by a few pictures. The result is *simplification*—everything on film and video is reduced to its simplest form. This is fine for relaxing, for not working, not learning. You sit back and let the images invade in a wash of thoughtlessness. As a thirteen-year-old client said to me recently, "I prefer TV to books because I don't have to *think*." We can get tired of thinking. The danger of watching as a steady diet for life is that we can lose the power to think. Read *Being There* by Jerzy Kosinski. As the audience becomes more passive, more manipulable, less imaginative and energetic, all systems will wind down to meet the population where it is. This has happened in American education. The rising tide of illiteracy, and, more important, of indifference, is signposted everywhere in the U.S. The decline of language is accompanied by an increase of violence. Language is power. To be inarticulate is to be frustrated and socially and politically helpless. Television is pushing us into a downward spiral of frustration and mindlessness. TV has made images of violence normal and acceptable. More than that, it has done violence to our potential for feeling, caring, thinking and creating.

In summary, then, reading nourishes literacy and the demand for literacy; television kills it. Reading increases activity, imagination and information; television increases passivity and dependence on the watching, viewer state of mind. The depressing, standardizing effect of TV is to decrease our tolerance for diversity, lower our understanding of print, impair our grasp of the humorous, the satirical, the critical. If we continue to watch TV, conformity and an ever-narrowing of views will be the order of the day. Whatever provokes thought, difference, individuality and change is at odds with the thrust of TV. Television strangles creativity, fosters impotence. In fact, I strongly suspect that chronic addictive watching of television would be found by long-term studies to lead to a reduced sex drive in males, to marital discord and a loss of family closeness and to a decrease of communication in the workplace. The problem with doing such research would be to find families in North America without TV sets for comparison. We have a TV set. But I never watch it—the only recent exceptions have been the U.S. presidential and Canadian party leaders' debates and Olympic ice skating—and the children are limited to one hour a day. This one hour is too much, but it is our compromise with other pressures. My view is that *whatever else they do is more valuable to children than watching the tube.*

1   C. S. Forester, "The Turn of the Tide," in *Some Things Fierce and Fatal*, ed. Joan Kahn (London: Bodley Head, 1971).

2   Ralph Gustafson, "The Newspaper," in *15 Canadian Poets X2*, ed. Gary Geddes (Toronto: Oxford University Press, 1988).

3   Charles Dickens, *A Tale of Two Cities* (London: Oxford University Press, 1949), pp. 1-3.

PART TWO

Reading for Time

CHAPTER FIVE

The Past

G regory Bateson, sometimes called the father of family therapy, was a pioneer in communication theory. He had a lot to say about feedback. He also gave story a central place in his view of how the world is organized—at least from a human point of view, which I suppose is the one we are stuck with until one or more E.T.s really come along. Story is basic to how human minds see their world and to how those minds work. I call this story-thinking. Here is a story Bateson liked to tell:

> A man wanted to know about mind, not in nature, but in his private large computer. He asked it (no doubt in his best Fortran), "Do you compute that you will ever think like a human being?" The machine then set to work to analyze its own computational habits. Finally, the machine printed its answer on a piece of paper, as such machines do. The man ran to get the answer and found, neatly typed, the words:
>
> THAT REMINDS ME OF A STORY

Bateson goes on to give his definition of story:

> A story is a little knot or complex of that species of connectedness which we call *relevance*. In the 1960s, students were fighting for "relevance," and I would assume that any A is relevant to any B if both A and B are parts or components of the same "story."

Again we face connectedness at more than one level:

First, connection between A and B by virtue of their being components in the same story.

And then, connectedness between people in that all think in terms of stories. (For surely the computer was right. This is indeed how people think.)

Now I want to show that whatever the word story means in the story which I told you, the fact of thinking in terms of stories does not isolate human beings as something separate from the starfish and the sea anemones, the coconut palms and the primroses. Rather, if the world be connected, if I am at all fundamentally right in what I am saying, then *thinking in terms of stories* must be shared by all mind or minds, whether ours or those of redwood forests and sea anemones.

Context and relevance must be characteristic not only of all so-called behavior (those stories which are projected out into "action"), but also of all those internal stories, the sequences of the building up of the sea anemone. Its embryology must be somehow made of the stuff of stories.[1]

In other words, Bateson sees story as a form of all organic organization. All organisms grow into their own story, which contains their history and their very nature, shape, form and function. This idea of connectedness is very basic to story. It is by linking bits of information together that we organize the past. It is by linking bits of the story to our own lives that we grow and develop our own life stories.

Memory and Story

As we move through life we record our experiences by turning them into language and into pictures called images. These images are

organized by sets of labels, like the words underneath cartoons. We
do not consciously remember everything. Sometimes we are surprised at what we can remember. In memory, the images are connected like events and characters in a story. Wilder Penfield, the
great Canadian neurosurgeon, working on epileptics, discovered
while he was doing open brain surgery that by placing his electrode
in certain locations of the brain he could trigger streams of memory
that the patient had no knowledge of remembering. Penfield was
poking around with his electrodes in order to map precisely the language "place" in the brain, since he and others thought at the time
that language had such an exact location. His reason for going on
this search was that when he performed surgery to relieve the symptoms of violent cases of epilepsy, he wanted to avoid damaging the
most important part of the brain, the part that made language possible. He, his colleagues and the patient were quite impressed when
they uncovered this memory bank that had preserved with startling
clarity apparently forgotten material—here is Penfield's comment,
in which he looks back to the early days of this discovery:

> On the first occasion, when one of these "flashbacks" was
> reported to me by a conscious patient (1933), I was incredu-
> lous. On each subsequent occasion, I marvelled. For exam-
> ple, when a mother told me she was suddenly aware, as my
> electrode touched the cortex, of being in her kitchen listen-
> ing to the voice of her little boy who was playing outside in
> the yard. She was aware of the neighborhood noises, such
> as passing motor cars, that might mean danger to him.
>
> A young man stated he was sitting at a baseball game
> in a small town and watching a little boy crawl under the
> fence to join the audience. Another was in a concert hall
> listening to music. "An orchestration," he explained. He

could hear the different instruments. All these were unimportant events, but recalled with complete detail.[2]

Memory is terribly important to the management of our lives. It gives us the store of learned information that helps us to manage the present, to know what to do and how to do it, to know what to avoid or seek and to know what we don't know. Memory helps us to plan our future. We could not anticipate or be safe without memory. Memory includes of course what we have read, what has impressed us. The stories that have gripped us have blended with our own lived experience and become part of our experience record. Children are capable of grasping the import of memory in their lives and relationships in early years. Here is Sarah's story, which did not set out to be *about* memory, but which shows clearly that she is fully aware that remembering and holding on to memories connects her to those she loves:

THE DIARY

Dad and I went to the store on Jan. 26. It is my birthday next week and while I wasn't looking he bought my present.

"What is that?" I asked as we were going out of the store.

"Oh, nothing," Dad said.

I was sure that it was my present but I wasn't sure what. My birthday was one week away. The next day was Monday.

I got up, got dressed and went downstairs and ate my breakfast. And went outside to chase the bus.

At school everybody gave me my birthday spankings because next week is my birthday. "Today I brought cookies, Miss Brook." I said.

"Good! When do you want to give them out?" Miss Brook asked. "Oh, I think this afternoon." I said.

Days past quickly and then it was time for my birthday. I invited, Donna, Connie and Christine.

Mom baked strawberry cake! That's my favourite kind of cake. After lunch, and the cake, I got to open my birthday presents!

From Donna I got a yellow Wild Puffalump. From Connie, I got a stuffed cat and from Christine I got a BIG doll from Old Boy. But best of all, I got a Diary from my Dad! Inside it said "Dear Sarah. This is what you have been waiting for. Remember! I got it while you weren't looking! Love Dad."

"Thanks Dad," and carefully wrote at the bottom of the diary, "Yes I do remember."

Think about the number of sensory impressions you get in one day, the smells, sights, sounds, feelings, events, words, surprises, disappointments, thoughts—just in one day. It would be impossible to record them as individual items. I remember a store—interesting word, that—we used to visit on our way to our cottage in Apsley, Ontario. We called it "The Place." This store was on the county road, a great barn of a place, like an airplane hangar, run by two colourful characters out of folklore, a father and his giant adult son. They sold hardware, army surplus goods, china, cottage stuff, fireplaces, dried food, tools, knives, axes, guns, lights, lamps, repellent, games, tents, tarps, cutlery, watches—in short, it seemed, everything and all in one room. It was bewildering to go into this place. So much clutter and congestion was there, you could hardly get in the door. To move down an aisle, you had to remove something out of your way. Goods were piled up to the dark, cavernous ceiling. Ladders, ropes, cans and stoves competed with hundreds of rifles, clothes, ropes, toys, radios, boxes of nails, screws, toilet fixtures and batteries, and stuff crammed over and under counters and glass cases and hanging from beams. Locks and bolts of every kind, farm and sports gear, pots and pans piled in mountains, new and used together, seemed to take on a kind of creeping, encroaching life of imperceptible movement, like a slowly flooding lake. Just looking around was confusing and exhausting, and the reason this place was both wonderful and bizarre was that there was no apparent order or organization to anything. It was a nightmare of merchandise, only less orderly than a nightmare.

One day I came into The Place and found the old man going around with a bit of paper attached to a clipboard. "What are you doing?" I asked. "Taking inventory," he replied. "The government wants me to count every nail, but I tell 'em, if you wants to do it, you come on in and do it, but if I do it, I just gets it approximate." I sometimes think that if I go mad, my mind will be like the inside of The Place, and I won't know where anything is. What was missing in that store was story. Oh, the raw material was there all right, like the experiences of life, but it had accumulated randomly. Story organizes, connects, links together and makes things, memories, findable. When you refer to a place in a novel and need to help someone else to recall it, you talk as though the book is a map, and give a how-to-get-there description. "You know that part where they are playing chess and the chauffeur comes in?" "Not clearly." "It's after the storm and she's had a bath and is sitting in his wife's robe, by the fire." "Do you mean just before the wife phones from the hospital with the news?" We are picking our way through mapped history, connected and organized into a coherent sequence of events. We see how one piece is related to another, how the puzzle takes shape as the pieces, recognized by their complementary shapes, begin to form a whole. This is how millions of individual items are storied into memory.

How this is done by our brains remains a mystery, about which we are just beginning to make some interesting guesses.

THE MYTH OF THE UNCHANGEABLE PAST

In George Orwell's *Nineteen Eighty-Four*, the hero, Winston, works for the Ministry of Truth. The business of this ministry is rewriting history according to the political needs of the present—in other words, lying. What makes this revision lying, a deliberate deception and not simply the open revision of history, is the lie that it is not happening. Rewriting history goes on in our world all the time as new information, new understandings and different points of view come into play. Every new book on the Spanish Armada or the Second World War gives a somewhat different version of it and broadens the picture. These new versions do not, however, wipe out the earlier ones and pretend they never existed. The Ministry of Truth on the other hand, asks people to deny the reality of their own experience, to pretend that the past never existed, except in the minds of the mad and the deceived. Not only are people asked to believe something new, they are required to forget the truths of yesterday. One efficient way to drive people crazy is to deny the reality of their own knowledge of experience. Those neo-Nazis who wish to deny the experience of the Holocaust are operating on the same principle as the government of Orwell's Big Brother: There is no truth but what Big Brother says is the truth, even if his truth denies the memory and experience of others. Only those who were not in the death camps can say there were no death camps.

We normally live our lives as though there is only one version of the past, the true one, the one we recorded at the time and that settled down into being the permanent, unchangeable memory. There is a good example of such a memory in Dickens' novel *Little Dorrit*:

There was the dreary Sunday of his childhood, when he sat
with his hands before him, scared out of his senses by a
horrible tract which commenced business with the poor
child by asking him in its title, why he was going to
Perdition?—a piece of curiosity that he really in a frock
and drawers was not in a condition to satisfy—and which,
for the further attraction of his infant mind, had a paren-
thesis in every other line with some such hiccupping reference as 2 Ep. Thess. c. iii, v. 6 & 7. There was the sleepy
Sunday of his boyhood, when, like a military deserter, he
was marched to chapel by a picquet of teachers three
times a day, morally handcuffed to another boy; and when
he would willingly have bartered two meals of indigestible
sermon for another ounce or two of inferior mutton at his
scanty dinner in the flesh.[3]

This idea that the past is unchangeable is a myth. The memory
stream of images and sounds that Penfield uncovered may not
change in its details, but the meaning, the understanding, the
interpretation of them as part of a larger life can change. The
changes might be better or worse. The charming old square, or the
little pub where we had lunch, has gone forever, erased by a tow-
ering white office building and a multi-storied parking lot. The
slum where I grew up, with the rubble-filled backyard where rats
from the nearby sewer sometimes played, has been buried under
a row of attractive red brick town houses with cedar doors and bay
windows.

Three months ago I painted my kitchen, and now visitors can't
remember the shabby yellow woodwork. Some insist I have had new
cabinets built. We can alter the past and we can do it for our own
mental health and general well-being. In fact, most psychotherapy is

based on exploring the past with a view to changing it. We alter the past by seeing it differently.

Reading to Remember

Before we can change the past we have to remember it, and we want to do so without open brain surgery. Most of us have memories we have repressed, buried, because the affect, the emotion associated with the experience, was too painful in some way to cope with. I have found with my clients that the most common painful experience in memory is a childhood humiliation, usually associated with school, since that is where children normally spend most of their time. School is the child's world, what adults call for themselves the "real world." It is here that the values of home, the support and reinforcement of home, the love and trust of home, are tested. Here is the land of competition, of public scrutiny, of peers', that is, strangers', approval or rejection. In school, the child is exposed and vulnerable. And here is the place where any achievement that is going to be made takes place. The well-loved child knows that mother will love whatever she does, approve of all her efforts. Winning praise abroad, winning high marks and public recognition, is a very different matter from being told once again by doting parents what a wonderful child I am. For that reason the humiliation that comes from being disgraced in front of one's peers in school is especially hurtful. The consequence of this hurt is that the humiliated individual buries the memory associated with the hurt feeling. Not always. In those families where the trust level is very high and communication is encouraged and modelled by parents, children may discuss the event and its attendant pain soon after it happens. It is then brought into consciousness and "storied," normalized and shared as family history, and so becomes part of the open record of the child's experience. It does not need to be hidden. On the other hand, the family may be one where the humiliation experienced at school will be reinforced. Instead of expressing love, sympathy, or support for the child and indignation at the teacher, the parents may direct their anger at the child. The child's disgrace becomes the family's disgrace, and they blame the child for bringing the family into disrepute. I know one woman who always got punished at home for being punished in school—a double scoop of trouble. Such a family already feels insecure and too noticeable, of course, and is highly sensitive to public opinion. The child from such a family knows this and tries to keep her shame to herself. This shame and its suppressed anger are what will be carried into therapy years later.

The result of such repressed memory—remember, it was repressed, left out of the story, to avoid the emotional pain associated with it—is that the affect response, the pain reaction, is likely to be evoked without the victim's knowing the cause. In response to another child's humiliation, for instance, our victim, now an adult or parent, may explode in uncontrolled anger at the child or the teacher, or may feel fear or nausea at having to speak in public and not know why. The emotional response to the original event had a survival function—"void this situation from now on"—and since the event did not become changed by integration into a life story (because the context was repressed) the message remains unaltered in situations where it is no longer appropriate.

One of my clients, a professional man in his forties, held a position that required him to do a great deal of public speaking. He had developed a phobia about this part of his work and had begun to avoid situations requiring him to speak to large groups, and his career was suffering in consequence. It was this crisis that brought him into therapy. It is also interesting that this man had an intense dislike for anything sticky on his skin. The idea of getting jam or honey on his fingers created disgust in him, and imagining such stuff elsewhere on his body made him wriggle and cringe with discomfort. When he read a story of a horrible death inflicted in the desert, where a victim was smeared all over with honey and tied down to be eaten by ants, his horror was at the smearing of the honey more than the bites of the ants. One of the stories of his childhood that emerged in therapy was this. When he was seven years old, he had put up his hand in class to be excused. The teacher ignored him, ignored his obvious distress, and waited so long that he had a loose bowel movement in his pants at his desk. Crying with shame and fear, he now got the teacher's attention. Her response to his plight was to shame him before the class and send him walking home in that condition, with feces running down his legs. This memory returned to him when he read about the humiliation suffered by one of the girls in Alice Munro's story about growing up in her novel *Who Do You Think You Are?*

It could have been worse. Disgrace was the easiest thing to come by. High school life was hazardous, in that harsh clean light, and nothing was ever forgotten. Rose could have been the girl who lost the Kotex. That was probably a country girl, carrying the Kotex in her pocket or in the back of her notebook, for use later in the day. Anybody who lived at a distance might have done that. Rose herself had done it. There was a Kotex dispenser in the girls' washroom but it was always empty, would swallow your dimes but disgorge nothing in return. There was the famous pact made by two country girls to seek out the janitor at lunchtime, ask him to fill it. No use.

"Which one of you is the one that needs it?" he said. They fled. They said his room under the stairs had an old grimy couch in it, and a cat's skeleton. They swore to it.

That Kotex must have fallen on the floor, maybe in the cloakroom, then been picked up and smuggled somehow into the trophy case in the main hall. There it came to public notice. Folding and carrying had spoiled its fresh look, rubbed its surface, so that it was possible to imagine it had been warmed against the body. A great scandal. In morning assembly, the Principal made reference to a disgusting object. He vowed to discover, expose, flog and expel, the culprit who had put it on view. Every girl in the school was denying knowledge of it. Theories abounded. Rose was afraid that she might be a leading candidate for ownership, so was relieved when responsibility was fixed on a big sullen country girl named Muriel Mason, who wore slub rayon housedresses to school, and had B.O.

"You got the rag on today, Muriel?" boys would say to her now, would call after her.

"If I was Muriel Mason I would want to kill myself," Rose heard a senior girl say to another on the stairs. "I would kill myself." She spoke not pityingly but impatiently. [4]

This book was given to my client because it dealt in part with marriage and divorce. Unpredictably, what he noticed most was this episode. His recall of his childhood humiliation did not explain everything, but it was an important discovery.

For children who have been unable to discuss their emotional pain, reading about the humiliation of others is a powerful normalizer of what seems like a uniquely horrible experience. A lonely child is made more lonely by such experiences. Literature is capable of producing the recognition that this kind of suffering is well known, recognized by someone else. Even more important, the writer never presents, cannot present, such a story without conveying some attitude toward it. So far as I can tell, the attitude is always one of sympathy for the child in the story or indignation at the insensitivity of peers or adults. So the story conveys a way of framing, seeing, understanding, organizing the pain into the larger picture of a life. The story provides a way of integrating the painful event into a life story. Not only does the reader feel known, understood and justified; she also can feel more control over the past. She has learned how to story the event and so become master of it instead of victim of it. Storying the event, that is, putting it into a context with commentary and feeling, is changing it and controlling it. Further, if the child can discuss the story with someone, he can talk about the self without confessing to the self-humiliation. For the writer, the act of writing, and for the reader, the act of reading, are controlling, active behaviours that move the sufferers out of the guilt state that comes with humiliation and into an understanding of how other people's insensitivity and cruelty turned the reader into a victim. Blaming the victim is a widespread response to children.

For adults who have repressed their memories for many years, reading can first trigger memory and then normalize and change the painful affect. Whenever I read the caning of David by the brutal Mr. Murdstone in Dickens' *David Copperfield*, I can't help thinking of my school days in England, where the custom was to punish boys by whipping them with a thin bamboo cane on the open palms of their hands, stretched out on command before the teacher. On one occasion a teacher, possessed of only the average amount of sadism common to that time and place, selected me as too noisy, talking, not listening. This was simply a false accusation on the particular occasion, and in my outrage at the injustice I stood and made an hysterical speech, a barely coherent tirade about being picked on, about injustice, a speech spluttering with tears of anger and frustration and with the passion of powerlessness. There must have been some undeniable authenticity in this outburst, because, to my amazement, I avoided, on that occasion, the beating, which left a child, I remember, with palms bruised and swollen in huge purple welts, so painful and stinging that he could not use his hands for many hours after.

David Copperfield bites his sadistic stepfather during a savage beating and as a result is sent away to a boarding school where his humiliation is completed. He must wear on his back a sign that reads, "Take care of him. He bites."

> What I suffered from that placard nobody can imagine. Whether it was possible for people to see me or not, I always fancied that somebody was reading it. It was no relief to turn round and find nobody; for wherever my back was, there I imagined somebody always to be. That cruel man with the wooden leg aggravated my sufferings. He was in authority, and, if he ever saw me leaning against a tree, or a wall, or the house, he roared out from his lodge-door in a stupendous voice, "Hallow, you sir! You Copperfield! Show that badge conspicuous, or I'll report you!" The playground was a bare gravelled yard, open to all the back of the house and the offices; and I knew that the servants read it, and the butcher read it, and the baker read it; that everybody, in a word, who came backwards and forwards to the house, of a morning when I was ordered to walk there, read that I was to be taken care of, for I bit. I recollect that I positively began to have a dread of myself, as a kind of wild boy who did bite.[5]

Another story of humiliation and sadism in connection with hands is told in W. O. Mitchell's novel *Who Has Seen the Wind*. In this episode, the teacher forces an ordeal upon a child that suggests a power struggle in which the boy's male strength, represented by his arms and hands, is proved to be weaker than the female teacher's authority. The sadistic-sexual connections are strongly suggested. Humiliation is a form of revenge that, while it focuses on one victim, may represent an attitude or feeling toward a large group, even a group as large as the opposite sex.

Miss MacDonald had taken off her glasses and was swinging them idly in a slow circle. Her face was intent, unpleasantly so. "Brian."

"Yes, Miss MacDonald."

"Did you say that you had washed your hands this morning?"

Brian felt a sudden flutter of panic at his heart.

"I have your name down on my list of those who washed their hands."

He wished that he had taken his hand down.

"Let me see them."

He held them out.

"Did you wash those this morning?"

"No," he said weakly.

"You said that you had."

"I didn't mean to, Miss MacDonald."

"Why did you put up your hand, then?"

"It-it just sort of went up."

She snorted. "Come up here." She rose from her desk and led him to the center of the room before the class, then turned to the other children with their expectant faces looking up to her.

"Here is a little boy who didn't wash his hands this morning." She paused. "That isn't so bad—sometimes all of

us forget. But when it's—when we are asked whether
or not we washed our hands, none of us"—She paused—
"*lie* about it."

The sibilance of pencils hissing over paper, the snuf-
fling, the whispering, the shuffling of feet, were stilled.
Someone giggled shrilly. Brian recognized that it was
Mariel Abercrombie.

"This boy did *not* wash his hands, and he *did* lie about
it," said Miss MacDonald. Brian looked down at the floor.

"Brian!"

He looked up to see that she was smiling. "Will you
hold up your *washed* hands for the class to see?"

He looked down at the floor; she hated him, he
supposed dully.

"Hold them up, Brian."

Head tilted forward, he raised his arms slowly, shoulder high, palms in. Miss MacDonald stepped before him
and turned the palms out to face the class. As she stepped
back, he missed the shielding of her body, and stood, a
small and abject soldier in the attitude of surrender with
thirty pair of eyes upon him.

"We'll just have you stand like that," said Miss
MacDonald in a kindly voice, "with your washed hands for
all the class to see. We don't want to have you think—it
isn't punishment," she hastened to say. "The Lord punishes
little boys who don't wash their hands and then say that
they did." [6]

When Brian is finally allowed to return to his seat, he faints in the aisle.

Dirty hands seem often to have given teachers opportunity to
humiliate a child. Here Hoda, from a poor immigrant family, is being

shamed, in Adele Wiseman's novel *Crackpot*. The children have been knitting to help the war effort.

"Two more squares for row four, from Hoda." Teacher held them up for all to see. "Honestly," she had a nice, friendly way of saying things that were going to make you feel bad, "honestly I don't know whether to add or subtract these from your score, row four. Perhaps it might help the war effort more if some people simply stopped knitting. The war might end sooner and our boys come home!"

The class tittered. Teacher waited a moment, then she said sadly, "It's not funny." The class went silent. Everyone knew that like many other teachers she had lost her sweetheart in the war...That was why you couldn't entirely blame teacher, when you were out of her reach.

But Hoda was well within reach, and aware now of a prolonged silence, with herself pinned at its centre. She had let the team down again. "I d-didn't kn-kn-know how to kn-kn-kn-it," she quavered finally, unable to look up.

"Neither did many others in the class," replied the teacher reasonably. "But they felt it was their duty to learn. And I suppose you don't know how to wash your hands, either? You were given a clean ball of wool. I can't even tell what colour these rags are. Class, can anyone tell me what colour this is?"

Yes they can, yes they can! Hoda knew they could. But no one spoke.

"No? Well, never mind." Teacher let out a mock little sigh.

"I do so wash my hands." The words were very deep and low from the effort of climbing past the tears in

Hoda's throat. "Only," there was genuine anguish in her voice, "things get dirty anyway."

"So I see," said the teacher gently, and smiled. This time the class laughed louder and craned to look at the fat girl who sat squirming in her rumpled, stained tunic and already grubby white blouse. Hoda opened up her quivering mouth and tried to pretend she was laughing too. The effect was grotesque and somehow irritated the teacher. She turned away abruptly. "All right, class, we've wasted enough time."[7]

The number of stories about the child's humiliation and sense of unfairness suggests just how common such experiences must be. For the adult who has repressed a memory of this kind, reading can be powerfully relevant. Very often, however, it requires some work to get in touch with the memory. You can try the following exercises for yourself. When you are reading fiction (or poetry) that evokes some affective (emotional) response, the memory associated with the response may be resistant to recall. The reader's response, your response, is undeniable, however. We all recognize the sweaty palms, the increased breathing and heart rate, the general edginess and heightened attention, or any of the other symptoms of fear, anger, pleasure, excitement, embarrassment, frustration, or sadness that can accompany reading. These are our clues to the relevance of the reading to ourselves. Normally we pass over these responses without even acknowledging them, except to be aware that the story or poem was "good" or "powerful" or "really got to me." Sometimes the power of a reading emerges in its full significance only years later. It is possible, though, to use these responses as sources of information and to go through the affect to memory, experience, or attitude, to use the reading deliberately and consciously to increase our self-awareness.

Here is a recently discovered poem by Lewis Carroll, author of the Alice books, written when he was thirteen:

The Fairy
I have a fairy by my side
    Which says I must not sleep,
When once in pain I loudly cried
    It said, "You must not weep."

If, full of mirth, I smile and grin,
    It says, "You must not laugh,"
When once I wished to drink some gin,
    It said, "You must not quaff."

When once a meal I wished to taste
    It said "You must not bite,"
When to the wars I went in haste,
    It said "You must not fight."

"What may I do?" At length I cried,
    Tired of the painful task,
The fairy quietly replied,
    And said "You must not ask."

Moral: "You mustn't." [8]

Though this poem comes from a Victorian child, many people who read it today identify with its picture of an intensely controlled and restricted childhood, a past that leaves a legacy requiring a lot of work to make it acceptable.

CHANGING ATTITUDES AND THE PRESENT

Although reading contributes to altering the way we look at ourselves in relation to others, there are one or two conditions of human response where we mustn't expect reading to produce instant revelation and radical change. The way we feel and think about most things constitutes our attitudes—the word literally means our posture, the direction we are facing. In adults, some beliefs are resistant to change through reading, and only over the long term and as part of a larger program aimed at change will reading be effective. Take the case of politics. Political beliefs are normally learned at home consciously and articulated repeatedly. From big Tories, little Tories come, and little Tories in their turn grow into big ones. Violent and radical severing of family bonds, as in the case of sexual abuse or physical assault, where the child is removed or alienated from parents, often alters this pattern, but for most people political beliefs are not open enough to permit the persuasive power of fiction to operate. Readers are more likely simply to reject what they don't agree with and refuse to read what does not confirm their views. The same is true of religion. This also is learned at home, and children will usually follow the same beliefs and position as their parents unless they are driven away, orphaned, or otherwise physically or emotionally exiled.

In the case of these belief systems or ideologies, only conversion will produce a radical change or about-face, like Paul's fit on the way to Damascus. There are several reasons for this. Religion, politics and table manners are learned early and continuously; they are habitually reinforced by elections, Sabbath rituals, group conviction, and fear of punishment for departing from the approved ways; there is usually little or no motivation for change, because one religion or party is not self-evidently better than another, not better enough to overcome the believer's attachment to his own; the belief system is reinforced by a community; for most people such beliefs are "surface" and less pressing than personal relations or individual feelings of self-esteem, except during elections and religious festivals. What reading does do in such cases is to reinforce already existing beliefs.

Another kind of behaviour that is not quickly changed by reading is what we call phobic behaviour, based on an irrational fear response that is learned or developed over a period of time. For some people it might be a fear of snakes, mice, dogs, or even cats. In the presence of the animal, the phobic panics, screams or freezes, runs away, and he avoids places where the horror is known to be. Other people might fear heights, closed spaces, open fields, rapid movement. I remember Cindy, who lived within walking distance of the counselling centre—only with the greatest effort, fighting off real panic, could she leave her home to get there. The effort was in fact too great to leave her much energy to work in the hour she spent after arriving, and then she still had to get home again. I agreed to make a house call and found her sitting in fear in her living room, rocking in a chair. Gradually we identified fears closer to home, a shadow that came down the stairs, a presence behind a door. Eventually, in a rush of memory, Cindy revealed a history of sexual abuse—she had been the child victim of an uncle's sick cruelty. The origins of fears are complex and often uncoverable only with difficulty. Still other people are afraid of flying, of situations requiring speaking in public, of social gatherings, crowds, being alone or eating in public.

Reading for phobics cannot be a short-term business, for the simple reason that reading makes its impact through cognition, through conscious thoughtful responses to information in the reading, buttressed by affective reactions or signals. Phobias produce a set of symptoms that are conditioned, immediate, hard to control and think about, like a reflex reaction, like sneezing. One look down at the tiny street, twenty stories below, or at the snake in the grass, or at the elevator doors closing, and the heart rate goes up, the palms go sweaty, the stomach aches and the breath comes short and fast.

Reading gets results by providing new, or new arrangements of, information that over time helps to change the relation between the reader and the reader's world. Reading can change behaviour, action, plans, by causing reassessment of the reader's own present behaviour when similarity or relevance is perceived in the story. For example, a student told me she was routinely visiting an elderly man in a nursing home as an act of kindness, taking him little gifts and conversing with him once a week. She had just been considering an end to these visits of charity—he was becoming difficult, complaining and making more demands of her time—when she read a short story, "Mice and Birds and Boy" by Elizabeth Taylor, that led her to look at the whole thing again, *seeing his position and point of view,* and thinking about ways to take some control so that she would not have to withdraw to protect herself—they would both lose if she did that. Another student, a mature mother of three, told a class of her peers that reading Bronwen Wallace's poem "The Woman in this Poem" made her feel "safe," because it gave permission for, validated, a number of scary parts of her own life about which she was uncomfortable—aging, having secret thoughts, indulging in fantasies.

Reading can be part of an ongoing life program, empowering the reader to rethink present coping strategies, to try out new behaviours, new moves. Reading can be part of the raising into consciousness of patterns of thought and action that have become mechanical and routine, with a view to changing them. Often, in our relationships, in our work and in our recreation we drop into habits of response that seem inevitable and entrapping. We find it hard to get outside of ourselves enough to see what we are doing, what we contribute to our situations. Most of us in Western society have more freedom and more control than we believe. We need other people's well-composed stories and insights to free us from our own habits, and we also need to see that we can read consciously, that there is a conversation between literature and life, our life. Once we understand that connection, we have opened a huge reservoir of help, of strength, for ourselves. We have, so far, devalued story and poem by believing that pleasure, delight and the imagination must be separate from work, use, seriousness and practicality. This split has seriously impoverished us. Reading is not necessary to our survival, if by survival we mean eating and staying warm. It is necessary to our larger survival, however, to an enriched, aware life in which we exercise some measure of control over our well-being, our creativity and our connection to everything around us.

1   Gregory Bateson, *Mind and Nature: A Necessary Unity* (New York: Bantam, 1980), p.14.

2   Wilder Penfield, *The Mystery of the Mind* (Princeton: Princeton University Press, 1975), pp. 21-22.

3   Charles Dickens, *Little Dorrit* (London: Oxford University Press, 1963), p. 29.

4   Alice Munro, *Who Do You Think You Are?* (Toronto: Macmillan, 1978), pp. 39-40.

5   Charles Dickens, *David Copperfield* (London: Oxford University Press, 1948), pp. 78-79.

6   W. O. Mitchell, *Who Has Seen the Wind* (Toronto: McClelland and Stewart-Bantam, 1982), pp. 87-89.

7   Adele Wiseman, *Crackpot* (Toronto: McClelland and Stewart, 1974), pp. 32-33.

8   Lewis Carroll, "The Fairy," reprinted in Morton N. Cohen, "Lewis Carroll and Victorian Morality," in *Sexuality and Victorian Literature*, ed. Don Richard Cox (Knoxville: University of Tennessee Press, 1984).

CHAPTER SIX

Reading, Feeling and Emotion

The weight of this sad time we must obey,
Speak what we feel, not what we ought to say.

King Lear

We live in a culture that seems to have declared war on feeling. Everything we do must be rational, have a logical, reasoned explanation. Teachers like their students to say "I think," not "I feel." We deny, repress, discount our feelings. This does not mean, of course, that we don't have feelings. We feel emotional responses continuously, but we are trained to ignore them. We are mostly insensitive to feelings in ourselves, our families and especially our children. Sylvan Tomkins, the father of much recent psychological research on emotion, understood that his work was pioneering:

> It is not just consciousness in general which has been neglected, but the role of affect has also been grossly underestimated. Indeed, we might speculate that the phenomena of consciousness might possibly never have been so neglected had the problem been restricted to determining what another human being thinks. It is rather knowing how he feels that has been most strikingly avoided. This is in part a consequence of the widespread taboos on affect which are learned in childhood.[1]

Feelings—sadness, anger, joy, fear, lust, embarrassment, shame, surprise, resentment, contempt, jealousy, tenderness and frustration—are very hard to describe in language, hard to talk and write about. This may be because in evolution, as human beings moved toward being two-legged rational creatures—*Homo sapiens*—they developed language *after* they had developed feelings. Feelings, in other words, are pre-linguistic; we feel before we "think" in language. Language is thought. Feeling is more basic, more connected to the animal part of us. Language seems to be best for describing the world outside ourselves; it does not seem well suited to describing our feelings. This is clear in many of our ordinary relations. We know how hard it is to say "I love you" in different ways, so we are encouraged by florists, candy-makers and jewellers to say it with flowers, chocolates and diamonds. In other words, we turn to our actions or behaviour to express ourselves. When we cannot verbalize anger, we yell, throw things, slam doors, or even commit worse violence. There is some suggestive evidence of a high degree of illiteracy among violent criminals.

The difficulty of expressing feeling seems to grow as we get older. New babies, as well as animals, have little problem in expressing their feelings directly without language. The discomfort of hunger, the pleasure of recognition, the growth of uncertainty and anxiety are well known to us. Smiles, wagging tails, cooing, purring, screaming, crying, howling are all direct expressions of feeling. As we grow up in our society, we are told not to cry (especially if we are male), and not to pout, and not to yell, and to wipe that smile off our faces! Since it is difficult to express our feelings verbally, and since feelings do not always fit the facts or lend much weight to argument, we gradually relegate them to some dark storehouse of forgotten parts of ourselves, like the dusty treasures of the past in Granny's attic. We delude ourselves that, shut up and locked securely in the dark, our feelings are safely under control, but in fact we are continuously haunted, influenced, changed by our feelings *especially when we do not acknowledge them.*

Adults have learned to rationalize. This means using the skill of argument as a form of reasoning in the service of making ourselves feel better, justifying ourselves, or explaining away. Psychotherapy is largely directed at penetrating the screen or armour of rationalization. The repression of real feeling and its associated memories means that we live a pretend life. It is tiring and stressful to be pretending all the time, to be keeping up a happy front while anger simmers away inside. The anger is not going to go away because we ignore it, any more than a hungry child will stop crying because we turn up the radio so we cannot hear him. The reason for this is of crucial importance here. Why is feeling so persistent, so nagging, that, do what we will, our power to rationalize, ignore, or distract will not overpower and eliminate it? The answer is that deep in the mid-brain, embedded in our most basic mechanisms for responding to the environment, is a set of signals to tell us that things are okay or not. In other words, *feeling* is primary instruction, and we ignore it at our peril. Feelings are body messages that indicate whether a stimulus in the environment is hostile, unknown, friendly, supportive, useful, boring (and therefore wasteful of valuable time), pleasurable, or requiring attention. The cry of the baby is not designed to make a mother think; it is matched to a discomfort response in the hearing of others, especially mother. The milk congestion in the mother's breast produces discomfort first, then possibly the thought that baby needs feeding. When the teacher walks down the aisle, Johnny stops talking and stares at his book. When an angry dog growls at me, I freeze to make myself invisible. The message is, first trust your feelings. But please note, this message is the very opposite of the one our culture preaches, teaches and advertises.

Most of what goes on in psychotherapy has as its goal the uncovering of feelings associated with painful memory, or of feelings that are not permitted, that habit has suppressed since childhood, when expressing certain feelings was not allowed. Many family taboos against feelings or expression of feelings have their roots in a simple-minded religious view. Honour father and mother gets translated into never show anger against them. Sexual taboos, religious in origin, mean sexual arousal or curiosity is bad, feeling the need to touch and be touched is wicked.

The disabling of feeling may have its roots elsewhere also, in a whole set of stereotypic images that the family conveys with almost religious conviction: Boys don't cry; it is not appropriate to show weakness; fear is shameful; our family has pride and dignity and never reveals its problems; never complain; accept your lot. Since emotion is primarily experienced in the face, a very common family message is "Keep a stiff upper lip." This means don't pout, don't smile, don't be sad, just bear it with a poker face. In adulthood this translates into a whole range of dysfunctions. Taboos around sexual feeling commonly lead to frigidity, guilt, impotence, or fear of the other sex, who threaten to awaken a forbidden arousal.

Showing affection, touching, kissing, hugging may be almost impossible or accompanied by great discomfort. The ability to be assertive, clear, outspoken, to ask for one's needs to be met and to express attitudes honestly, may be missing or may be so undeveloped that what emerges is aggression, yelling, screaming, or physical violence. This is because owning his feelings, having his emotions accepted and supported and understood even when they are negative (that is, anger, pain, loneliness, fear, even grief) can be denied to a child, because it is somehow offensive to an adult.

I remember one client who had been very close to a grandfather who died. She was not allowed to attend the funeral and was left in the care of a neighbour while the burial took place. When she cried, in sadness and frustration—maybe even in anger at her loss, the woman taking care of her slapped her and shut her in a room by herself. She was forbidden to cry. My client remembered all of this when she read the episode about Uncle Craig's funeral in Alice Munro's *Lives of Girls and Women:*

> "Your Uncle Craig died last night."
>
> My mother's voice, telling this, was almost shy.
>
> I was eating my favorite, surreptitious breakfast— Puffed Wheat drowned in black molasses—and sitting on the cement slab outside our door, in the morning sun. It was two days since I had returned from Jenkin's Bend and when she said *Uncle Craig* I thought of him as I had seen him, standing in the doorway, in his vest and shirtsleeves, benignly, perhaps impatiently, waving me off.
>
> The active verb confused me. He *died.* It sounded like something he willed to do, chose to do. As if he said, "Now I'll die." In that case it could not be so final. Yet I knew it was.[2]

Literature helps us to discover feeling, by expressing feeling for us. I have said that feelings are the hardest of human responses to put into language. Stories express feelings we recognize, and permit us to identify them, to experience them in language. Because they get expressed in language they become for readers, for you, *conscious;* you may now be *aware* of them. Sometimes writers, who specialize in language, talk about feelings directly. Here is an example, also from Alice Munro, of such a description:

> Being forgiven creates a peculiar shame. I felt hot, and not just from the blanket. I felt held close, stifled, as if it was not air I had to move and talk through in this world but something thick as cotton. This shame was physical, but

went far beyond sexual shame, my former shame of
nakedness; now it was as if not the naked body but all the
organs inside it—stomach, heart, lungs, liver—were laid
bare and helpless. The nearest thing to this that I had ever
known before was the feeling I got when I was tickled
beyond endurance—horrible, voluptuous feeling of exposure, of impotence, self-betrayal.[3]

The speaker does not try to explain this; she merely reports what the
feeling was like as precisely as possible. Shame is one of the associated
feelings of defeat and failure. It is physically characterized by blushing,
by downcast eyes, and by drooping head and shoulders. The embarrassment that comes from being "bad," condemned, or defeated is rooted in loss, in losing a struggle for some prize, and in powerlessness, in
being helpless and rendered impotent. Perhaps deep in our evolutionary past the prize was food, or a mate, or a piece of territory. Now the
prize might be a ribbon, a certificate, or a word of praise.

As for being helpless, it is difficult at first to understand why a
victim, say of rape or other assault, rendered helpless and forced to
submit to indignity, should feel shame. We can understand anger,
but shame? And yet victims of muggings and other crimes not sexual at all, often require therapy to adjust to their "defeat." Alice Munro
is choosing one example of an experience in which being forgiven
produces a feeling of shame. Del, the speaker, has bitten the arm of
her cousin Agnes and drawn blood. She is forgiven, excused for being
overwrought at Uncle Craig's funeral. We can speculate that being
forgiven involves first of all being condemned and then being treated as somehow not responsible, or weak and incompetent. In fact,
Del did win a kind of victory over her cousin. Tormented, bullied and
assaulted by Agnes, who is mildly sadistic, Del fought back. In some
other society or setting, she might have been applauded as a victor,

and she could have smiled, head held high, and strutted around the room. As it is, her behaviour produces shame in herself and outrage in others. Nice girls don't bite or even fight. Then she is forgiven. Now she has been defeated twice, rendered helpless twice, first by Agnes—whose superior size and strength could be resisted only by biting—and then by the adults who condemn and *forgive* her. So she gets forgiven, not praised. Now her helplessness is complete, *for there is no fighting back against forgiveness.* Jesus knew what a powerful weapon it was. The reader does not have to figure all this out in order to recognize and understand Del's response.

Nor do writers like Mice Munro need to know all the research and psychology about emotion and human development. They don't, by and large, concern themselves with high-speed laboratory films of facial expressions or with baby monkeys running to wire mesh mothers in animal labs in universities. Writers get their information from observing natural human (or animal) behaviour exactly and minutely, and from taking a clear route to their own feelings, which they have noted and recorded with precision. The fact that research usually and belatedly confirms what writers have observed simply shows how accurate the literary observation is and how powerfully and economically the information is transmitted to readers.

Not all feeling in literature is described directly like Del's. Some is implied by context. Readers provide the specifics from their own experience to fit the paradigm, the pattern of feeling provided by the writer. To stay with shame, for example, there are thousands of experiences, petty defeats, minor humiliations, that can be supplied by readers to fill the spaces provided by the writer. When a reader supplies these, she clarifies, makes conscious, and so gives voice, meaning and understanding to experiences that merely fester in chronic pain if left unexpressed. Writers provide language that can evoke feeling; we readers supply the experience.

Here is a famous passage from "Araby," one of James Joyce's best-known stories. The young adolescent boy who tells, or rather confesses, the story, is adoringly in love with a girl he hardly knows, and impetuously promises to bring her a gift from the bazaar called Araby. The uncle with whom he lives forgets or ignores his plea to be allowed to go to Araby on Saturday night and does not get home to give the boy any money until nine o'clock. When the boy gets to Araby it is all but closed down.

> Observing me, the young lady came over and asked me did I wish to buy anything. The tone of her voice was not encouraging; she seemed to have spoken to me out of a sense of duty. I looked humbly at the great jars that stood like eastern guards at either side of the dark entrance to the stall and murmured:
>
> —No, thank you.
>
> The young lady changed the position of one of the vases and went back to the two young men. They began to talk of the same subject. Once or twice the young lady glanced at me over her shoulder.
>
> I lingered before her stall, though I knew my stay was useless, to make my interest in her wares seem the more real. Then I turned away slowly and walked down the middle of the bazaar. I allowed the two pennies to fall against the sixpence in my pocket. I heard a voice call from one end of the gallery that the light was out. The upper part of the hall was now completely dark.
>
> Gazing up into the darkness I saw myself as a creature driven and derided by vanity; and my eyes burned with anguish and anger.[4]

Does this relate to you in any way? Can the story of a boy's bitter disappointment mean much to you? Ask yourself some questions like these. Can you remember your first infatuation, your first crush on someone you hardly knew? Did you want to impress, to please, to be chosen? Can you remember your first great disappointment? How old were you, and how did you feel? Who else was in the story, and what role did your relationship play in the sadness? Were you angry? Frustrated? Is there any part of you now that still feels what you felt then? In what ways are you still like the child you were then? How could you feel better, how would you like the story to have turned out? Did you ever have a great disillusionment, ever see suddenly behind the tinsel and the paint how shabby something was? How had you deluded yourself? What did you want to think, and why did thinking that, matter so much?

Now these are all universal questions describing universal experiences. The particular content must be supplied by you, and in supplying it you can rethink and reorganize your experience. Where memory is pleasant you can re-experience it. I will have much more to say about that soon. Where the past has been painful or confusing, you have the opportunity to review and change it.

Recently, a student running a seminar in a course I was teaching asked the class how they felt about Anne of Green Gables sitting on the station platform alone. You will remember that Anne has been sent for from the orphanage, is expected to be a boy to help with farmwork, and is waiting for "collection" at the railway station. To my surprise, I suddenly, involuntarily, recalled being evacuated from London at the start of the Second World War and sent to a rural village station by train. I later learned I was in East Anglia. My sister and I, and a trainload of other children, wrenched from our parents without preparation that I can recall (I was seven at the time), were unloaded in the country and awaited collection by rural families. We had luggage labels tied to our lapels. I and my sister were the last to be collected. I don't know if people just came in, looked over the motley crowd, and selected whom they wanted, or if we had already been assigned and our rural recipients simply arrived last to pick us up. I do know that the experience was one of the most painful, scary, depressing of my life, and I can recapture some of the hollow feeling, just here in the solar plexus, whenever I think of it, almost fifty years later. Strange to say, though, now that I have put this memory together with Anne on the station platform in Bright River, I feel better about what happened to me. I feel less individually, uniquely abused. I am able to think of all those Barnardo Homes boys who came to Canada and suffered, many of them, as little more than slave labourers in horrible circumstances. I have some insight into refugees treated like baggage. That experience of mine has a human history, can be shared and be a bond to others, and can be made into a discussible shape by a little description springing from the imagination of Lucy Maud Montgomery. Most readers will not have had such a close parallel to Anne's situation in the station. But Montgomery must have seen that the image of Anne alone on the platform could call forth a thousand similar feelings of aloneness and rejection in readers, as I discovered in my class. There is a little bit of orphan in each of us.

Not all feeling described in literature is presented directly. In fact, most literature presents actions, behaviours and events that indirectly suggest feelings. As I said before, feelings are hard to write about, hard to put into language, but all feelings are related to some experience, whether it's pain from hunger in a baby, joy in seeing an old friend, or fear of elevators from having been locked in a closet during childhood. Affect, feeling-emotion, does not just pop up for no reason. It is possible, and much easier, therefore, to describe actions and events and places that are associated with certain feelings. In fact, this is what literature mostly consists of, descriptions of possible life situations in which the appropriate feelings are supplied by the reader. Feelings always have a context.

I spent some time working with a client to uncover precisely what she felt like in her relation to the world, how it felt to be her. The closest we came after some time was "lonely." I then took her back to her childhood routines by means of mental visualization; I got her to go to her back door, be in her kitchen and so on. It was during my prompting about greeting mother that she pointed out the reality of the situation, a reality I had not been able to grasp before. She was alone. Mother was out, father was away. The house she came back to every day was silent and empty. She made her own snack; she turned on the TV; she sat alone and waited. This went on for years. This aloneness, then, was not merely loneliness, as I had mistakenly thought. She always felt some anxiety, fear, anticipation, expectancy, and underneath it all a sense of being neglected, of not being worthy, of not being cared for. Somehow she had come to believe that she was partly responsible for her own aloneness. If she had been "better" in some way, someone would have been there for her. And rather than staying out late or playing with friends, she was told she had to be home in order to wait. The house needed her to wait and hope and hurt. All of these feelings, not explored in words before and so not given a shape one could see, had a context and were evoked by returning to the context. This was her story.

Fiction is the best medium for providing contexts for feelings by using language the reader may not be able to supply for herself. The reader attaches emotional content to the words, and experiences what is important to *herself.* By providing a setting for the reader's feelings to surface, fiction makes possible an awareness of hidden parts of the self. For instance, a student whose brother had died in a car accident two years earlier, thought she had dealt with her grief, until she read "Particulars" by Bronwen Wallace, when she discovered that there were still a lot of feelings to sort out.

Here is a description from a short story called "A Christmas Carillon" by Hortense Calisher. The character Grorley has left his wife and children and is living alone, torn between his bachelor freedoms and his attachment to the security and comfort of family and home. Read this passage carefully, aloud if you can:

Thanksgiving Day was the worst. The day dawned oyster-pale and stayed that way. Grorley slept as late as he could, then went out for a walk. The streets were slack, without the twitch of crowds, and the houses had a tight look of inner concentration. He turned toward the streets which held only shops, and walked uptown as far as Rockefeller Center. The rink was open, with its usual cast of characters—ricocheting children, a satiny, professional twirler from the Ice Show, and several solemn old men who skated upright in some Euclidean absorption of their own. Except for a few couples strolling along in the twin featurelessness of love, the crowd around the rink was type-cast too. Here, it told itself, it participated in life, here in this flying spectacle of flag and stone it could not possibly be alone. With set, shy smiles, it glanced sideways at its neighbors, rounded its shoulders to the wind, turned up its collar, and leaned closer to the musical bonfire of the square. Grorley straightened up, turned on his heel, smoothed down his collar, and walked rapidly toward Sixth Avenue. He filled himself full of ham and eggs in one of the quick-order places that had no season, taxied home, downed a drink, swallowed two Seconal tablets, and went to bed.[5]

How do you feel about Grorley? Are you sad or sorry for him? Are you repelled by him? Is he self-indulgent? Is he a coward or a hero? What is he looking for? Is there anything scary or repugnant for you here? Are you glad you are not Grorley?

Your answers depend entirely on who you are and what experience of life you bring to the writing. The feelings you experience, if any, in response to the reading, are not right or wrong—they are part of your way of understanding the passage and a help to understanding yourself. Look again. What feelings can you find in the passage? Strangely enough, feelings are not explained there. The feelings are in the reader.

I tried this on a class of mine and found a very wide range of responses. One girl felt very strongly the coldness and isolation of the scene. Another felt it was awful to be on the outside looking in, the houses all turned inwards on Thanksgiving—a bad day not to have company, family, or home. Still another young man became quite angry at Grorley, was disgusted with him and felt he was a "wimp." This student is a very intelligent, ambitious, hard-driving fellow who clearly believes in control, in making things work, in not avoiding challenges. I have no doubt that underneath so much competence is a fear of passivity, of loss of control, of loneliness or helplessness. I will say more about these fears in the chapter on aging.

Here is another passage, the opening one from *Love, Infidelity and Drinking to Forget*, a lovely, rich novel about life in rural New Brunswick by an American, Elizabeth Gundy. The novel opens and closes with good-byes. Read and think about the following passage before answering the questions. Visualize the scene, let yourself be there, stand in a corner on the sidewalk, unnoticed by Sara, Carol, Daniel and the others. Watch what happens and then take off with Daniel and Sara.

The houseplants were spread on the sidewalk like a flower show, along with a mounting collection of unessentials that wouldn't fit in the truck—picture frames, floor lamps, kitchen table, wok, and his armchair.

He strapped her easel and paintings on top of the truck. She kissed her friends good-bye one last time.

"Carol…Vito…Judy…" she cried.

"Sara…Daniel…"

He got behind the wheel. Sara extended her arms through the truck's open window.

"Call," cried Carol.

"There aren't any phones up there…"

"If you need anything…" wailed Judy, forcing the wok through the open window onto Sara's lap.

He started the motor, and the truck moved down Christopher Street. "Write," cried Sara. "Keep us up to date…" They headed toward Hudson Street, out of sight, out of earshot.

She's sad, thought Daniel. But she's prepared to the teeth. Her purse bulged with papers—Canadian immigration certificates, birth certificates, dental X rays, the cats' rabies inoculation declaration, her Bloomingdale's charge plate, and the master code of their cartons which would now have to be changed to delete the floor lamp, kitchen table, and his armchair.[6]

Permit your feelings to flow into consciousness. Does the passage disturb you at all? Do you feel excited or happy? Confused? Uncomfortable? Dislocated? Certainly "moving" is one of life's most stressful events. Can you remember moving, how sad you felt? My worst memories of moving are from childhood. Almost nothing seemed more unsettling and sickening than sitting in an empty house, waiting for the moving van, or pulling up to a building in an entirely strange district or town, or packing up all one's possessions that seemed to belong permanently in their old places. It is possible, I think, to break a heart saying good-bye. The passage I have quoted does not really describe any feelings. Yet it provides a framework, a colouring book for the reader to paint in feelings from personal experience. In doing this, in calling up feelings and memoried experience to activate the writing, to illustrate the text, the reader is able to re-experience his own life in a slightly altered way, a way that can give new insight into old material. Memory does this by reappearing dressed in the new language provided by the writer. The reader's experience is necessary to give life to the writer's suit of clothes, and, in turn, the reader's experience is brought to life, to the surface, by the language, the clothing that the reader is forced to put on in the act of reading.

To use a different analogy, the writing is like a hand puppet and the reader is like a hand. The puppet comes to life only on the moving hand, but the hand is motivated to do what it does by the character, shape and demands of the puppet, and the performance is limited by the experience, skill and imagination of the hand's owner. All fiction and poetry therefore is a vehicle for experiencing feeling, whether it describes feeling directly or not. The reason for this is that all places, characters and events can be potential settings for feelings to be supplied by the reader. Since feelings are hard to verbalize, the physical or social settings for them are provided instead, and the feelings are *experienced* anew, without description. These feelings can then be used by the reader for understanding attitudes, values, the personal past, relationships and so on.

Catharsis

More than two thousand years ago, Aristotle described the powerful effect of tragedy, performed in the theatre, on its viewers. Remember that printing had not been invented, most people could not read and theatre was the only vehicle for the transmission of dramatized literature. For this reason, tragedy was serious business; it contained philosophic, moral and religious teaching and dealt with matters of life, death and fate. Aristotle pointed out in *The Poetics* that a person watching tragedy sees in the action on stage an imitation of life, a situation that, because it is based on human experience, can be recognized. The language, the behaviours, the props and scenery work in conjunction with the recognition of human suffering, confusion and struggle, to produce feelings in the audience, feelings that today we call being "moved." Aristotle identified these feelings as pity and fear. I think these emotions arise out of compassion for someone we recognize as like ourselves and fear that what we see could happen to us. Aristotle explained that experiencing these emotions leads to their "purgation," a relief from them in some way that he does not explain, but that he calls "catharsis."

By now we have developed a psychological language that helps us to map and visualize how this purgation or relief, this catharsis, can work. Human beings are equipped with emotions, affects, that are basic to their functioning and to their survival. We experience fear to keep us from dangers; anger to protect us against threats; joy to reward and so motivate us; and compassion to link us to others because we cannot make it alone, to name only a few of the primary affects. As we grow up, we are socialized and taught to repress, even avoid, certain affects. We bury our fear and we harden our hearts. This is not good for us. The buried or disregarded affects continue to work in us, but if they are unacknowledged their effect is toxic and produces deflections and diversions of feeling that lessen our control, our clarity and our efficiency. By seeing tragedy we are confronting, experiencing consciously, our emotional life, so that we become freer from the hidden power our secret fears have over us. Our frozen emotions are melted.

Aristotle has less to say about comedy, but basically it works in the same way. By seeing the ludicrous, the weakness of human folly, the obscurity of mistakes we recognize, we experience the pleasure and relief of acknowledging our own frailties, our own mistakes, and we laugh because it's not us in that particular pickle but it could be, or it has been and we have survived.

We can't go to the theatre all the time, and it isn't open night and day. It doesn't stage what we happen to need, as though by magic. The performance proceeds through the play at its own speed, not at ours. We can't review it, except by returning to the theatre for the next performance, or by memory, or by reading the play script. To read the play is the same thing as reading a story, except that if we have seen the play we will read it influenced in our imagining by the voice, tone, accent, gesture, characterization, setting and costume of the production we saw. But a powerful drama that speaks to us personally can, of course, be very powerful indeed. It makes us witnesses of an actual event.

Imagine that a couple who have lost a teenage daughter are watching a production of *King Lear* and seeing at the end of the play the king holding Cordelia, of three daughters his one loyal, loving child, dead in his arms. This would be painful for such an audience, heart-wrenching in the extreme. Remember also that in our culture we are not supposed to express strong emotion in public. We suppress or hide our tears and swallow our sobs, burying our faces in our handkerchiefs or tissues or waiting till we have recovered before going into the theatre lobby. This inhibition makes the pain of catharsis more difficult for us. Imagine that adult children of a chronically alcoholic mother are seeing a production of Eugene O'Neill's *A Long Day's Journey into Night,* about the anguish and conflict of a family trying to cope with a severe addiction problem. How would they feel? What produces such strong emotional reactions in the viewer?

We have already seen how emotion or affect can be repressed from the training we received as children. We also know that emotion is very difficult to speak about, to put into language, because it originates in pre-language centres of the brain that can operate to influence our behaviour without the benefit of language. Language is, however, the most important tool human beings possess for producing consciousness. Language, in other words, is an organized report of what is going on—a report that can be stored in memory and retrieved by hearing or reading other relevant language cues. To get from the feeling-producing parts of the brain into the conscious, knowing, reporting, organizing parts of the brain, where information is labelled, recognized, sorted and filed; to cross between these parts, human beings use language as their most efficient agent. The brain sends messages very rapidly back and forth.

What happens in catharsis is something like this: the viewer (or reader) recognizes a situation that approximates some personal, emotionally charged experience. He is willing to stretch the personal experience to fit the viewed performance because of the need to have the personal experience recognized and understood. By this I mean that important emotional experience is easier to bear if it is shared, recognized by the playwright or novelist. The reader's need to be not alone and to be understood is a powerful incentive to apply his personal experience generously so that it will connect to what is being seen. The play takes the emotional experience of the audience and organizes and describes it in language. Then it can be *consciously* known by the audience *in a way not previously achieved.* The audience now know *their own* experience much better, more fully, more consciously, and in a language that makes the experience more "discussible," seeable, manageable and so controllable. In other words, the code that is language, applied to emotion or feeling that was before simply disturbing—and that controlled the reader/viewer—now makes possible some kind of process that puts the "I" in charge. This recognition/control experience produces the relief that Aristotle describes.

Is the pain of recognition worth the relief? Would it be better to keep painful emotion buried and avoid it? It is fair to say that the fear of this pain keeps a great many people from both psychotherapy and reading. They know they carry around painful memories, feelings, hurts and wounds from experiences and relationships. They greatly fear the pain of recognizing the experiences and the associated feelings. Grownups may even have been taught as children not to cry, not to be sad, not to be hurt. Many parents tell their children that their suffering hurts them, the parents, too much, so please don't do it. "I can't stand to see you cry!" People trained like this work very hard to control the pain so that it does not surface or emerge into consciousness. This is hard work. They must be on guard at all times, warding off reminders, avoiding various intimacies and closenesses, interrupting the speech of others lest something be said that will evoke their buried pain. They intellectualize what they read and what they see, to keep from feeling-recognition.

Even university English departments, where people read a lot of literature designed to evoke personal feelings, are well stocked with sensitive, hurt individuals who in spite of their talent and a love of language must rationalize and intellectualize literature so that it can be disarmed of its affect. People who are able to suppress feeling believe they are very much in control of everything. Indeed, control and even bullying can become characteristic of the personality of such people. They insist on having their own way. In reality, however, they are being controlled by their unacknowledged, unexpressed and unrecognized pain-emotion. It is a bit like having a treasure that you believe is the source of your power and influence, but that demands so much guarding, protection, anxiety and management that it really controls you, like the precious ring that is Sméagol the Gollum's obsession in *The Hobbit* by J. R. R. Tolkien.

For these reasons it does make sense for human beings to find some way to articulate and so process their experiences. Writers help us to do this by putting into language situations we can recognize. Books speak, give voice, for us. Our catharsis is part gratitude, part relief at the communion of recognition, at not being as alone as we thought we were, at having language provide a form and shape, a container, for our emotion and pain. *The language of the play completes the feedback loop from our emotions to our consciousness.* The couple whose teenage daughter died in a car accident may appear to have little in common with the ancient and legendary King Lear, but when he, rocking his dead child Cordelia in his arms, utters his last words to her—

> Why should a dog, a horse, a rat, have life,
> And thou no breath at all? Thou'lt come no more,
> Never, never, never, never, never.
> Pray you undo this button. Thank you, sir.
> Do you see this? Look on her! Look her lips,
> Look there, look there—[7]

and then dies of a shattered heart, a broken old man, what must they feel? Lear has given voice to their great pain, has publicly expressed their depthless grief. They are helped to know how they feel and so can be more whole. They are less alone, and are placed in touch with a universal suffering, a larger order that crosses time and space, and a language that gives expression to the breaking heart.

Shakespeare's greatness rests precisely on his ability to write such lines, to imagine such suffering and give it voice. Even more amazing to me is Shakespeare's awareness of precisely how literature works upon his audiences, as he explains in *Hamlet*. Shakespeare shows us that he understood better how readers read than do most critics today.

Hamlet finds out that his father has been murdered by his uncle, now king and married to Hamlet's mother, the widow of the murdered king. Hamlet moves slowly toward the revenge demanded by his father's ghost. To test the truth of his uncle's guilt, he uses the mirror of fiction. He commissions a play that will reenact the crime. His uncle, in the audience, should respond so as to reveal his identification with the characters and events in the play:

> I have heard
> That guilty creatures, sitting at a play,
> Have by the very cunning of the scene
> Been struck so to the soul that presently
> They have proclaim'd their malefactions;
> For murther, though it have no tongue, will speak
> With most miraculous organ. I'll have these players
> Play something like the murther of my father
> Before mine uncle. I'll observe his looks;
> I'll tent him to the quick. If he but blench,
> I know my course.[8]

Shakespeare was obviously fully conscious of the connections between theatre and life and of the usefulness of literature in baring secrets of the soul. For Hamlet, the point about the play is that it is public. Had he given the king the play to read privately, the king's response would have been at least as strong, but unwitnessed, and Hamlet needs proof, witnesses.

The most convenient way to experience catharsis is by reading fiction and poetry. To read a novel in which the reader loses the sense of separateness, lives with the characters, becomes part of their life and setting, laughs and cries with them and takes on a life in the fiction; to do this can often lead to a catharsis at the conclusion of the novel, when it is sadly, reluctantly, gratefully closed and put away. The reader feels a great sense of loss, a grieving, but at the same time he feels a profound sense of pleasure, perhaps awe, at having been enabled to share the life of imaginary figures to whom he has grown close. This closeness comes from the reader's willingness to role-play the parts in the book and in so doing to experience emotions appropriate to the characters and situations.

Let us take an example. Jane Eyre is an orphan in the famous novel of that name by Charlotte Brontë. Jane is ten, a foster child in her aunt's house, where there are three cousins whom their mother spoils relentlessly. Uncle, who might have been kind, has died. Jane is barely tolerated, abused emotionally and physically, tyrannized by her cousin John. Her life seems to be a continual misery. She is treated with contempt, even by the servants, and is threatened with being turned over to the poorhouse. She has no choice, in the harsh world of the novel, but to endure as best she can in the house. The novel begins with one more cold rejection by her aunt, who is pampering the other three children. Jane has no hope of receiving affection, or even a kind word, from that quarter. She takes refuge in another room with a book from the bookcase. The incidents that follow are really a climax to her life at her aunt's. Books seem to have been Jane's one route to another life. How many adults have told me they survived the intense suffering of their childhood by reading! Jane is attacked by her eleven-year-old cousin John and told she must not touch "his" books, which of course he doesn't read. Instead, he throws the books at her after hitting her with his fist.

> …the volume was flung, it hit me, and I fell, striking my head against the door and cutting it. The cut bled, the pain was sharp: my terror had passed its climax; other feelings succeeded.
>
> "Wicked and cruel boy!" I said. "You are like a murderer—you are like a slave-driver—you are like the Roman emperors!"
>
> I had read Goldsmith's "History of Rome," and had formed my opinion of Nero, Caligula, &c. Also I had drawn parallels in silence, which I never thought thus to have declared aloud.
>
> "What! what!" he cried. "Did she say that to me? Did you hear her, Eliza and Georgiana? Won't I tell mamma? but first—"
>
> He ran headlong at me: I felt him grasp my hair and my shoulder: he had closed with a desperate thing. I really saw in him a tyrant: a murderer. I felt a drop or two of blood from my head trickle down my neck, and was sensible of somewhat pungent suffering: these sensations for the time predominated over fear, and I received him in frantic sort. I don't very well know what I did with my hands, but he called me "Rat! rat!" and bellowed out aloud. Aid was near him: Eliza and Georgiana had run for Mrs. Reed, who was gone upstairs; she now came upon the scene, followed by Bessie and her maid Abbot. We were parted. I heard the words:—"Dear! dear! What a fury to fly at Master John!"
>
> "Did ever anybody see such a picture of passion!" Then Mrs. Reed subjoined:—"Take her away to the red-room, and

lock her in there." Four hands were immediately laid upon me, and I was borne upstairs.[9]

Locked in the red-room, where her uncle had died, Jane becomes hysterically ill, and her illness leads to her removal from the house.

My reactions to this story, if I examine them, are a mixture of admiration at the writing, amazement at the callousness and inhuman coldness of the Reed family, anger at and dislike of the pretension and snobbishness of the middle-class world they represent, indignation that a child should be so treated, a desire to protect and revenge Jane, and wonder at her courage.

A similar episode in *Oliver Twist* comes to mind. Oliver, tormented beyond his endurance by a much bigger boy, Noah Claypole, finally turns violent and attacks his persecutor:

A minute ago, the boy had looked the quiet, mild, dejected creature that harsh treatment had made him. But his spirit was roused; the cruel insult to his dead mother had set his blood on fire. His breast heaved; his attitude was erect; his eye bright and vivid; his whole person changed, as he stood glaring over the cowardly tormentor who now lay crouching at his feet; and defied him with an energy he had never known before.[10]

These episodes remind me of my five minutes as hero, when I lost all control and attacked my persecutor, the school bully, in a Cambridge schoolyard, a place where an evacuee from London was as odd as an alien from outer space. Obviously, the experience is more widespread than I had thought—but I wish I had known that then, had been in a slightly wider world that had included Jane Eyre and Oliver Twist.

Not everyone reads this the same way, however. My client is adopted. She is now in her middle twenties. After her adoption, three children were born to her adoptive parents, making her the oldest child. Such a situation is not at all uncommon. The impression I had was that Tess, the adopted child, gradually became more and more emotionally neglected, while attention and affection were given freely to the "natural" kids. In fact, she seemed to become a kind of domestic servant, a substitute mother, whose role was to help raise the other children. I gave *Jane Eyre* to Tess with dramatic results. Tess had received two dominant messages in her childhood. One was to honour and respect her parents, to whom she must be eternally grateful because they had "chosen" her, and so proved how much they loved her and how lucky she was. Of course, the behaviour in the home didn't seem to support the idea that her parents loved her, and the confusion eventually brought her into therapy. Before this she had not been able to talk about the situation at home without appearing resentful, ungrateful and complaining, and this was not allowed. The second message was that since she was so lucky she must never feel sorry for herself. Now the ability to be sorry for oneself, to be sad for one's own suffering, can certainly be overdone, but not to be able to feel this at all is to have shut down an important part of the feeling apparatus. Empathy consists of making links between one's own suffering and that of others.

Tess was stuck and living with a set of rules that had shut her emotions off from her consciousness. The opening chapters of *Jane Eyre* moved her very powerfully. We were able to talk about how it felt to be Jane, how unfair and unjust her aunt and cousins were to her, how lonely she must have been, and how she was caught between the rules of gratitude, with their corollary, the fear of being totally outcast and alone, and the unexpressed knowledge of her own unhappiness. The adult Jane, who tells the story of Jane Eyre, describes a much more brutal and open situation, a more black and white one, than Tess could lay claim to. In a way, the degree of caring that Tess actually received made it harder for her to acknowledge her feelings. By talking first about the novel, Tess was eventually able to sort out her real feelings about her childhood and admit the truth about how her parents felt and behaved without feeling wicked for betraying them. Of course *Jane Eyre* helped me to understand what we were talking about, since I had never been in Tess' situation. Jane spoke for Tess, in extreme terms, yes, but so clearly that Tess could not escape some of the images and their application to her.

It is interesting to see how many children have felt at some time or other that they might somehow be in the wrong family, might have been secretly adopted or simply unwanted or a mistake. *Jane Eyre* appeals to the indignant, sometimes rejected, criticized, unfairly treated child in most of us, and enables us to get in touch with that child we carry with us who suffered in shame, who did not have the words, and who was tied up in a web of rules designed to protect our parents and keep us "seen but not heard." Literature helps us to be heard.

1   Sylvan Tomkins, *Affect, Imagery, Consciousness* (New York: Springer, 1962), 1:5.

2   Alice Munro, *Lives of Girls and Women* (New York: McGraw-Hill Ryerson, 1971), p. 45.

3   Munro, *Lives of Girls and Women*, p. 57.

4   James Joyce, "Araby," in *Dubliners* (Harmondsworth: Penguin, 1976).

5   Hortense Calisher, "A Christmas Carillon," in *Family: Stories from the Interior*, ed. Geri Giebel Chavis (Saint Paul, Minn.: Graywolf Press, 1987).

6   Elizabeth Gundy, *Love, Infidelity and Drinking to Forget* (Garden City, N.Y.: Dial Press, 1984), p.1.

7   William Shakespeare, *King Lear*, V. iii, in *The Complete Works* (Harmondsworth: Penguin, 1969).

8   William Shakespeare, *Hamlet*, II.ii. ed. L. Kittredge (Boston: Ginn, 1939).

9   Charlotte Brontë, *Jane Eyre* (New York: Norton, 1971), pp. 8-9.

10   Charles Dickens, *Oliver Twist* (London: Oxford University Press, 1949), pp.41-42.

CHAPTER SEVEN

The Truth that Lies Ahead

We have seen how reading literature can change the way we look at the past and the way we manage our behaviour and our relationships in the present. Can reading help us to manage the future? How do we think about the future, and how does it affect how we feel now? How is it possible to think about events and possibilities that have not happened yet? How do people get to imagine and project things to do or make, places to visit, people they would like to meet or plan to meet?

We are composed of a blend of our genetic programs—our raw material, so to speak—and of everything that has happened to us— how our raw material has been processed. Whatever has happened to us, whatever we have done, will have some influence on what we do in the future. If we have been bitten once by a dog as a child, we are likely to try to avoid getting bitten a second time. When she was a child, my wife was bitten on the face by a German Shepherd dog. In addition to the bite, she had several stitches to endure, so the entire incident became an elaborate, painful, scary life event, a land-mark event. As a result, though she still likes some dogs, including our own Airedale, Guy, she won't go near a German Shepherd. Her fear became breed-specific.

Eddie Greenspan, the well-known lawyer, reports that since his childhood bite by a dog he cannot abide any dog and will go blocks out of his way to avoid one. He says that Stephen King's *Cujo* is too horrific for him to read. We can all think of things that scare us, and some of us can trace these to specific events in our lives. Others have forgotten or don't want to think about the origin of their fears. But whether we remember or not, those fears will influence our thinking and our planning, as will the joys, the sadnesses, the surprises and excitements of the past.

Since the past is so powerful in influencing our future, if we change it, say by reading and so rethinking past experiences, then we can also change the future. Let me give you one example of this; and remember, a good deal of psychotherapy is aimed at changing the past in order to liberate the present and the future. This story is about Libby. She had been a client for some time, suffering from an extremely poor self-image, even self-dislike. Libby was prone to proving her worthlessness by going to bed with any male who asked her. She had been married several times, the first time when she was fifteen and pregnant. Now, in her late thirties, with three grown children, she wanted to change, to take control of her life and fulfill her potential for success, both economic and relational. If someone has learned to be self-condemning, it is important to find and identify the sources of this labelling so that the "I," in this case my client, can learn to separate herself from the labels and change her way of thinking about herself and her behaviour. You are not "bad" just because others say you are "bad." In other words, as long as you think the label is *you*, you will have a hard time getting rid of it—it becomes tattoo, not sticky peel-off.

In working with Libby, I discovered that her mother had not wanted her, had deeply resented the domestic role for which she had had to give up a career. This woman experienced extreme problems with her own femaleness and sexuality, and, above all, seemed to *take no pleasure* in her female child and conveyed this to her. If Libby could learn that this was part of the origin of her problem, then she could be free to unlearn it and think of herself differently. To put it another way, she might have to "lose" her deceased mother's version of her in order to gain her "self." This can be very difficult, because in rejecting a parent's version of oneself, the grown child may feel disloyal, may be rejecting the parent. If I think I have to reject my parent in order to love myself, I am caught in a dilemma.

In the long process of exploring her past and supporting the independent, creative, individual side of Libby, I had from time to time given her various books I thought were relevant. Libby made all the excuses that I have come to recognize as signalling a lack of readiness in the client, or of relevance, interest, or applicability in the readings. She was too busy; she was so tired at night she could not read; she was so distressed in her latest affair she forgot all about it; and so on. Then, late in our relationship, in one of our last sessions, I gave her Charlotte Vale Allen's *Daddy's Girl*. I have given many clients this book to read, and keep several copies in my office. The author, a Canadian journalist and writer who lives in New York, tells the story of her growing up as the incest victim of a domineering father, who regularly sexually abused his daughter and forced her into a variety of sexual services that left her feeling used, nauseated, contaminated, confused and rejected. I shall have more to say about sexual abuse and incest in the chapter on women's issues. For now, I want to tell you that Libby, for the first time, felt some real energy and excitement at seeing her *feelings* described in print. She discovered from reading this book that circumstances can make a person a victim, make her feel unwanted, rejected, valueless. I had been telling Libby that *it was not her fault* her mother did not like her or want her or had emotionally abused her. Now, here was powerful confirmation of such a possibility in her reading about another child who, through entirely no fault of her own, finds herself selected for a special kind of victimization. The book made believable through reading *experience*, the cruelty that can be inflicted on an innocent child.

Libby read about herself when she read about Charlotte locking herself in the bathroom, hiding in closets, becoming a sexual automaton, getting sick, feeling like dirt. She could now believe that she had truly been unlucky, an innocent victim. She had read a story that touched her own history closely enough that she could see the hurt child in the story as a sad and victimized other person and as herself; she could now therefore begin to see herself as not guilty, and could separate herself from the distorted parenting of her childhood.

How did this discovery, prepared for by previous counselling, free Libby to live differently in the future? By changing her self-image, and by re-knowing the past in ways for which she did not have to feel like a bad or disgusting person, she could imagine a future under the *control* of a talented, able, okay self. She could plan to do things that would now be possible because it would be appropriate for her to succeed. She could now take over her life. By redefining the past with the help of reading, she could feedforward information to design a future.

FEEDFORWARD

Monica was a student in my literature survey course. She came from a profoundly troubled home, felt overresponsible and trapped. Her situation seriously affected her work and interfered with her reading. Monica had grown up knowing a lot of pain. She revealed some of this pain after she was invited to respond personally to the literature in her program. One of her assignments was to read *Lady Chatterley's Lover* by D. H. Lawrence. She wrote, "What I admire about Connie Chatterley is her courage to be free, to do what she wants and to live her own life." Some time after this, Monica came to tell me that she had been accepted in the flight training program of the Canadian Armed Forces. She had decided to take over her own life.

Leonard was nineteen, a homosexual who lived with his mother after his parents were divorced. He had not spoken to his father in two years, was convinced his father hated him and would despise him forever if he were to find out about Len's sexual orientation. Leonard condemned himself and was embarrassed at his closeness to his mother, so he tended to fight with her. I wanted Leonard to tell his father how he felt without regard to the consequences—after all, they could not be more estranged than they were in Len's mind already. I asked Len to read a short story from *The Red Pony* by John Steinbeck. In this story, the boy Jody suffers a lot of disappointment with respect to adult males. His father is a tyrant who appears to be insensitive and does not hide his contempt for his aging father-in-law, a grandfather whom Jody reveres. Jody feels alone and betrayed—he does not have the father he wants. I think what I wanted was to open up to Len questions about fathers, maleness and communication. Len read the story and became very angry as we discussed it. Adults, he said, were just brutal, boring, stupid clods who had no right to have children they could abuse.

Len decided to tell his father how he felt, how he had always been ignored, was not good enough, was just not *known!* His father had not tried to see him for two years! What kind of father was he? Len phoned his father and they met for lunch. At first his father was defensive, but finally he just listened. He had thought Len hated him for leaving his mother. He felt that if he tried to be with Len, he would just be rejected all the time. He did not care about Len's sexual feelings, he just wanted Len to understand why he had to leave home. They decided to meet for lunch once a week to talk about their lives.

These cases are examples of feedforward. First, let's take a closer look at feedback. The best example of a simple feedback system is the common household thermostat, which is called in engineering a "servomechanism." The thermostat functions mechanically in response to the environment. It has "set" points. If the temperature drops below a certain set point, the "on," the thermostat permits the completion of a loop that activates the heat system, which drives up the temperature of the air, which in turn has the effect of breaking a loop in the thermostat so that the heat goes off. The goal of the thermostat—the name means "heat-static"—is to keep things on an even keel, to prevent radical change. It responds to the environment, permits temperature rise, but only to the extent of restoring conditions to a previously "agreed upon" setting, what we might call normal.

I had a friend who went away on a three-week trip leaving things in his apartment in the control of his thermostat. Something went wrong. When he returned, he opened his door on what had become a sauna. The fish were cooked in the aquarium, the fridge had broken down from overwork and his food had rotted, plaster had dried and cracked, and furniture, hot to the touch, was coming apart. The thermostat had become unresponsive to feedback.

What the thermostat should be "reading" and responding to in the environment is information—information that it acts upon. Radar and sonar operate on similar principles. A signal is sent out, and then returns conveying information about the environment. As a consequence of this feedback, the signal sender-reader might do any one of a number of things depending on some short- or long-term goal. For instance, it might be necessary to change course, increase speed, send a message, or become quiet. In the cowboy movies I used to watch, when the hero was hiding behind a rock and wanted to know where the bad guy was, he would put his hat on a stick and raise it up a little till it was visible; then the bad guy would shoot at it and so give away his position. This information was then used by the hero to do something.

Human beings use feedback constantly to modify present behaviour; we look and listen a lot, and respond, not always appropriately, but always. We feel material and buy or reject it; we squeeze fruit; we stroke each other; we feel our skis moving too fast and spread our feet into a snowplow. I write till the ink runs out, and then I see the faint symbols and change pens. Or *we read,* and we think and feel about what we read, and this may or may not affect our behaviour—though it very often affects our *perception,* which in turn affects our behaviour *pervasively.* The words of the story are a coded signal requiring decoding. We activate the code, which in turn activates a recall/recognition process in our brains. We feedback information to and from the literature in a looping pattern.

Human beings, indeed all creatures and in a sense even plants, depend on memory to survive. This is what is meant in biology by adaptation. Over time, as the environment changes, responding organisms in the environment also change to fit into it. The goal is always survival, peace, balance. The moth changes its colouring; species change their diets. Today we see humans changing their eating habits in response to pollution, chemical additives, lack of exercise.

We use information from the past to alter our behaviour in the future in order to improve our chances of survival. Feedforward is using the information from past experience to plan an action in the future. If you try to open a door and find it locked, you are getting feedback. Your action on the door, twisting and pulling, fails to open it. Failure is a crucial source of feedforward information. If you decide to go and get the key to open the door, you are incorporating the failure information into a feedforward system, planning a successful action in the future, imagining a next try. The feedback ("door locked") makes it possible to take future action ("get key"). Planning and imagining a future become possible.

I have chosen to use opening a door as my example quite deliberately. People who read speak of having doors opened to them, doors of insight, doors of perception, doors of imagination. Reading about the actions and situations of other people helps us not only to review the past and think about it differently, but also to see new possibilities, new ways of doing things. We think about how we might change a relationship, how we might hurdle a problem; we speculate about how we would handle loss, grief, or seduction. Reading stories about what hasn't happened to us yet can inoculate us to future problems by giving us practice, safe, imaginary practice, at being in the problem now. "What if?" reading helps us to experience what might be and prepares us for what may come. A very powerful recent example of this is Jacobo Timerman's story of being imprisoned and tortured in Argentina, *Prisoner Without a Name, Cell Without a Number.* When I read this I kept thinking, over and over again, I could be in prison, this could happen to me, how would I handle this? In fact, the author claims that one of his purposes in writing the story is to prepare readers for just such a misfortune:

> Although I cannot transmit the magnitude of that pain, I can perhaps offer some advice to those who will suffer torture in the future. The human being will continue to be tortured in different countries, under different regimes. In the year and a half I spent under house arrest I devoted much thought to my attitude during torture sessions and during the period of solitary confinement. I realized that, instinctively, I'd developed an attitude of absolute passivity. Some fought against being carried to the torture tables; others begged not to be tortured; others insulted their torturers. I represented sheer passivity. Because my eyes were blindfolded, I was led by the hand. And I went. The silence was part of the terror. Yet I did not utter a word. I was told

to undress. And I did so, passively. I was told, when I sat on a bed, to lie down. And, passively, I did so. This passivity, I believe, preserved a great deal of energy and left me with all my strength to withstand the torture. I felt I was becoming a vegetable, casting aside all logical emotions and sensations—fear, hatred, vengeance—for any emotion or sensation meant wasting useless energy.

In my opinion, this is sound advice. Once it's been determined that a human being is to be tortured, nothing can prevent that torture from taking place. And it's best to allow yourself to be led meekly toward pain and through pain, rather than to struggle resolutely as if you were a normal human being. The vegetable attitude can save a life.

I had a similar experience during those long days of solitary confinement. More than once I was brusquely awakened by someone shouting: "Think. Don't sleep, think." But I refused to think. I behaved as if my mind were occupied with infinite diverse tasks. Concrete, specific tasks, chores. To think meant becoming conscious of what was happening to me, imagining what might be happening to my wife and children; to think meant trying to work out how to relieve this situation, how to wedge an opening in my relationship with the jailers. In that solitary universe of the tortured, any attempt to relate to reality was an immense painful effort leading to nothing.[1]

IMMUNIZATION

In 1965 or thereabouts, Martin Seligman was doing psychological research on conditioned responses with dogs, when he made his first discovery of *learned helplessness*.[2] He had been giving electric shocks to dogs who were restrained in some kind of apparatus that made it impossible to escape or avoid the shock. The dogs quickly learned that nothing they could do would help them to avoid the discomfort. After some sessions of this treatment, the dogs were transferred to a shuttle box where on one side they received shocks, but if they jumped over a low partition they could escape the shocks and so be free of pain. To Seligman's surprise, the dogs trained first in inescapable shock did not try to escape. They simply lay down and whined, they gave up, despaired, or, as Seligman described it, they "wilted."

This led to a series of experiments that produced some now famous results. Dogs trained *first* in a shock-escapable setting will continue to escape even after a period of training in a non-escapable-shock situation. It is as though, having first learned that something they could do would improve their situation, they did not forget this, even when they had to endure a period of inescapable, unalterable discomfort. Their early success in escaping shock seemed to have *immunized* them against future despair. This observation about dogs was subsequently confirmed by research on rats, cats, fish and people. The theory of learned helplessness revealed that when creatures *believe* that nothing they can do will affect the outcome of a situation in which they are hurting, they are rendered passive. Believing themselves to be helpless, people will endure suffering that could in fact be avoided or stopped by appropriate action. Moreover, such learned helplessness is transferred to other situations requiring cognitive problem solving. Students finding themselves unable to control a pain stimulus in an experiment have diminished problem-solving skills in a cognitive test that follows the experiment. Our belief that we are helpless seems to become general and render us more helpless in a wider circle of challenges.

DEPRESSION

In human beings, helplessness leads to depression, a mind-set that seems to say, "Okay, I give in—I can't control this situation—nothing I do will make any difference—I'm just going to try not to feel, not to think—be numb." This shutting down can lead to loss of appetite; to excessive sleeping or loss of sleep and to lack of motivation in work, sex and play.

ANXIETY

Related to that on helplessness is the research on unpredictability. It seems that the natural tendency of human beings (and other animals) is to use experience to make predictions. We try to organize our world and our responses to it by seeing patterns of predictability that will make our behaviour safe and give us control of our environment. "Whenever I crayon on the wall, Mom gets mad, so I better not crayon on the wall and just do it in the colouring book." One way to make people anxious and prone to ulcers is to place them in a situation in which events happen with no pattern, no predictability, and so make planning impossible. This seems to render people not only helpless ("Nothing I can do will change this bad thing happening to me") but also anxious ("Nothing I can do will assure these good things or prevent these bad things happening to me"). Good and bad outcomes are independent of my action. If this is what is learned, a state of chronic anxiety develops and often produces what we have now come to identify as stress-related diseases.

It is also possible of course to have too much predictability, too much of a good thing. An environment that is too risk-free prevents us from using our problem-solving skills, renders us passive and non-adaptive, overrelaxed and so non-creative. The attempt to control everything non-human as well as human can render us helpless in the long run. Too many rules, too much law and order, too much insulation from weather, crop failure, discomfort and so on can render us helpless, so that when our controlling systems break down, as break down they will, we will be unable to help ourselves. Overreliance on electric power, calculators, physicians, politicians, automobiles can lead to helplessness.

One other piece of research from Seligman is worth noting. Dogs were placed in a harness that caused them, when they turned their heads, to activate a device that shocked them. They learned to hold their heads very still. The implication for human behaviour seems to me to be this. If we come to believe not only that we are helpless to control outcomes, but also that any action we take will make matters worse *because we are failures,* then we will completely lose the ability to take action for our own well-being.

CURE AND PREVENTION

The role of literature reading as an aid in altering a person's belief in his own power to change and control his life is discussed in detail throughout this book. For now, I want to summarize the implications of the learned helplessness theory for reading.

Seligman cured his helpless dogs by physically dragging them on a leash from the shock area of the box, where they lay in pain, across to the safe no-shock area. If he did this enough, up to 250 times, the dogs eventually learned to do it for themselves. In trying to motivate human beings who believe themselves helpless, the therapist obviously cannot drag her clients from home, to work, to the store. But as part of her treatment of non-active clients she can intervene by giving them reading. Reading does not require leaving home, does not demand physical activity or social interaction and does not appear to be a scary challenge to action for someone who feels unmotivated. If a person will agree to go so far in therapy as to read, the activity has started. By presenting her client with stories that move from "I know how you feel" onto "Look, this is how I did it," she enables him to play out *cognitively,* in a belief system, the *possibility* of acting to take control of his life. Remember, it is the *belief* that one is helpless that leads to inaction.

When the dog is dragged to safety, it has not volunteered to save itself, but it is being shown the *experience* of getting to safety— a movement it eventually undertakes for itself. Similarly, the reader, being engaged cognitively and affectively with the story and its fictional, active characters, imagines he is saving himself, in the guise of his borrowed fictional roles, and so experiences a sense of action. As I have said, this is part of a *cure,* a reinforcement of a generalized program to motivate the helpless.

Even more interesting is the use and role of reading in the *prevention* of helplessness. Literature offers to readers, from childhood to advanced age, a multitude of models of action, problem solving, survival and courage. Nobody can possibly encounter in personal life enough experience to cope with even a small variety of frustrating situations. Even more to the point, nobody can escape the limitations *of her own experience,* her one story with her one way of seeing it, without the help of other stories. These other stories show the reader, first, that there are other stories. There is not just one way of seeing or coping or not coping. Children trapped in extremely controlling family systems, or in poverty, can easily feel helpless and grow up feeling helpless, in a cycle of seemingly inescapable repetition. Reading could greatly assist such children, yet sadly it is precisely these children who are least likely to get it.

Other stories offer other simulated experiences of surviving, of being in control. In addition, since the story is managed by the author, given a shape, order, outcome, resolution, there is a sense of control and order experienced in the reading itself. Reading is not only a voluntary action, it is an action whereby the reader admits the possibility that she will take action in her own life, simply by trying it out first in fiction. It is practice for life. Even enduring, not giving up hope, just holding on, as described by Jacobo Timerman in his book, or by Arthur Koestler in *Darkness at Noon,* is a form of action that can help us. Fiction can be a powerful tool for immunizing, and that is why, in experienced readers, new real-life situations often call up something that has been read and stored in the past, and that now acts, benignly, to help to make sense of the present.

MOVING ON

Using literature to help us to manage our future lives is pleasant, appropriate and easy. In decoding an author's story we must make it ours, that is, we must produce some set of responses in order to make sense of what we read. The roles we play in living through the story are the rehearsal for future coping, or for future creativity. When the most famous redhead in the world, Anne of Green Gables, experiences the death of Matthew, her beloved adoptive father and her champion, she does so for millions of readers around the world. All those children who read this fear the death of their parents, their grandparents and others they love. Most never speak about it. The parents are not comfortable talking about their own deaths; it seems like bad taste for children to do so. But that does not mean they don't fear the loss and experience anxiety. Anne grieves and cries and mourns, and Anne survives and grows up. It is possible to survive, it is possible to feel the worst pain and still prevail.

Some time ago I gave a novel called *Beat the Turtle Drum* by Constance C. Greene to our two younger children, then about ten and four. The family in this story includes two sisters, and quite near the end the younger falls out of a tree and is killed. This sudden death is a shock and I felt it. So did the elder girl. She talked about it; she talked about feeling responsible and worried all the time about her sister's well-being, and finally she talked about how she would feel if her little sister were to die.

In the days when Charles Dickens wrote about the death of Little Nell in *The Old Curiosity Shop,* more children died in England than do today. The death of a child was less surprising, more commonplace and so more integrated into the ordinary life of the population. The frequency of infant and child death led, however, to widespread parental and family anxiety. Every birth and every child was at risk. Readers treated Nell's death as a personal loss, in fact begging Dickens, as though he were God, not to write her death. Dickens knew that she had to die for his artistic purposes, knew that children died every day, and knew that his readers needed her death though they wanted her to live "happily ever after," so he made her immortal by killing her. Here his goal was to sensitize his audience to the value of children, who were often invisible or brutalized in nineteenth-century industrial England. Rather than being overwhelmed by suffering, his audience was in danger of becoming insensitive to and closed off from the plight of children. The danger was (and is) that a Disney, fantasy, pretend world, in feeding the desire to escape from real suffering, would blind the population to the visible suffering around them. The opposite of Little Nell is Peter Pan, precisely the kind of sugar-coated fantasy Dickens wanted to avoid.

Death and aging too have until very recently been taboo subjects, and literature has been a powerful antidote to this silence. Heaven and angels and sweet eternal bliss in the arms of the best Father of all, no longer seem as available as solaces and rewards as once they did. Fiction can help us confront our own fears in the present and give us some immunization for the future.

I still have a book in my possession inscribed, "Gerry Hynes to Joe Gold at Xmas 1954-55." Gerry was my roommate in my last year at university in England. His character will be more fully described in my memoirs, should they ever be written. Gerry knew I was going to the U.S., and to prepare me he gave me a book, *Americans in Glasshouses* by Leslie James, that satirizes everybody. This book turned out to be important to me. After the war and during the McCarthy years, which coincided with my undergraduate years, people and things American were extremely unpopular in Britain. Americans had power, money, influence, and were throwing it around. They also had right-wing notions not much liked in postwar socialist England. The GIs had not been very welcome as temporary residents. They were better fed and clothed than we were. Their money attracted English women. They were like tourists in a Third World country. Now that the war was over, they were less admirable than ever.

I was going to study and teach in Wisconsin, U.S.A., and I was going with some very negative attitudes. I thought large cars were vulgar and unnecessary and felt angry when one occasionally jammed up a tiny, ancient street in a small English town, as I had seen happen in Stratford. I had no concept of American space and distances, of American climate, of American diversity. I was set for some shocks, and I was likely to take with me attitudes that would get me into a lot of trouble. Gerry's gift helped me to laugh at Americans, and this laughter greatly diffused my anger and prejudice. It made me see that others—the author—could know a lot more about America and still laugh at it, laugh at it in the context of a world full of laughable cultural peculiarities, of which the American was only one. Here is an example of what I read:

> Even beauty is statistically measured in America. The lines, or curves, of Jane Russell have made her the most beautiful girl in her age-group. When Americans want to say a girl is pretty, they shun poetic imagery and say,

"She's a perfect 36!" (Footnote: No one could ever think of applying this term to the average British girl.) One frequently overhears an American man saying to another: "Who was *that pretty number* I saw you with last night?"

Englishmen do not always understand the American quest for numerical certainty. They are often shocked by Americans who respond to a politely vague invitation to "come to dinner some time" by asking "When?"

Unlike the British—who devised the rules for cricket so that matches could end without either side winning—Americans want to be sure what goes on. They want to know who wins and "what the score is." They even plan, build, name and number their streets consistently. This is rightly regarded as unimaginative in England, where half of the streets are named High Street, a quarter are not named at all, and the rest are given names in duplicate—so that going to dinner at a friend's house is a quiz or puzzle rather than an occasion for eating. (*See* Eat, American Tendency to.)[3]

Because I was able to imagine America as a place where I might be amused, where I could be interested and intrigued, where I could compare my own experience with the author's, I was able to look forward more agreeably than before—to *feedforward* more positively. This is one of the great virtues of travel literature, especially travel fiction or biography. We can prepare for what we will see—we can expect and become familiar with and be less anxious and alien. By feeling ourselves into a story we can be part of an imaginative feed-forward experience. This is one example of literature providing us with new *experience for our own future* by giving us someone else's past, for presumably the author has been where we are going.

Is it possible that reading a book could cause a person to emigrate, actually to choose another country in which to make a home? Not long ago I was having lunch with Sean Virgo, a writer of Irish extraction who has chosen to make his home in Canada. Quite casually, as we talked of our respective lives as children and our chosen country of adoption, Sean let drop that he had come to Canada as a result of reading Grey Owl. I was astonished, and immediately confessed that I too had been powerfully and permanently hooked by Grey Owl's extraordinary stories of the Canadian wilderness. Indeed, as a sickly child in crowded, foggy London, a city choking on its pollution and bombed to rubble near where I lived, I read everything Canadian I could get my hands on. Was it possible, I asked Sean, that Canada was littered, so to speak, with men who had been boys when Grey Owl was a celebrity in England and who had "read" their way to Canada? Should we put out a call and see if we could start a Grey Owl club for aging romantics who had grown up on *Pilgrims of the Wild*?

Grey Owl, whose real name was Archibald Stansfeld Belaney, is one of the most intriguing writers in Canadian history, one of those extremely eccentric late English colonials who adopted a new identity in worlds totally alien to the civilized, formal repression of the England they left. Grey Owl became an Ojibwa and did his damnedest to lose himself and every trace of his background in a new identity as an Indian guide, hunter and trapper in Northern Ontario. Grey Owl's achievement was not merely that he turned conservationist and helped to save the beaver from extinction in Canada. He translated Ojibwa and wilderness values, the feel of life in the Canadian bush, to people, both in Canada and in England. He has lived in memory under something of a cloud ever since he managed to hoodwink the English by his assumed identity, even fooling royalty with his noble "savage" performance. He is not a favourite with the native population either, I suppose because as the most famous Indian in Ontario, he wasn't Indian at all.

Some summers ago, I was lazing in bed on a Sunday morning, musing aloud that I wanted to go on a holiday, was yearning for the northern pine forests and lakes and was tired of Algonquin Park and its one million Toronto campers. "What happens if you turn the map over?" my wife asked. I leaped out of bed for a map of Ontario and raced back with it. "The road leads to a gigantic network of lakes at Temagami," I told her. "Isn't that the place Grey Owl went to?" she asked. I stared at her with my mouth open. I had not thought of Grey Owl since I was a school-boy, and I felt excited and ashamed at having forgotten the power of his influence. A few days later we arrived at Temagami to start a perennial love affair with Grey Owl's country and the myths and heritage of the Ojibwa people of Bear Island, whose land it is and whose rights are still not recognized.

The story of Grey Owl's work has even now not been properly told. That is the subject of another book and a special enthusiasm of mine. For now, let me say that the stories Grey Owl told gave visions of a freer, purer, more untamed world, a world not merely of adventure but of challenge. For me, he wrote about living at the threshold of what mattered, where to hide feeling, instinct and talent could mean death. The world I inhabited seemed unreal by comparison. Beatrix Potter would not appeal again. Here is a passage of Grey Owl's writing that records the hours that changed his life. Prompted by his wife, the writer describes his conversion from alien, hunter, exploiter to a different vision, of fellowship, caretakership, that would change his life and the lives of others, even mine. Imagine how odd, how gripping, how liberating this writing must have been to a child having difficulty breathing, cooped up in a London rain, waiting for winter and childhood to pass. My body was in that

London bedroom, but my mind was on Lake Temagami, a place where I would actually canoe, forty years later.

> Whilst making a set at an old, renovated beaver house where I knew the female to be, I heard faintly the thin piping voices of kitten beavers. In apparent clumsiness, I allowed my paddle to drop with a rattle on the canoe gunnell with the intention of hiding the sound, but Anahareo had heard it and begged me to lift the trap, and allow the baby beaver to have their mother and live. I felt a momentary pang myself, as I had never before killed a beaver at this time on that account, but continued with my work. We needed the money.
>
> The next morning I lifted the bodies of three drowned beaver. The mother was missing however, one trap being unaccounted for. I found where the chain had been broken, and dragged for the body unsuccessfully, later breaking the dam and partly draining the pond, but without avail. She would be the largest and most valuable, so I bemoaned my loss and forgot the life that had been destroyed for nothing, and the helpless kittens left to starve. After a whole day spent in a fruitless search, I removed all traps and equipment and proceeded to camp, having no intention whatever of returning; but the next day, after skinning and stretching the catch, for no reason at all I changed my mind. So inauspiciously do important events intrude themselves into our lives. I portaged back to the ruined pond that would never again be good for anything, and we paddled over to the old beaver house in an effort to discover if the female had succeeded in getting back there, but could find no indication either by sight or sound of her presence.

So we turned to go, finally and for good. As we were leaving I heard behind me a light splash, and looking back saw what appeared to be a muskrat lying on top of the water alongside the house. Determined to make this wasted day pay, I threw up my gun, and standing up in the canoe to get a better aim, prepared to shoot. At that distance a man could never miss, and my finger was about to press the trigger when the creature gave a low cry, and at the same instant I saw, right in my line of fire another, who gave out the same peculiar call. They could both be gotten with the one charge of shot. They gave voice again, and this time the sound was unmistakeable—they were young beaver! I lowered my gun and said, "There are your kittens."

The instinct of a woman spoke out at once. "Let us save them," cried Anahareo excitedly, and then in a lower voice, "It is up to us, after what we've done." And truly what had been done here looked now to be an act of brutal savagery. And with some confused thought of giving back what I had taken, some dim idea of atonement, I answered,

"Yes; we have to, Let's take them home." It seemed the only fitting thing to do.

This was not such an easy matter as the kittens were well able to take care of themselves in the water, being older than I had thought. By the exercise of considerable patience and ingenuity we eventually caught them, and dropped them aboard, two funny-looking furry creatures with little scaly tails and exaggerated hind feet, that weighed less than half a pound apiece, and that tramped sedately up and down the bottom of the canoe with that steady, persistent, purposeful walk that we were later to know so well. We looked at them in a kind of dumbfounded bewilderment, feeling much as if we had caught a pair of white elephants, hardly knowing what to do with them.[4]

So we can see how reading can serve the process of feedforward. The reader's mind uses reading experience to plan and imagine ahead. I was able to leave the confines of my physical environment and imagine how it would be to move to a new world. I could place myself in that world and use my knowledge to alter the future. Just as a reader can remake the past, so he can make outcomes different from what they might have been. We are not as helpless as we sometimes think. Reading for the future is one more possibility in the struggle for control of your own life. Do it!

1   Jacobo Timerman, *Prisoner Without a Name, Cell Without a Number,* tr. Toby Talbot (New York: Alfred A. Knopf, 1981), pp. 34-35.

2   Martin E. P. Seligman, *Helplessness* (San Francisco: W. H. Freeman, 1975).

3   Leslie James, *Americans in Glasshouses* (London: Falcon Press, 1950), p.13.

4   Grey Owl, *Pilgrims of the Wild* (Toronto: Macmillan, 1934), pp. 27-29. This book is available in a Penguin edition.

PART THREE

Growing Through Reading

CHAPTER EIGHT

Literature and Human Developement

When you stop to think of it, children have a pretty hard time, one way or another. The hoops they have to jump through just never stop coming. We celebrate various graduations. My daughter wanted a party when she graduated from primary piano to level one. What is more surprising to me than graduation is that children ever make it to school at all. What I mean is that, given that there is so much to learn, given all the tasks that face children and all that is expected of them, it is amazing that most of them don't go bananas, or just resign. As a matter of fact, the experts tell us that there is such a thing as infant suicide and that children can lose the will to live. The most important support system for a child's survival is sensitive, loving, caring, knowledgeable, non-paranoid parenting. This is easy to say, hard to do. Reading, literature, can greatly help both parents and child. Let's look at some of the child's tasks.

First, there is breathing. Nothing to it, you say. Ask an emphysemic or an asthmatic if there is nothing to it! It's the first thing you have to do on being born, and it remains *the* number one priority for life. An infant must avoid getting smothered or choked. Then it has to eat; again, a straightforward matter of opening its mouth and sucking? No; since this is not paradise, the food supply, often as not, is not there just when you want it. Mother gets delayed, the babysitter forgets, the formula runs out, the phone is ringing, the bottle is too hot or cold, and vigorous self-expression may be necessary to get results. Or perhaps mom or dad has read a self-help book that says ignore baby's crying unless it's on schedule. Here Greenwich *Mean* Time takes on rich new significance. If baby gets hungry on a personal, erratic, biological schedule that violates the theory, then tough on baby.

The number of anxieties is beginning to pile up, and we've hardly begun to cope with life's stresses. What about all the sounds? What are the giants babbling about? Why do they yell at me when I smile? Now I have to learn to walk, but I keep falling down. I'm scared and frustrated. I must learn to talk or I'll never take care of myself. What about pooping? Mother is having fits because baby is not toilet trained. Baby has accidents. Baby wets the bed. Baby is afraid of the dark. Baby sees monsters in the closet. Baby has to learn that he is separate and alone. He has a name, an address and even a phone number. These will soon have to be memorized. Please notice that so far we have not even left the house. Let's not!

Outside is traffic, more noise, animals, strangers, lostness, weather, ice or sun, rain or wind and the need for special and more and more clothing, where I live, anyway. Outside there are a million threats to survival. The world is a terrifying place. It must be ordered, organized, controlled and made safer. It must be managed. All these masses of information, transmitted from outside through the senses and by internal circuits from biological drives and feelings, amount to chaos. The information that reaches consciousness must be arranged into manageable packages for convenience, must be filed and stored for future reference, since surviving depends on stored information. Confusion must be unscrambled, sorted into thinkable and related units. The best method human beings have evolved for organizing large amounts of sensory information is storymaking. This is learned in childhood and is an indispensable aid in helping children cope.

First the child must learn language. Stories follow. The floods of strange information about the world, family, place and self must be storied into sense. To put this more accurately, the responses, feelings, attitudes of the child must be storied. The child learns to query: Who am I in relation to all this that is not-I?[1] What does love, parent, brother, dream, pain, even death, mean? How can I think about it? How can I talk about it? What do the rules mean? What about my emotions—anger, fear, excitement, curiosity—are they okay? What rules am I breaking? Will I be punished? Why is the grownup angry at me? Will I die? Stories are the most helpful tools a child has for sorting all this out. Stories have authority. Stories normalize. Stories model behaviour and feeling. Stories model the power to make stories—a power that children must develop in order to manage their own particular individual worlds, the ones seen through their own unique eyes.

Sentences follow the shape of story. The earliest games have simple story shapes. "All gone," which is what adults say to children, is a story about food, or "Hello, Matthew" is a story that tells of a meeting. Learning sentences in infancy is learning the beginnings of story power. Very quickly the world and our responses to it can be shifted into story form and so made controllable. One night I was driving my daughter Sarah, who was seven at the time, to her music lesson along a dark country road, in wintry weather. We passed an old farmhouse, almost totally dark. "That looks like a haunted house," I said. We both started making haunted house noises, howling and moaning and hooting like tortured owls. Feeling that I ought to make this "all right," I said, "And they all lived happily ever after." After a few seconds of silence, from the dimness of the passenger seat, Sarah said, "That was a very short story." Children recognize, at about age five, the formulas and conventions of storytelling. They need to cut their teeth on Mother Goose. Let's look at some of the rich information contained in nursery rhymes.

Children begin their association with literature long before they can read. Poetry and story can be transmitted by an adult, building on the sound base acquired through learning adult speech. Traditionally, this transmission of literature was done by the mother, who spent the most time with the child—hence, "mother tongue." Children can, in my view, get a good foundation for reading by hearing nursery rhymes. Since literature is based upon sound, it is necessary for good readers to be able to hear the words, the rhythms of phrases, in their heads as they read. The earliest rhymes and word games are accompanied by movement—baby is held and rocked, joggled, dandled, or patted. The association of pleasurable body sensations with language and rhythm helps to give a value to words, long before their meaning is deciphered. The words don't even have to make sense.

> This little pig went to market,
> This little pig stayed at home,
> This little pig had roast beef,
> This little pig had none,
> And this little pig cried wee, wee, wee
> All the way home.

This is played on five toes with a tickle at the end for the noisy pig. Parents who play games like this with their children are conveying several important messages:

1. I choose to spend time playing with you.

2. I like your toes.

3. Toes can be pigs (metaphor).

4. Language can be fun, play.

5. Stories can be physically felt.

6. I am sharing a tradition of literature with you.

7. I enjoy your pleasure.

8. I respect your intelligence.

9. I like to be a baby too.

10. I like to say poems.

Some rhymes are vivid nonsense that helps us to imagine unlikely events and combinations and that conveys the simplest bare bones of story and fantasy:

> Hey diddle, diddle,
> The cat and the fiddle,
> The cow jumped over the moon;
> The little dog laughed
> To see such fun,
> And the dish ran away with the spoon.

I recently published a paper in a scholarly journal, and at the head of it I quoted the last two lines of this rhyme:

> Humpty-Dumpty sat on a wall,
> Humpty-Dumpty had a great fall,
> All the King's horses and all the King's men
> Couldn't put Humpty together again.

I wanted to encapsulate my point that traditional literary criticism, with its royal authority to tell people what and how to read, was shattered forever, no matter how many experts tried to stick it back together. The wisdom and usefulness of nursery rhymes are lasting.

Other rhymes clearly teach lessons that are useful to the child's life, without having recourse to a boring lecture. In providing instructive, painless, delightful narrative, these rhymes sow the seeds of a perception of the usefulness of literature and its life applications:

Ding, Dong, Bell,
Pussy's in the well.
Who put her in?
Little Johnny Green.
Who pulled her out?
Little Tommy Stout.
What a naughty boy was that
to try to drown poor pussy cat,
Who never did him any harm,
and killed the mice in his father's barn.

How much more effective this model is for being kind to animals and not tormenting the cat, than a verbal or physical assault on the child, which teaches him only that violence and browbeating are authorized. Children, it seems, have always been fond of persecuting cats—more than one rhyme is devoted to this subject:

I love little pussy, her coat is so warm,
and if I don't hurt her, she'll do me no harm.

It's better to transmit these nursery rhymes not entirely from memory, but often with the aid of a book, so that the value and authority of the book are present from the start, and so that the magic remains in the book, where it will eventually be available to the child even in mother's or father's absence.

Nursery rhymes can convey all the moods, styles and affects that we later encounter in more elaborate literature. I have always loved the hint of mystery and the sinister in this one:

> There was a crooked man,
> And he walked a crooked mile,
> He found a crooked sixpence
> against a crooked stile;
> He bought a crooked cat,
> which caught a crooked mouse,
> And they all lived together
> in a little crooked house;

and in this one:

> I do not like thee, Doctor Fell,
> The reason why I cannot tell;
> But this I know, and know full well,
> I do not like thee, Doctor Fell.

How clearly this conveys the intuition children have about whom to trust, an intuition we try to reason out of ourselves as we get older. Perhaps we need our childhood instincts. Best of all on this subject, that sense of the nagging or haunting thought, presence, or atmosphere that we ignore at our peril, is this:

> As I was going up the stair
> I met a man who wasn't there,

He wasn't there again today,
I wish that he would go away!

There are rhymes of instruction, about domestic life, parental authority and what is expected of us:

Three little kittens, they lost their mittens
And they began to cry.
What, lost your mittens, you naughty kittens
Then you shall have no pie.

Fortunately, they find their mittens. I am always losing mine. Nursery rhymes are the first body of literature we learn and remember, and our remembering them illustrates the cumulative and informing power of literature. It is strangely satisfying to go to Gloucester, where Dr. Foster went and stepped in a very deep puddle, or to find oneself travelling through Banbury Cross, as my family and I did last summer, even though one does not see a fine lady on a white horse.

From about the age of five on, children are ready for fairy tales. Here begins their real acquaintance with the magical world of the whole history of human imagination. There are fairy tales and folk tales from every language, some going back thousands of years. These stories do a great many things children need to have done for them. Fairy tales may be divided into five kinds. One deals with family relations; a second presents the encounter with the world outside and all its dangers; a third deals with growing up; the fourth deals with emotions and sexuality; and the fifth explores the formation of personal identity. In one way or another all the child's deepest fears and confusions lie within and across these boundaries. I include death under growing up, which involves learning to age and preparing for final leave-taking.

Of course, to get what they need in the way of satisfaction and experience from books, children will have to be read to. Hearing stories is the way human beings in more primitive days obtained their experience of literature, and still do in some places. Children should never be read down to, any more than they should be talked down to. If they don't understand something, they will ask and so give you the opportunity to interact personally, give you the chance to show what reading will be possible. Children who are read to, model on their parents' reading. They want to be able to unravel the mysteries of decoding print, the way you can.

I have taught my children to read by phonic method, which is the natural way of reading and follows the origin of language learning. There is no point in being rigid about this, though a flexible mix of sound, sight and even touch is best. Nothing equals the satisfaction of seeing the look of wonder and dawning excitement when the magic of sound codes in writing suddenly gleams through the fog of mystery. The sense of looming power is wonderful to behold in the child's eyes.

The best teachers I ever had were those who read to us and read well, with pleasure and animation. Most of the adults I know still love to hear stories read aloud. Dickens filled theatres on both sides of the Atlantic with the brilliance of his dramatic readings. And audiences will still gather to enjoy storytellers weaving their magic.

As the mind of the child grows, more and more connections are made between mystery objects—mom and dad, mouth and spoon, cat and purr, shout and fear, dark and sleep, and millions of other relations—and lead to millions of questions. Here is a sample list of typical questions the child would ask if he had the language and syntax to do so:

1. When they go to change my diaper, why does Mom (or Dad or Sister) wrinkle up her nose and look angry at me? If I have done something wrong, how will I ever find out what it is?

2. Why are they angry if I don't like something they give me to eat?

3. Why am I hungry? How come food isn't there, just when I need it?

4. Am I wicked for hating Dad when he yells for Mom and she is cuddling me?

5. How can I not be afraid? I must try not to, because I get called names for being afraid, yet there are so many things to be afraid of.

6. How will I ever survive all the danger in the world?

7. How will I ever remember all the things not to touch?

8. Why is it wrong to play with my genitals when it feels so good?

9. Why do I have to wear clothes all the time?

10. How can I arrange to watch Mum every second, so she won't leave me?

11. If my parents die, who will look after me?

12. What if Dad (or Mom) does not come home?

13. Why are little girls (boys) different?

14. Who am I, how did I get here, did they want me, am I adopted, can I be sent away and what is death? (These are all part of one question—the first part.)

15. Grandma and death and me—if she dies, why won't I die?

16. Will I ever be beautiful?

17. Will I ever be clever enough not to get so many things wrong? (I must be really stupid!)

18. Will I ever grow up? (Because there are so many dangers and things to learn, I'll never make it!)

19. How can I trust grownups when they break promises?

20. How can I be good, be honest, and still be myself, when I can't tell the truth about how I feel and I can't do what I really want?

The first and best stories that deal with all these doubts, fears, hopes and desires are fairy tales. The child's mind does not function on the basis of our logic, or grownup rationalization. The abstract language preferred by Western adults means nothing to the child. Adults try as much as possible to avoid metaphor, though they are never wholly successful. Let's make up a story, with two versions. One will satisfy modern grownups, the other children or preliterate cultures.

Once upon a time, there was a beautiful land, covered with groves of trees, which grew and blossomed in the sun. The spirits of the trees sang with pleasure as they moved in the wind and felt the rain feed their roots and branches. Because the trees were happy, they put forth leaves to shade the workers in the fields between them, and they sheltered the birds, who made beautiful music for the people of that land. One day, men came from afar, who saw the trees and saw that they would make good houses, ships, factories and paper where the men came from, and saw that they themselves could get rich selling them. "What use are these?" they asked. "They take up space that you could grow food on." "We have enough corn," said the people, "and the spirits of the trees bless us with shade and song and beauty." "Nonsense," said the strangers, "you can sell your extra corn and get rich and buy guns and machines and take holidays. Get out of our way." So they brought in more men and machines and they cut down all the trees and left the land bare. The birds went away and all was silent. The spirits of the trees were very angry with the people who had allowed this to happen, and they wandered restlessly about the land causing great winds to blow. They blew the land until only rocks were left, and they blew the dust into the sea. The people could grow no food and so they starved or left, and the land became a desert, where vultures flew and waited for more death.

It is also possible to tell the story like this:

In the past, Ethiopia (or the Queen Charlotte Islands, or Brazil, or Nebraska, or Temagami) was well covered with arboreal protection. Industrial demand for hardwood and pulp made lumbering an attractive short-term solution for unemployment and cash shortage in hard-pressed, expansionist economies. The harvesting of large quantities of timber left the land exposed to accelerated soil erosion. Absence of reforestation left the problem unattended. Those who settled on the cleared land found no employment in agriculture, the soil now being too poor. With the supply of wood now gone and unreplenished, no local industry was viable, and the land was now too inhospitable for tourism or other compatible development. Soil erosion and ecological imbalance thus led to desert conditions, climate change and long-term economic decline.

The changed language of version two makes no more sense than the animated language of version one. Version one is more sensible, graspable, visualizable, imaginable. But version two is what our technocrats prefer as more real. The language has been *abstracted*, changed from concrete images like birds, spirits, blowing, to concepts like soil erosion. Children prefer concrete images because they have not yet learned the language of abstraction. When they do they will have lost a powerful human response-code for describing and making sense of their world, *unless they can keep it alive through story.* Fiction, even adult fiction, helps us to imagine the world and our relation to it, helps to translate it into sense, into order, into the knowable. Fiction is a means of describing the world in *human terms,* or of humanizing it.

The logic of children does make sense. In fact sometimes it makes more sense than our logic, and children have to learn nonsense to deal with us. Sarah, at eight, was helping her mother to cook the other day. Reading the recipe, she suddenly exclaimed, "Oh dear, this recipe calls for two *egg whites* and we only have brown eggs." Of course egg white is like *Snow White,* simply the name for something white. Since the egg white is not white until it is cooked, the mistake was not one of observation, but of language, adult language. Fairy tales are true to the life observation of children, to their intuition and feeling about the life they *know.* If fairy tales seem silly or unrealistic to adults, it is because adults have exchanged their imaginative power grounded in sensory and emotional whole experience for an educated faith-knowing not founded upon experience. Yet for much of the time, the earth we walk on is flat, not round; and there are people and places that make us feel uncomfortable, try as we will to reason ourselves out of what part of us knows. Jesus knew this value of stories as related to experience very well, and put his moral instruction into story form. "Those who have ears to hear, let them hear." The rest must live in the prison of literalism, of the letter, of rationalized logic divorced from human feeling and observation.

The problem is well illustrated by the story of the emperor with no clothes. Only the child, innocent of adult games of conformity to authorized versions, and true to his own personal view, yells out the truth. His imagination, the power to see and understand, has not been corrupted by social lying. The kind of attitude exposed in the Hans Christian Andersen story is the kind that prevailed in Nazi Germany, among the millions who "didn't know" or didn't want to know, and that still prevails among the Holocaust revisionists who say it never happened. This is adult madness indeed. By all means, let us stay children, at least to the extent of being true to the knowledge of our own real-life observations.

Speaking of authorized versions, the history of the English Bible is very instructive. I guess everyone has heard of the Authorized Version of the Bible, called the A.V., or the King James Bible. This book is a translation of earlier Bibles written in Hebrew, Aramaic, Greek and Latin. The work was done by a committee of bishops called to the job by King James I of England. What is interesting is the reluctance of those who were involved. The entire enterprise was really a rearguard action against unauthorized translation. For a long time, the only Bibles had been in Greek and, more especially, in Latin. The priests were supposed to be able to read the Latin and tell everyone in the parish what it said. People who could not read for themselves (and few could read at all, let alone Latin) were supposed to trust the priests to tell them exactly what was said. Even when the priests could read Latin, and many of them could not, there was nothing to prevent them from offering, and everything to encourage them to offer, their own versions of what the Bible said. Then, in the fourteenth and fifteenth centuries, a number of Bibles in the vernacular, that is, in native, contemporary languages, began to appear in Europe—in German, French and English. Translations were officially banned in England, and these books had to be bootlegged into the country.

The majority of senior churchmen did not want a translation at all. The Latin version kept the power to interpret in the hands of the Church and out of the hands and minds of the great unwashed multitude. So popular, widespread and irresistible was the desire to have these unofficial Bibles that it was finally considered politic to have just one authorized, standard and uniform version placed in every church—hence, the A.V. The bishops' fears that every man and woman would be his or her own priest were in fact well founded. What followed the English Bible was a great increase in diversity of religious opinion. John Bunyan's *The Pilgrim's Progress* was one outcome, said to be the most widely read book in the world at one time. Dozens of new sects emerged, focused on points of doctrine and interpretation. Following the translation of the Bible, the English novel developed, and with it a secular morality. Freedom meant variety, diversity and conflict. It is always thus. To be free is more disturbing, troubling and demanding than to be managed and controlled by external authority.

The illiterate people who were waiting for the power to read and a book to read from were like children dependent on adult authority. The authorized version of Western, rational, technocratic consumerism is at war with imagination, magic, diversity and individualism. The logic of the fairy tale is not authorized. In fact, its disturbing messages are threatening to many adults. This conflict is neatly summarized by Charles Dickens in his novel of modern industrialism, *Hard Times,* which begins in a state classroom. Sissy Jupe is a child from a circus, the fringe element of society. Her unauthorized family lifestyle is in conflict with most of the Victorian codes, in dress, behaviour, language and morality. The circus is unsettled, unstable and earthy. Sissy Jupe knows horses firsthand, knows what they *feel* like, smell like, act like. She knows their variety, of colour, shape, size and temperament. But she cannot define a horse in the manner of a dictionary. In this world, all the children have a number, rather than a name. Sissy Jupe is girl number twenty.

> "...Give me your definition of a horse."
> (Sissy Jupe thrown into the greatest alarm by this demand.)
>   "Girl number twenty unable to define a horse!" said Mr. Gradgrind, for the general behoof of all the little pitchers. "Girl number twenty possessed of no facts, in reference to one of the commonest of animals! Some boy's definition of a horse. Bitzer, yours."
>
>   "Quadruped. Graminivorous. Forty teeth, namely twenty-four grinders, four eye-teeth, and twelve incisive. Sheds coat in the spring; in marshy countries, sheds hoofs, too. Hoofs hard, but requiring to be shod with iron. Age known by marks in mouth." Thus (and much more) Bitzer.
>   "Now girl number twenty," said Mr. Gradgrind. "You know what a horse is."[2]

If you condemn this kind of insane literalism—this belief that metaphor, fiction, imagery, is false, while "facts" are true—perhaps you should look around you a little more closely. Victorianism is still very much with us. We are still banning erotica, pulling Harry Potter from school libraries, dominating poverty-stricken Third World countries, advocating white racial superiority, ripping off native people, censoring films, teaching girls in school how to wash their hair, and giving rapists ninety days in jail to be served on weekends. The Victorian age is alive and well and living in North America.

Fairy tales do not accept the tyranny of factual logic. In them, people die and return to life. Is this true to experience in any sense?

Do we ever die to one life and emerge to a different one? Do we get reborn into different life stages? Does divorce feel like a death, and is remarriage ever a rebirth? Did your own life ever change so dramatically that you felt reborn? There are many readers who will say yes to all these questions, who will recognize a time when they felt renewed and the past seemed like a dream or another life. Anne Shirley is reborn in Prince Edward Island and acquires a new name, Anne of Green Gables. Sarah is reborn in the Bible when she conceives Isaac. Red Riding Rood is reborn. The language of fairy tales speaks to the truth of *felt* experience. To limit language to one meaning only is to destroy it.

Children do not have abstract language for the emotions—ferocity, savagery, lust, cunning, anxiety, timidity and so on. Animals serve very well to embody these emotions; because they are more instinctual and direct in their behaviour, they can carry or represent the emotions the child feels but cannot name in other ways. By recognizing a *behaviour* instead of an abstract name, the child can know it and so place and control the feeling, "handle" it in his mind. Animal figures act as counters or tokens, as emblems. The need to *concretize* is basic to human thinking. It is the source of the power and importance of poetry. It is the opposite of what adults come to know as "bullshit"—especially abstract political and academic "bullshit." Children are extremely effective "bullshit" detectors. Here is William Blake's poem on the tiger—lovely spelling and all:

The Tyger

Tyger! Tyger! burning bright
In the forests of the night,
What immortal hand or eye
Could frame thy fearful symmetry?

In what distant deeps or skies
Burnt the fire of thine eyes?
On what wings dare he aspire?
What the hand dare seize the fire?

And what shoulder, & what art,
Could twist the sinews of thy heart?
And when thy heart began to beat,
What dread hand? & what dread feet?

What the hammer? what the chain?
In what furnace was thy brain?
What the anvil? what dread grasp
Dare its deadly terrors clasp?

When the stars threw down their spears,
And water'd heaven with their tears,
Did he smile his work to see?
Did he who made the Lamb make thee?

Tyger! Tyger! burning bright
In the forests of the night,
What immortal hand or eye
Dare frame thy fearful symmetry?[3]

Children respond very strongly to the powerful rhythm and imagery of the tiger burning bright and understand this poem perfectly, even if they don't know the meaning of "immortal" and "symmetry." Those words are for literate grownups and literary critics, to show them that Blake means business and that it is okay to read this poem to children. Adults tend, I am afraid, to deprive children of what they need unless they feel certain that their own values and beliefs are being implanted in children at the same time. Literature has long been seen as something for adults to use in their indoctrination of children.

Tigers and lions are normally ferocious and very scary. So are bears. So are the forests where they live. "Goldilocks and the Three Bears" shows us a curious little girl getting into someone else's family where she does not belong and disrupting their way of life. This is the way foster children often feel, not really wanted and not fitting in. There is great danger in this apparently friendly and cozy little home. Not all bears are teddy bears. The wolf also is a very dangerous and savage creature, as cunning as a fox, but bigger and more powerful and, like a big dog, deceptively friendly and playful.

The wolf is always male in literature, always dangerous, especially when he lies in your bed replacing the known and nurturing. Once the child takes on a parenting role and is old enough to nurse grandma, the wolf is a threat. Finding the right mate is an awesome task, and from the time a child knows she must one day marry, a certain anxiety is normal. Mummy and Daddy sleep together, but finding anyone else she could possibly manage sleeping with safely, let alone happily, seems hopeless, an unthinkable idea. Fortunately, Red Riding Hood survives her scariest experience and presumably grows up normal. Perhaps out of all those unpleasant little boys who call names and pull hair and steal hats off heads and throw them in the mud, one will grow into a protective and caring hunter, and, like Daddy, will take care of her and become a suitable mate.

Geese and mice are silly, gentle, helpless creatures, as we are a lot of the time. The child feels powerless, or enslaved like Cinderella. Doing domestic chores and getting them right seems a hopeless and thankless task sometimes. Siblings seem to do nothing. Someone else is mother's or father's favourite. Will I ever grow up? Will I ever be properly valued? Will my beauty ever be noticed? Because the child cannot express these feelings does not mean they are not there. Not only are the feelings inarticulate, unlanguaged; they are deeply buried, even forbidden. Many children are not allowed to express or show anger. They are supposed to be grateful. They are urged to think of those poorer and more hungry and more overworked than themselves. They are made to feel like "bad" people if they complain. They are supposed to be thrilled to wash dishes. They must smile, not frown.

I remember the most utterly terrifying story of my childhood was a Victorian tale in which a little girl, who was bad-tempered and always stamped her foot in anger, eventually stamped her foot and caused the ground to open and swallow her up so that she was never seen again. What could be more monstrous than to be so alienated and insensitive to childhood feelings that adults invent tales designed solely to control child behaviour? It is hardly surprising that we have a whole history of sickness and delinquency among children, when much of adult motivation has been to minimize the inconvenience they cause rather than to enjoy them, share with them and learn from them. We need children to tell us that the emperor has no clothes, more than ever today, when the emperor has television on his side.

To beat the odds, children need magic, fairy godmothers and animals that talk and care. Parents are not all good, despite the advertising they do. Mothers can be witches. Fathers can be cruel and indifferent. Children survive emotionally with help from stories that make a kind of hopeful sense of their fears and concerns. Hansel and Gretel survive, using their own wits and imagination. Siblings must often rely on each other. Cinderella triumphs, with the help of her fairy godmother. Mice can become horses, just as little girls can be mothers and masters of their own fates. Little boys can climb up beanstalks, grow higher and defeat giants. David slew Goliath. Jack killed the giant. Beowulf killed Grendel. There is hope. There are models. Without such stories, where is hope to be found?

There must be models beyond our parents. Stories have authority and are not limited by the special interests of our own families. Someone else, from outside, who does not know us personally, must tell us what we can apply to ourselves. The best stories are *disinterested*. They apply to us as if by magic. Children *recognize* parts of themselves in stories without having to be literary critics. Snow White is connected to a much larger world than the one defined by her vicious stepmother and her weak father. There are other forces on her side. Fairy tales connect children to larger worlds and bring centuries of folk wisdom, the accumulated store of lived experience, into a shape that can be grasped and remembered.

Giving a child the gift of story, story that does not shrink from the ugly, painful, or frightening, is the best gift of all. Certainly it is the most lasting, that will help make sense and order out of the chaotic clutter of experiences that victimize and make one feel helpless. These stories stay with people a lifetime and continue to assist them in organizing the relationships and disappointments of life, which often seem incomprehensible.

In answer to "why me?" or "poor me," stories say, you are not alone; they say "poor everybody," but also "brave everybody." Not all the world is your enemy. They teach harmony and honesty. They say we are related to animals, who can be our friends if we trust and care for them. They say children do have power to grow and learn. They tell us that other children were thought simple and stupid and proved to be wise and successful. They show us that parents don't know everything and can be surprised and remorseful. They play out our suppressed desire for revenge. They give us hope. They connect us with the past—once upon a time—and give us cultural roots.

Stories are the best of our heritage, the gift of minds that stay alive in us and help us to survive. Children need these stories. We all need them. If we deny them, forget them, prettify or launder or ban them, we are in deep trouble. A culture that forgets or distorts its folk tales and fairy tales, that is too smart and too grown up, too rational and too technological to bother with such stuff, is already on the slope of its own decline. Our species survival kit includes stories. Without them, we are lost in a forest, or in a desert rather, stripped of magic, of animals, of children who can serve us. As Michael Ende teaches us in his modern moral fairy tale *Momo,* children can help us to survive; we need their vision, their imagination, their play to keep us in touch with our own needs. But children can be mentally crushed. When children are seen as little producers and consumers in training, it's game over for humankind.

How About Here and Now?

The literature of fairy tales is timeless. It deals with times and places delocalized, non-historical, applicable everywhere. This is possible because these stories speak to the inner, universal child, to states and conditions of childhood that know no boundaries of time or place. Fears of big people, of the dark, of being deserted, of being hungry or neglected are no different among children around the world, among children now and two hundred years ago—or even a thousand years ago, when some of these stories first appeared. Indeed, the presence of similar stories around the world, or similar versions of the same story, shows us how universal are the concerns and the fears that are dealt with in them.

The hopes, delights and excitements of children are more primal, less culture-influenced and socialized, than those of adults, because there has been less time to learn these influences. One child is more like another across cultures than one adult is like another. It would be much harder to adopt an adult than a child, because children are not yet culturally set in their ways of thinking and behaving. A child up to the age of seven or thereabouts can learn a new language, new food tastes, new behaviours and beliefs fairly easily. Fairy tales speak to those universals, that still-to-be-formed part of the child who has not yet fully learned the prejudices and values of her culture.

There is, however, in every child, a "local" person, someone learning her "context." A context is the pattern of surroundings that gives shape, colour and texture to particular items. Think of context as background, like the overall pattern of a carpet on which some special design stands out, or like the face as context for a particular nose, or like this sentence in the context of this chapter. The context for the child becomes more and more important from about the age of seven on. School, home, the language she learns, the foods favoured by the culture, clothing, religion, lifestyles and degrees of privacy, health care and grooming, life cycle events and the responses to them, and the style of behaviour among family members—all of these influences take on greater force as the child reaches what is in our society grades two, three and four.

An increase in language ability greatly enhances the interaction between the child and the environment. A child who reads a lot is socially privileged by the acquisition of language and life information. Reading, if it did nothing else, would increase the child's knowledge of how to describe the world and her feelings about the world. With more language, a child is more visible, being more articulate, more expressive, more influential, more interactive, and therefore more powerful. Because of these qualities, the child gets more feedback, more response and more attention. This in turn leads to more self-esteem and curiosity and so on to increasing levels of effectiveness. With language, the child becomes an influential member of the family in "adult" matters. It is primarily through language that the child makes the transition toward adult concerns and relationships. Discussions about politics, holidays, moving, or major purchases can involve an articulate child.

In our culture enormous importance is attached to formal education. Most of the child's waking life is spent in an educational institution during all the formative years, from six to eighteen, and for about fifteen percent of the population, until twenty-two or twenty-three years of age. We judge almost everything according to school performance. We look to a child's school grades as a sign of adjustment, mental health, social comfort, intelligence and coping skills. Friendships form at school. Teacher approval is crucial to self-approval. All of this is founded, in our world, in our literate society, on language. Self-expression is crucial to school performance. I predict that as we turn our research interests more and more to language or its lack as a component in crime, delinquency, depression and running away among school populations, we will find a significant difference in language skills between achievement and failure, both social and academic.

But reading for children does a great deal more than provide more language. Children have to cope with the here and now of their context, their social, familial, community life, their emerging friendships and rivalries and their own encounter with rules or inhibitions. As children grow and go to school and take in more information they become aware of similarities and differences. They learn where and how they live in comparison to others and that not everyone lives the same way. If they are poor, they learn *that*. If they live in an apartment, they learn *that*. In fairy tales we do not read about traffic, rock and roll, air pollution, drug abuse and AIDS. Urban life has produced danger, pressure, crowdedness, and noise that was once unimaginable. The child needs help with all of this, help in sorting it out and normalizing it. So we turn to modern children's literature to assist us in raising our children. It is important to our survival that children grow up learning—by reading—of the alternatives to concrete wastelands, polluted air and Disney World's artificial birds.

Judy Blume's books for early readers, *Tales of a Fourth Grade Nothing* and *Superfudge,* are about some of the frustrations and embarrassments of having a younger sibling. More important, though, than the foreground struggles of life for a nine-year-old, and all the challenges of growing up, is the background information, the context, that the reader must absorb with the stories to get to the point. This family lives in New York City, so we get to read about muggings, elevators and apartment life, Central Park as the nearest and only bit of country to remind one of another world, and the business and money pressures that Daddy feels working for an advertising agency.

A child of eight begins to share family anxiety about money and unemployment, about paying the bills and planning ahead. A child of eight becomes aware of the dangers of the street, of strangers, of traffic, of getting lost or getting hurt. These books are valuable encounters, not only with thoughts and feelings, but with the struggle to cope with an environment. Judy Blume often deals with power. The child who must obey parents without agreeing or understanding is encouraged by reading of another child who can model some internal independence, or who can reinforce, justify, the private thoughts of a reader-child who might otherwise have guilt about rebellious thoughts.

> I ran to my room and slammed the door. I watched Dribble walk around on his favorite rock. "My mother's the meanest mother in the whole world!" I told my turtle. "She loves Fudge more than me. She doesn't even love me anymore. She doesn't even like me. Maybe I'm not her real

son. Maybe somebody left me in a basket on her doorstep.
My real mother's probably a beautiful princess. I'll bet
she'd like to have me back. Nobody needs me around
here...that's for sure!"[4]

The child must retain some rebellion, some independence, to grow
up normally, able to take care of himself. A child who submitted
totally would be broken, helpless, a ready candidate for any repressive cult or dictator. If Judy Blume is mildly subversive on behalf of
children, it is because they need such allies to survive. Heaven protect us from too obedient children. Fortunately, many parents usually know instinctively the importance of some resistance in their children and will slightly smile or shake the head in wonder at the rebellious, pert, or talkative child. This signal the child picks up instantly
like a Geiger counter and thinks, "It's okay to argue, but I'd better
not go too far." Parental approval or criticism is not enough for a
child of eight and up, who knows by now that parents are biased,
either besotted with adoration or hung up about particular irritants.
There are different rules in different homes, and children see these,
talk about them and have to make sense of them. They need an outside view, something in print, by a stranger, that has the ring of
impersonal authority. The energy of fiction to empower readers is
awesome.

Here is a passage from an adult novel, David Lodge's *Out of the
Shelter,* about a boy who grows up in England during the war:

A big bang woke him. There was a buzzing in his ears, and
although Jill was still in bed beside him it was as if she was
crying a long way away. The first thing he did was to pull
up his pyjama trousers. Some dirt had fallen on his head.
The electric light was swinging in the air, throwing wild

shadows over the walls and roof. The two mothers were standing at the bottom of the steps.

—Jack, Auntie Nora was shouting, are you all right Jack? Jack? Oh my God! She went up the steps, tripped, and crawled out of the shelter, calling Jack.

—Nora, don't, be careful, his mother said. He saw her make the sign of the cross and her lips moving silently as she closed her eyes tight.

—Mummy! Daddy! Jill wailed, hugging her doll. Where's my Daddy?

Timothy started to cry too, not knowing why. Jill jumped out of bed and ran to the steps. His mother opened her eyes.

—Jill! Come back!

But Jill was already through the door at the top of the steps. His mother scrambled after her. Timothy was frightened. He would be left on his own.

—Mum! he shrieked.

She stopped and turned round, saying something, but he couldn't hear. There was a loud whistling noise and a flash and a roar and just before the light went out his mother seemed to be flying across the shelter towards him. He felt her body fall across his and cried out because she had hurt him but he couldn't hear his own voice because of the buzzing in his ears. A lot more dirt had fallen on the bed. It was pitch dark and he was very frightened. Then he felt his mother move and her arms tighten around him. She was saying something but he couldn't hear properly. Then he could hear as if she was a long way away. She was saying:

—Timothy, are you all right, Timothy? She was crying.[5]

I lived through the Second World War in London, England, and experienced raids night after night, first in the Anderson shelter dug in the yard, and later in a shelter that was a table of steel inside the house. Mostly I have kept the experience to myself. I don't mean the events—they are well known; I mean the felt experience, the terror, anxiety, frustration—how it came through the senses. I think I buried a lot of it inside me somewhere. Sometimes one has to wait forty years or longer to find expression for one's life. Lodge's novel, which is founded on personal experience by a writer of about my age, was just such an experience for me when I read it recently. I was strongly moved by it, but more, I was grateful for it. The expression, the novel, sometimes gives a shape, a form, to experience that we recognize as our own. The novel is then a gift, a creating of the reader's reality, existence, history. The pieces of my past, my life, that were lying around in a puzzling mess—unexpressed, unformed, vaguely felt—are gathered together and given recognizable and storable shape. This is a priceless gift—a gift to the reader of part of the reader's life. Now I can say, if you want to know some of how it felt to be me as a twelve-year-old in England in 1944 and 1945, read *Out of the Shelter.*

Of all the books I have used with research in reader response, none seems to have been more important, to Canadian readers anyway, than *Anne of Green Gables,* the first of the series of Anne books by L. M. Montgomery. There are many strange ways, surprising ways, in which Anne has given strength, support, even survival to female readers. My explanation for the extraordinary influence of this book is that Anne is a model of female resilience in and from a time when many repressive rules were applied both to children and to women, so that female children were particularly "put down." Anne is a rebel, a poet, a model of survival. She starts out as an orphan of dubious origin, in itself a black mark, and by chance is rescued by an elderly couple, brother and sister. From then on, her own wit, language and wisdom save her. She has red hair, once upon a time another obstacle to popularity. She is impulsive, irrepressible, and something of a misfit in the staid Island community that becomes her home. But she talks her way out of dilemmas and into the reader's heart. A good deal of what she has learned came from books that helped her to survive. Anne shows her readers that it is okay to be female and smart. It is valuable to have "imagination." It is possible to overcome great hardship. It is satisfying to love nature, beauty and language. It is all right to be different. Here is a typical passage from *Anne:*

> "I never say any prayers," announced Anne.
>
> Marilla looked horrified astonishment.
>
> "Why, Anne, what do you mean? Were you never taught to say your prayers? God always wants little girls to say their prayers. Don't you know who God is, Anne?"
>
> "'God is a spirit, infinite, eternal and unchangeable, in His being, wisdom, power, holiness, justice, goodness, and truth,'" responded Anne promptly and glibly.
>
> Marilla looked rather relieved.
>
> "So you do know something then, thank goodness! You're not quite a heathen. Where did you learn that?"
>
> "Oh, at the asylum Sunday-school. They made us learn the whole catechism. I liked it pretty well. There's something splendid about some of the words. 'Infinite, eternal and unchangeable.' Isn't that grand? It has such a roll to it—just like a big organ playing. You couldn't quite call it poetry, I suppose, but it sounds a lot like it, doesn't it?"
>
> "We're not talking about poetry, Anne—we are talking about saying your prayers. Don't you know it's a terrible

wicked thing not to say your prayers every night? I'm afraid you are a very bad little girl."

"You'd find it easier to be bad than good if you had red hair," said Anne reproachfully. "People who haven't red hair don't know what trouble is. Mrs. Thomas told me that God made my hair red *on purpose*, and I've never cared about Him since. And anyhow I'd always be too tired at night to bother saying prayers. People who have to look after twins can't be expected to say their prayers. Now, do you honestly think they can?"

Manila decided that Anne's religious training must be begun at once. Plainly there was no time to be lost.

"You must say your prayers while you are under my roof, Anne."

"Why, of course, if you want me to," assented Anne cheerfully. "I'd do anything to oblige you. But you'll have to tell me what to say for this once. After I get into bed I'll imagine out a real nice prayer to say always. I believe that it will be quite interesting, now that I come to think of it."

"You must kneel down," said Marilla in embarrassment.

Anne knelt at Marilla's knee and looked up gravely.

"Why must people kneel down to pray? If I really wanted to pray I'll tell you what I'd do. I'd go out into a great big field all alone or into the deep, deep woods, and I'd look up into the sky—up-up-up—into that lovely blue sky that looks as if there was no end to its blueness. And then I'd just *feel* a prayer. Well, I'm ready. What am I to say?"[6]

We see Anne through her encounter with death and grief, love and disappointment, rejection and victory. Anne is a great heroine who has helped millions of readers to cope with what seemed like insurmountable difficulties. I shall have more to say about Anne later on.

Children need fantasy for a number of reasons. The power to fantasize is really the ability to imagine arrangements in time and space that violate the normal, the ordinary, or the observable. The familiar is altered so as to be odd, unlikely, or against the laws of physics, chemistry, or biology. In ordinary life children don't fly, animals don't speak and we cannot move ourselves through walls and across time warps. In our imaginations, however, we can. Otherwise perfectly sane people talk to their cats and dogs, and some even claim their pets talk back. Some people even talk to their plants. At Halloween we dress up and pretend to be other people, to live in other times. People visit medieval castles to relive other times or enjoy glimpses of them—once upon a time. In dreams, we fly.

The brain power we have to dream, which violates the logic of nine-to-five, of the familiar, of the routine, is part of our power to think creatively. We could not make new things, invent new devices, design new interiors, unless we were able to imagine doing so, unless we were able somehow to see our creations even before they are there. We rearrange our environment and our relation to it through a brain power that works first in our heads. It is essential to our survival, individually and as a species, to cultivate and nurture our imaginations. Most human activity takes place in the mind, and a small portion of this gets translated into action. To peel an orange we first imagine ourselves eating the inside. To buy a car, we first imagine ourselves driving it. To set a mousetrap, we imagine a mouse getting caught in it. We use our ability to imagine the not-yet-happened, the not-yet-invented, the not-yet-related in order to cope, survive, surmount difficulties. That is how we cross rivers, fly in the sky, get married, choose houses, books, jobs and holidays. If we do not encourage a degree of fantasy in children, we are depriving them of brain power, an ability they need to manage their own lives and to contribute to the life of the species. If we were imprisoned entirely in the confines of the here and now, we could not get out, we could not solve our problems, we could not find alternatives.

A great many people in our society are underprivileged by being underimaginative. They go to others in a whole range of areas to assist them in imagining alternatives to their present situations. There are now consultants to help business people imagine. Often this is thought to be information-seeking. In fact, in the areas of finance, personnel relations and personal relations, career planning, personal appearance, recreation, home design, the experts help people to *think differently* about how to do things. A great deal of information is not new to clients. In counselling, for instance, it is the client who has all the information. Ninety-five percent of the information I work with as a therapist is provided by the clients, on whom I am totally dependent to do the work. What I do is to help them to rearrange, reshape, re-examine the information. Einstein *imagined* old questions about the observed world in new ways. The rest of us have to learn to do this all the time. Fiction is a powerful and rich source of new ways to think about our lives and relationships.

For now, I want to suggest that we can help children to grow up creatively, ensuring that they are well provided with coping skills, through reading. Charles Dickens said of reading avidly when he was a child, it "kept alive my fancy." What are the threats to fancy or imagination for the child? Dickens' childhood was in many respects bleak and unstable. A child who lives in depressed economic conditions, who cannot travel, whose home is not filled with a variety of exotic or curious objects, whose parents and friends have themselves limited language and few stories to tell, such a child *especially needs fiction.* Yet this is the child least likely to get it.

Reading about other places, about heroes, about adventures makes possible the hope and idea of an alternative life. To imagine another, a freer, more colourful, world is to have another existence, a richer, alternative existence that makes the present more endurable and makes change of the present more possible. To be an illiterate slave to the present is to live in despair, hopelessly, mechanically. Children need models other than their parents. They benefit from being able to imagine different lives. Think about who you are and who you have become and about the best features of your life. Did your favourite and most memorable childhood reading have any bearing on that, any connection with it? Children need imaginative escape from the limitation of their real surroundings. Mental, social and even physical illness can result from being helplessly trapped, hopelessly locked into routines. Sadly enough, it is children who are already under-privileged—who are poor or illiterate, or who are new immigrants—who have the hardest time acquiring what they need most, fiction and reading skill, the imaginative life. For a poor child to read only about the life of the rich is not, of course, particularly helpful. One of the best ways to get rid of the distractions or limitations of social context in literature is to write about animals. Much of Aesop's power comes from his stories' freedom from a social context that would prejudice the response. We are left with behaviours that we can recognize in anyone, from any class or part of town. The fox that covets the grapes, the tortoise and the hare, the lion and the mice all interest us as portrayals of universal attitudes. Much more interesting are animals that take on entire lifestyles and personalities. Here is one of my favourite passages from all literature:

"This has been a wonderful day!" said he, as the Rat
shoved off and took to the sculls again. "Do you know I've
never been in a boat before in all my life."

"What?" cried the Rat, open-mouthed: "Never been in a—you never—well I—What have you been doing, then?"

"Is it so nice as all that?" asked the Mole shyly, though he was quite prepared to believe it as he leant back in his seat and surveyed the cushions, the oars, the rowlocks and all the fascinating fittings, and felt the boat sway lightly under him.

"Nice? It's the only thing," said the Water Rat solemnly, as he leant forward for his stroke. "Believe me, my young friend, there is nothing—absolutely nothing—half so much worth doing as simply messing about in boats. Simply messing," he went on dreamily: ''messing—about—in—boats;

"Look ahead, Rat!" cried the Mole suddenly.

It was too late. The boat struck the bank full tilt. The dreamer, the joyous oarsman, lay on his back at the bottom of the boat, his heels in the air.

"—about in boats—or *with* boats," the Rat went on composedly, picking himself up with a pleasant laugh. "In or out of 'em, it doesn't matter. Nothing seems really to matter, that's the charm of it. Whether you get away, or whether you don't; whether you arrive at your destination or whether you reach somewhere else, or whether you never get anywhere at all, you're always busy, and you never do anything in particular; and when you've done it there's always something else to do, and you can do it if you like, but you'd much better not. Look here! If you've really nothing else on hand this morning, supposing we drop down the river together, and have a long day of it?"[7]

This book, *The Wind in the Willows* by Kenneth Grahame, and this passage of writing, carried all the wonders of another world to me, and it did so without showing me a class or place I could never attain. Disguising these tastes and attitudes in animal costumes *neutralized* them for me and made it possible for me to yearn for the country, for boats, rivers and trees, as pure feeling, unconfused desire. In reality, I felt like Mole, shut up in dingy London suburbs, dying in smoke and dirt and noise, or so it seemed to me. When Mole gets out of his hole, out of his chores and his cramped space, and wriggles on the grass in the sunshine and finds it "delicious," I, too, feel the intensity of this contact, I also long for the sensation of warm sun and cool green grass on my skin. Are children closer to the "earth," I wonder, are they natural ecologists, natural conservers of natural beauty? Children need books that express their own feelings back to them, that give voice and language to deep and perhaps only dimly felt needs. Children have in any case a certain natural rapport with the images of animals that makes these images ideal vehicles for the transmission of feelings and life events. Animals are dependant, not very articulate, shy and timid, greedy for affection.

Charlotte's Web by E. B. White introduces the issue of death and loss in a sufficiently distanced way that the issue can be felt and approached *to the degree that the child reader permits.* We can apply Marx's economic dictum very well to reading—from each according to his abilities, to each according to his needs. The beauty of reading of this kind is that the child regulates, turns the dial up or down on, the amount of response and interaction required. Not only does Lewis Carroll's *Alice in Wonderland* capture the wonderful rapport that children feel with animals in an adult world (a world so confusing it must seem crazy to a child half of the time); it also has two other powerful ways of expressing for the child reader. One is Alice's extraordinary discovery that she can become very, very small, like a mouse, or very, very big, like a giant. Children know very well how it feels to be insignificant, small, helpless, unnoticed, a little thing of no account. Alice *shows* how it feels without becoming all technical, psychological and theoretical about it. She simply is, on occasion, very small. Similarly, the child knows how awkward and uncontrolled her body feels as it grows and grows and grows. Clothes don't fit any more and toys and places that seemed quite suitable before now seem impossibly puny and cramped. The box that we once hid inside is now good only for storing dolls in.

When my daughter Sarah was seven, I gave her an attractive child's book called *Big Sarah's Little Boots* by Paulette Bourgeois. This book focuses on the theme of growing physically larger and saying goodbye to smaller things one has loved, like the boots you outgrow. Of course, in this case the common name Sarah reinforced the recognition-comfort that my child experienced—the "I understand how you feel" that the book tells the child as she decodes the language and internalizes the story, makes it her story. We can use literature to help children normalize confusing feelings about their physical growth.

These feelings of body strangeness and awkwardness are particularly strong during the period around puberty, just before the onset of sexual maturity and characteristically at the age of eleven or twelve, sometimes a bit later. The chemical changes required to produce sexual development and reproductive capability are usually accompanied by body, mood, hair and emotion changes that can be very confusing. There are swings between laughter and tears, feeling grown up and feeling helplessly childish, between being confident and anxious, gregarious and hermit-like. Our culture is virtually without ritual ceremony to normalize and integrate into the community the child-becoming-adult. Bar and Bat Mitzvah for Jewish boys and girls and Confirmation in churches are the only remnants of earlier ceremonies. The child needs to feel normal and approved, recognized and understood, especially at this time of biological stress. If the child cannot get the necessary sympathy and support at home, why not provide it from literature? Better to admit that we as parents cannot do enough, have not the time and patience or even the necessary skill, and so turn to books for help. Books, stories, can act as peers, friends and parents by speaking to children about themselves. Alice says to the child, "See, I know just how you feel sometimes, and it comes out all right in the end—you'll be normal like me." Here once again is the comfort of that larger world that *normalizes*—a process that I have mentioned often and that matters a great deal. I'll bet the question I hear most often from clients is, "Am I normal?" This is, of course, the core message of Hans Christian Andersen's ugly duckling story. Conveniently, the ugly duckling turns out to be beautiful in the right context. I say "conveniently," because the challenge in ordinary life may be to come to terms with being not beautiful in a world of very narrow standards of beauty. Can we love those who are not lovely on the outside, the elephant man, the multiple sclerosis victim? These are the issues Andersen skirts. Still, his message is important—there is a context where you can fit in.

The other quality that *Alice* has in outstanding degree, more than any other children's book before or since, is a recognition of how confusing and fascinating *language itself* can be, and how much fun it can be also. The "mock turtle," the "bread and butter flies," and the "long tale" the mouse tells are all part of an educational romp into the fun and puzzle of words—the magic world of language-power for children. Alice, like Anne, is very good at language. This has three clear results for the reader. First, the hero who speaks well, clearly and effectively speaks for us. We recognize the emotion—say, anger, sadness, or frustration—of the character, and we feel it also, and then the character articulates the right words to give expression to the emotion, and so relieves both herself and us. Instead of feeling merely baffled, tongue-tied, or shy, instead of going away wishing we had said this or that, we get to enjoy and savour the exactness of the written words. The second benefit is that not only are we deeply satisfied and motivated to learn new words, phrases, syntax, styles and tones of expression, we are also taught how and when to use them— the text provides us with eloquent models. The third power comes from the context in which this effective speech takes place. By reading Anne, or Alice, or Rat or Badger in *The Wind in the Willows*, a child learns that words can have power to change the context, that violence, screaming, raving, or running away need not be the only response. It is possible to change context and behaviour by language. Anne manages her life through language. Alice finds out about herself and her world through language. This happens in the process of engaging the reader in the pleasure of story. Here the message—say, that Anne survives and triumphs—is not separable from the means of conveying the message.

1   Identity is formed by separation, differentiating. P. D. Eastman's *Are You My Mother?* is an example of a book very helpful to young children in dealing with identity formation.

2   Charles Dickens, *Hard Times* (London: Oxford University Press, 1955), pp. 4-5.

3   William Blake, "The Tyger," in *William Blake*, ed. J. Bronowski (Harmondsworth: Penguin, 1910).

4   Judy Blume, *Tales of a Fourth Grade Nothing* (New York: Dell, 1972), p.38.

5   David Lodge, *Out of the Shelter* (Harmondsworth: Penguin, 1985), pp. 12-13.

6   L. M. Montgomery, *Anne of Green Gables* (Toronto: McClelland-Bantam, (n.d.), pp. 50-51.

7   Kenneth Grahame, *The Wind in the Willows* (New York: Signet, 1969), pp. 30-31.

CHAPTER NINE

Growing Up Sane

I t ought to be easy to go crazy during adolescence. The conflicts and the confusions multiply. Today on the radio I heard a former alcoholic young man explain that his incurable alcoholic father used to warn him of the dangers of drinking, and beat him up regularly. The violent actions did not speak louder than the words, but they did create confusion, anger and mistrust, so that the heir to the behaviour did not know what to believe. Adolescents are required to carry increased responsibility, learn more rules and accept more adult information as they grow up. Yet in our society they are lied to on a regular basis. On the one hand they learn that alcohol is bad for them, and on the other that alcohol is part of the good life; they are told to be good, kind, generous and selfless and to be ambitious, ruthless, competitive and rich; they learn that happiness consists of higher values, religion, culture and service, but also that what counts is fast cars, faster sex, and half-million-dollar houses; they are taught to be real, honest, sincere, authentic, but also to digest a steady diet of *Survivor, Friends, The Practice,* and *The Sopranos.* Television, just about all of it, has an ulterior motive: it traps in order to sell; its goal is commerce—not improved relationships, not mental health, not happier human development, not world peace, not planetary survival, but simply increased material consumption.

We parents have ulterior motives also. We want to preserve power, law and order in the home. We want budgetary restraint, freedom from anxiety, peace, quiet and privacy. Adolescents are in conflict with all of these goals. They want attention, freedom, mobility, money, support, approval, noise, space, friends and their own power. All this is natural and may be anticipated, though the degree of discomfort in families can vary.

School, which is where our children spend most of their waking hours, also has ulterior motives. Agenda number one, the stated objective, is to educate our children for life, learning, growing, self-development, livelihood and creativity. The unstated agenda is much like that of the home, only more powerfully so—to produce the greatest convenience for administrators, teachers and governments; to avoid hassle, discomfort and controversy; to produce conformity and uniformity among children; and to inculcate the values of the society that foots the bill and pays the salaries, no matter what those values are. I will have more to say about this later, in the chapter on education.

There you have it—the makings of teenage rebellion. Inside the adolescent are biological, inherent, inherited and social needs to grow, sort out the true from the false, make sincere friendships, discover individuality (identity), express and receive love and caring and express the self. The most powerful instrument for expressing the self in relation to the world that is not-self is language. Language is the primary human strategy evolved for organizing experience. Story is the basic unit for packaging the language. So beyond the home, beyond the school and beyond television, where can the adolescent turn for help in growing up? Right, to story-books. Literature, though it must compromise with publishers, markets, social tastes and values, economics and so on, is still the most free of all media. Literature is the most complex and therefore most interesting form of story, the most generous in permitting individual reader responses, the most sincere in being at its best an individual writer's version of the world, and the most private, portable, accessible and time-manageable of information packages. Here is the source, an almost unlimited resource, of alternative information for adolescents.

There probably isn't a more pressing concern for teenagers than sex. Their biology makes sure of that. Each of us is formed by a minute but pervasive program built into our genetic makeup, the basic cell material from which we develop. With only very slight variation this program contains an instruction to reproduce itself; it does not want to get lost or wasted. One of its devices is to make some other human beings, usually of the other gender, attractive to us, by shape, size, smell, texture and smile. The object of this attractiveness is reproduction, and to make sure we don't try for contact once and then give up we are blessed, or at least stuck with, a lot of incidental rewards: intense genital and nervous system arousal and pleasure; affection and reassurance; companionship; team-power and children whom we try to influence. For cultural and social reasons, sex has become layered over by rules, taboos, goals, fears and punishments, to offset the appeal of too strong rewards.

I met a seventeen-year-old client recently who told me he was terrified of sex. He explained his fear as the result of a health studies class on sex in high school. All they taught him about were diseases and pregnancy. He knew a great deal about AIDS, venereal disease, herpes. Apparently, about love, pleasure, or the naturalness of sex, no words had been exchanged. Here is a passage from David Lodge's *Out of the Shelter* that describes precisely the power of fiction to educate, liberate and normalize the stress, embarrassments and confusion about sex:

> He recalled his guilt over what he had done with Jill when
> they were five, and how he had been too ashamed to
> confess it, and wondered for years afterwards whether
> all his confessions had been void because of that one

suppression of the truth, and all his communions sacrilegious. Until one day he was reading a book, a grown-up's book he had taken at random from the shelves of the local library, and started to read. And there suddenly was the whole episode, as if the writer were describing himself and Jill—the two children left alone in the house, I'll show you mine if you'll show me yours, and the boy looking but not wanting to show his own, it was all exactly as it had happened. And although it was only a story, it showed that other children had done the same thing. And it wasn't described as anything very awful, or surprising, but as if it were quite ordinary. The relief had been tremendous. He was not alone. He belonged to a community, curious about the bodies of the opposite sex. It had been quite easy, then, to mention the business with Jill in a general confession he made during a school retreat, and the priest had made no comment.[1]

What books, then, should I give my young client? I gave him *Tex* by S. E. Hinton. It has an absentee father, as my young man had, and some conflict with a brother, which he recognized. There is an episode where Tex is pounced upon for shoplifting—a scary experience shared by my reader, but of which he did not tell me until he had read the novel. The question of sex did not come up. J. D. Salinger's *The Catcher in the Rye* would be a good one, but mostly because it would allow him to recognize the feeling of being an oddball, weird and different, which is so common to mid-adolescence. For an English reader, eighteen-year-old Terrence, Sue Townsend's *The Secret Diary of Adrian Mole, Aged 13 3/4* was extremely helpful. He had long been uncomfortable with guilt about his sexual feelings, his romantic yearnings and his resentment of his divorced mother's boyfriends, who came and slept over fairly frequently, forming a kind of serial intrusion on family privacy. Terrence never knew, in his early teens, whom he would find in the kitchen making breakfast and wearing the familiar courtesy towel-robe. Like many characters in books that help children cope, Adrian Mole survives a great deal of confusion, disappointment and growing pains. He struggles with schoolyard romance and lives to tell the tale. Terrence could see the humour of this book and so was enabled to convert some of his own painful memories into amusing ones. He gained reassurance from discovering that his history was *normal,* even if it was not *common.* Here is a powerful distinction for educators and therapists. What is unusual can still be "normal," that is, within the realm of ordinary, believable, manageable human experience.

Readers have varieties of experience that, especially for the young, can seem quite peculiar, frighteningly "different." The narrower the child's experience, the more there is to be frightened of. Reading helps extend this experience. Even when a story shows different traits and problems from the reader's, the story character proves that being different and being frightened is *normal,* and that one can get through life stages.

It's a sad thing that children are sometimes denied approval for finding what they need in books. One seventeen-year-old girl, Wendy, read Margaret Laurence's *The Diviners,* a long, rich novel that has a lot to say about a mother-daughter relationship, about love and feeling. Wendy was excited to see that love and sex can be beautiful and powerful and that mothers have needs and feelings daughters often don't know about. She tried to talk to her mother about what she had discovered, about how wonderful the novel was, and she tried to express some of her responses, her feelings, about guys and parental approval and about how sex with a guy you love might be okay. Mom was shocked. She read the book. Whatever she really felt we'll never know. What she did was to go to the school board and explain that obscene material encouraging sex between unmarried persons was being prescribed in the curriculum. A great hubbub followed. In other words, some parents want the material most valuable to actual adolescent readers banned because they do not want to confront the reality of their children's needs. A similar thing happened to Judy Blume's books. A very sensible mother, offended that a teacher was denying this material to her daughter, went out and bought the books and gave them to her. What about all the mothers who don't know the value of such reading, or who can't afford the books?

Adolescents need tons of information. They also have a way of finding it. Research I did a few years ago shows that adolescence is the time when people read the most, read quite a lot in fact. This is true even for those who as adults read very little. Adolescents are not much taken care of by parents—they have to get ready to be wholly independent. Adults often aren't much help. It also happens that children go through adolescence when parents are most involved in their own careers and mid-life issues. The enormous resource of reading is what comes to the rescue. I knew a boy who was a true male Cinderella. He was adopted. When his parents began to have children naturally, he became more and more emotionally excluded until he felt like an exploited stranger. He was extremely reluctant to admit these feelings, but he showed me who he was by sending me his three favourite books, the treasures of his own bookshelf. I read these books and they sent a powerful and clear message to me. I saw who he was and what he was trying to tell me. One book was Jean C. George's *River Rats, Inc.,* a wonderful adventure about two boys striking out on their own. The second was Cynthia Voigt's *A Solitary Blue.* Here again a rejected, lonely boy tries to win his mother's love and attention and fails. The boy in the story survives with his father's help and the friendship of an orphan family from school. The third book was also about rejects, children who don't belong, who aren't wanted and who have to make it by themselves. My client would communicate to me only in this dramatic way. By sharing reading interests he was able to point me clearly towards how he felt and saw himself, without condemning his adoptive parents. These readings undoubtedly showed him that surviving his pain and loneliness was possible.

My gift to him was *I Am David* by Anne Holm, one of my favourites. David escapes from a terrible prison camp somewhere in southeastern Europe and sets out to find his Danish mother, whom he has never seen. It is a wonderful story of a boy's suffering and survival. Readers are often stirred by it and enabled to see their own plights in a different light and with a different kind and degree of self-pity. They can take courage from David's example and hope from his survival. This kind of recognition of character-who-is-oneself makes an acceptance of one's own situation possible, and acceptance, in turn, makes action and planning possible.

When I gave my gift to Andy, several messages were transmitted. Without discussing the meaning of *his* books, without interpreting them or him, without exposing his private pain to discussion, I showed him that I understood and recognized how he felt by matching a similar book to his own. Second, I showed respect both for his reading and for the *process* by which he was choosing to pursue his therapy. Third, I helped to normalize his experience of being lonely and rejected, because while he might have said to himself that his finding books "about him" was a freaky accident, I was saying to him, no, what you experience is widespread and well known.

I should also point out that there were strict rules in his family that prevented him from revealing feelings, complaining, expressing pain, or exposing family problems. Reading can provide a person from such a background with feedback for feeling, in a silent, private and secret way. By giving Andy *I Am David*, I joined him in a scheme to assist his own growth and coping skills, without breaking the family rules or coming into open conflict with his family. In this kind of situation, stories can be the means of exploring the truth of feeling and experience in spite of family fears and restrictions. We are not told what Rapunzel did with herself all day locked up in her tower, besides brushing her hair. I hope she survived and extended her world by reading, while she waited for rescue.

As we enter middle and late adolescence, we become aware of many confusions in our search for the answer to "Who am I?" We run into racial bigotry and prejudices about groups of people, the "other sex," other colours of skin, other customs. Once upon a time—perhaps still in other cultures—children had adventures and excitements, challenges that had to be met, just by the nature of the way they lived. Boys and girls had tests to pass to mark their coming of age, after which they joined the community of adults as full members. Children learned to hunt, or performed feats of courage, skill and endurance in the process of living. The need for personal testing, the need to explore one's own skills, courage, resourcefulness, is still there, though the opportunity for such discoveries is not so obvious in a modern, civilized culture. Braving the elements, avoiding wild beasts, combating hunger are not necessary for most of us. Some of our need is taken up in sports, in camping, canoeing, learning to drive, passing exams. Our minds, our biological inheritance, do not change at the same pace as our housing designs or school systems, our agriculture or transportation systems. We are fascinated by animals, even extinct animals like dinosaurs, or by storms, or we like climbing trees and rocks because our central nervous systems carry messages from long ago, before the wheel was invented.

Reading can provide a valuable way for young people to search their own responses to adventure, to danger and to the emotions that arise in dangerous situations. If we don't get scared, we don't know how to deal with our fear. "The boy who went out in search of the shivers" in the fairy tale was suffering from a serious disability— a lack of affect. He knew that he had to acquire the fear feeling. The books that fired my imagination as a child are hardly fashionable now. Many had to do with the war and military exploits. The Biggles books about a fighter pilot were my favourites, and I simply vacuumed my way through them all. Percy F. Westerman was a similar case, but more boring and sombre. Much of what was popular then had a fiercely colonial, racist quality. Rider Haggard's *King Solomon's Mines* was a favourite. Rudyard Kipling's short stories were favourites, and later the boy in me responded to Ian Fleming's James Bond novels.

Mark Twain's *Huckleberry Finn* provides among other things a fine sense of danger and adventure for North American children, as the white boy tries to assist in his black friend's escape from slavery. John Wyndham's novels, which often focus on children in science fiction fantasy situations, can be extremely exciting. Stories of great feats or adventures of real-life experience, like Joshua Slocum's *Sailing Alone Around the World,* provide young readers with models of courage, endurance and resourcefulness. Books like these show us that people who live dangerous lives, sometimes by chance, also have inner lives that assist them in surviving. We learn that it is possible to feel afraid and behave courageously at the same time. When I was a school-boy, I fell in love with the writing of James Thurber. His story "The Secret Life of Walter Mitty" revealed that a fantasy life was a well-known human trait, that imagination could be more real and urgent than our daily chores and that people do live more than one life at the same time. They are almost never the robots they sometimes appear to be. Several students have told me that "Walter Mitty" is their favourite story because they daydream and have felt guilty about it.

Teenagers, young men and women, are part of a larger world than their families provide. They are connected to the natural world, to plants, flowers, trees and animals, to lakes and streams and land and to climate. They are fascinated to explore these links, to see how their environment affects their lives. They are concerned about ecology, nuclear threat, pollution, and their food and drink. Here is a poem by Matthew Arnold that has a profound effect upon young people who are up to reading it:

Dover Beach
The sea is calm tonight.
The tide is full, the moon lies fair
Upon the straits—on the French coast the light
Gleams and is gone; the cliffs of England stand,
Glimmering and vast, out in the tranquil bay.
Come to the window, sweet is the night air!
Only, from the long line of spray
Where the sea meets the moon-blanched land,
Listen! you hear the grating roar
Of pebbles which the waves draw back, and fling,
At their return, up the high strand,
Begin, and cease, and then again begin,
With tremulous cadence slow, and bring
The eternal note of sadness in.
Sophocles long ago
Heard it on the Aegean, and it brought
Into his mind the turbid ebb and flow
Of human misery; we

Find also in the sound a thought,
Hearing it by this distant northern sea.

The Sea of Faith
Was once, too, at the full, and round earth's shore
Lay like the folds of a bright girdle furled.
But now I only hear
Its melancholy, long, withdrawing roar,
Retreating, to the breath
Of the night wind, down the vast edges drear
And naked shingles of the world.
Ah, love, let us be true
To one another! for the world, which seems
To lie before us like a land of dreams,
So various, so beautiful, so new,
Hath really neither joy, nor love, nor light,
Nor certitude, nor peace, nor help for pain;
And we are here as on a darkling plain
Swept with confused alarms of struggle and flight,
Where ignorant armies clash by night.[2]

Most readers don't try to be literary critics and don't need to be. They respond to mood, they feel a sense of what they read. The sense or meaning of the words depends on the way the reader *feels*. Different readers feel different emotions from the words and so the words are different for them. One student found this poem extremely valuable. She decided that the poem was about loneliness. The world is a great big hostile, lonely place. No one understands, she said, what it's like to feel like the only person in the world, looking out over a huge plain that you have to cross alone. Only love, special love with one particular person, can get you through this ordeal. This girl found it amazing that someone a long time ago had recognized this, someone knew and could write down exactly how it felt. A writer could cry out to a loved one, let us be true to one another because no one else can be trusted. The need for a true friend is very strong in adolescence and is not to be treated lightly by adults, who have learned much more self-reliance. Something else very important happened here, though: the student I'm talking about discovered she had links, feeling and thinking links, with a man who wrote over a hundred years ago. Loneliness is intensified when connections to the past are missing. The fact that people used to feel as we do and survived, and that they have bequeathed their world to us in their writing—this discovery gives hope and helps readers to see that perhaps the horrors we face are simply our version of past horrors that others have overcome. Connecting to the past helps us to survive. This is a very important argument, a "roots" argument, for reading literature from the past.

It's easy to forget that literature is our *major* link to the past, to its thinking, feeling, manners, rules, religions, customs, language and attitudes. Movies and TV did not exist when Matthew Arnold wrote "Dover Beach." We are not going to be shipwrecked in galleons as Defoe's Robinson Crusoe was, or sent to Australia or America for stealing ribbons in a London market, like his Moll Flanders. Or take the story of the Australian penal colony, Van Diemen's Land, described by Marcus Clarke in *For the Term of his Natural Life*—a gripping, grim tale from 1874. Literature extends our consciousness across space and across time. The record of what life was once like is in literature.

Young people can take a great deal of comfort in seeing that their feelings and experiences not only are "normal" for today but have a well-established lineage, a link across time. To feel at home on this planet, among people, individuals need to feel part of a long continuity. It is easier to grow up, have children and die if millions of others have done so before. To feel brand-new, alien, suddenly *here*— like transplants from outer space—would be utterly lonely. And nothing can give us the sense of belonging, nothing passes on the life line, the rope to which we can safely hold, as actively and effectively as literature. Without the stories, the past is silent.

The completion of the growing-up process is signalled by the young adult's desire to form a union with another person and start a family of her own. Many people do get married before they are adult, and the statistics show that this does not make for lasting marital unions. Ideally, the young adult should have achieved a sufficient degree of independence, a sense of self-reliance that welcomes the responsibility of adult decision making. It is helpful also to have some career direction that will make the future predictable, at least up to a point. To choose a partner for life requires the ability to identify, through self-knowledge, the tastes, preferences and attitudes that will be the basis for partnership. To create a story with another person means that one's own story must be pretty well in place. Children and teenagers have to be self-centred, since it takes most of their time and energy to grow up. To divert much of this energy into forming a relationship is difficult at best, and almost impossible if one partner, let alone both, has a set of tasks remaining to be completed.

Take sexuality as an example. The issue here is not primarily genital or even glandular. The experience of gender differences, personal, social, biological, goes far beyond the physical. Sexual information for adolescents is largely theoretical. The sexual experience of masturbation, which is available and uncovers feelings and fantasies in the individual, remains solitary. Petting is experimental, body-discovering, both one's own and another's. But what is the other sex really like? How do I make approaches? What is right, safe, appropriate? Who controls what happens? What does it feel like to be him or her? What is expected of me? Am I in love? Am I just being used? The reading that will help teenagers through all this has to focus on all these discoveries, has to show that all the fears, ignorance and strong feelings are normal. Reading that shows adult union and adult love issues will not be understood, or at least will be converted by the adolescent reader into what he needs for now. When we reach young adulthood, however, and begin to think in terms of lasting relationships, parenting and mutual sexual responses, we need reading to help us to imagine what this might be like. We need to extend our concerns to moral issues, social issues, conflict and harmony. Let me illustrate.

There are two images around sex that stick in my mind from my boyhood. One is Jane Russell's cleavage in the movie *The Outlaw*. Jane's claim to movie fame, at least before she costarred with Marilyn Monroe, was her exceptionally large bosom. It first claimed public attention in an otherwise completely forgettable western, *The Outlaw*, with its notorious episode wherein Jane saves a feverish cowboy's life by sleeping with him. The logic of this never quite got through to me, so my fantasizing about this episode was always spoiled by an element of confusion as to the likelihood of sexual lifesaving. None of that really prevented me from having an obsession with the picture, however. I, and an equally information-starved group of friends, managed to get to see this film—which shows how tame it must have been—and what we held our breath for was a two-second shot of Jane Russell's breasts as she leaned forward in a loose blouse. We had never seen a braless woman, let alone a naked one; we had never imagined feminine beauty on such a scale. Since these were the days when you could stay in the cinema and watch again and again the continuously running feature and shorts, we patiently sat through ninety more minutes of boredom to get a second dazed, momentary look at Jane's pendant frontage. We were not interested in love, in relationship, in mutual sympathy and understanding—like Captain Friday we just wanted the facts. We were starved for information—visual information, statistical information, practical information and information about feelings and what grownups did when they did "it." Did women like it? Did babies get made every time?

The Outlaw was a daring film for its era, an era when Paris was still the wicked city, the only one, and topless waitresses were even less imaginable than unrationed steak. Information was hard to come by. Parents were (and often are to this day) not much help. They live secret lives. Many don't talk about sexual matters or their own feelings. And as for school, ha! You might wait forever, it seemed, to pry information out of the educational system. There, all the good bits were removed even from Shakespeare. The schools taught nothing. Where were we to get the information? In occupied Europe, as I understand from the movies, families could huddle in basements and secretly listen to the BBC and Radio Free Europe giving their versions of the war. There was nothing equivalent in sexual matters for English adolescents, who huddled together to exchange false folklore, most of which they had invented. I can even remember one occasion when a group of male adolescents gathered round a fifteen-year-old sex maniac to listen open-mouthed and wide-eyed to a reading of his own lurid story about a wedding night, and how we marvelled at his knowledge and talent. That's how desperate we were.

The other image I remember can be quoted below. It is one episode, a few words really, from Lawrence's *Lady Chatterley's Lover*:

And afterwards, when they had been quite still,
the woman had to uncover the man again, to look at
the mystery of the phallos.

"And now he's tiny, and soft like a little bud of
life!" she said, taking the soft small penis in her hand.
"Isn't he somehow lovely! so on his own, so strange! And
so innocent! And he comes so far into me! You must never
insult him, you know. He's mine too. He's not only yours.
He's mine! And so lovely and innocent!" And she held the
penis soft in her hand.

He laughed.

"Blest be the tie that binds our hearts in kindred love,"
he said.

"Of course!" she said. "Even when he's soft and
little I feel my heart simply tied to him. And how lovely
your hair is here! quite, quite different!"[3]

What interests me now about this is that nothing else about the
novel stayed with me. When I read the novel again as a teacher, I was
amazed at its richness and complexity.

We find in our reading what we need at a particular time. We
focus our attention on the things that seem important to us where
we are in our own development. This does not always go reliably by
age, either—we might be a very enlightened fifteen or a very sheltered and naive twenty-five. The contrast between my concerns at
fourteen, picking through *Lady Chatterley* for the interesting bits, and
those of a young adult woman interested in the dynamics of mate
selection, is well illustrated by what a student wrote about the novel
a few years ago. The student told me frankly in her essay that
Lawrence's novel brought her to the full and honest realization that
her sexual experiences had been a self-betrayal. She wrote, "Having
sex with someone you don't love is the most powerful experience I
can imagine and denying your true feelings makes it even worse. Sex
becomes exactly what Lawrence was protesting against, merely a

mechanical act." For her, Lawrence was a very important reading experience. It clarified her past feelings and forced her to go over them so that she could sort out what mattered to her. It gave support to her own view that love is an essential ingredient for sexual intimacy. The novel was an *authority* for a view that was natural to her— it gave her courage and justification she could use to help her to stand her ground in the future. Lawrence gave a context in a powerful story about love that the student could use to clarify and organize her own feelings and beliefs. Her thoughts and feelings were not just peculiar to her, nor were they trivial and nasty, best pushed out of sight in a world that celebrates casual sex in a flood of advertising and pop movies.

These concerns about what matters in relations, how we feel and how this compares with what a spouse feels, are exactly appropriate to a time of life when we must form new relations and make adult decisions. Where will we get help? How can we know what we think if we don't have feedback? Whom can we talk to? Who will talk to us? We are not likely to talk to parents who have not been forthcoming on subjects such as their own sexuality or their own relations. Besides, they are only one couple; what if they are peculiar, too? We can talk to friends, sometimes frankly, but how much do they know? Literature is our richest resource. Interesting novels and poetry show us how complete strangers think and behave, and fiction is capable of speaking *for us,* as it did for the student I just mentioned.

One young woman explained to me how important Ernest Hemingway's *A Farewell to Arms* had been to her in young adulthood. The novel is a pretty gloomy picture of an attempt by a young soldier and a nurse to run away from war and live a blissful life of love in neutral Switzerland. Their love is perfect, idyllic, but Catherine dies in childbirth and Henry walks off in the rain. Cynthia read this novel and loved it, devoured it and related to it. Her friends found it depressing. She told me she found it depressing, too, but this did not bother her. The more the hero suffered, she said, the more she loved it. We live in a world of hype, of youth worship, of carefree beauty on the beach, of beer ads that promise happiness, of Disney happy endings. Our world can be, in its cheerfulness, a terrifying place. As a young woman said to her mother in a recent episode of a soap opera in what was supposed to be an emotional confrontation between the two, "Please, Mother, you'll ruin my makeup." My daughter, who was watching, said, "That's sick!" In many ways we do live in a sick society, and many of our problems—broken families, crime, inequality—stem, I think, from a deep sickness that comes from living with lies and deception. Many people attempt to shut down feeling and pain by drink, drugs, travel, food, sex and even religion. This evasion leads to a cycle of desperation. Only the knowledge of ourselves and our relations to life can heal us. Literature is one aid, one path through the maze. When we are brave enough to confront our realities, our fears, the fragile quality of life, the vulnerability of our loved ones to disease and accident, our fear of loss, then we realize that there is something obscene about the unrelenting jolliness of a sitcom world.

Adolescents, who must prepare for adulthood, pay a very high price for being amused by trivia all the time. There is an insulting quality to entertainment that feeds back to us images of false gaiety, that denies our real feelings and anxieties. We need to be known, to be recognized, and for that reason literature is now more important than ever. We need to see our fears expressed and understood, even realized and played out, so that our deep selves are validated by the story. The novel gives us credit for being able to see the sadness of life even as we survive it. Fiction respects us. *We can handle it!* But we need *to practice,* we need to feel and discuss what can happen, how it can feel. Cynthia was flattered and enlightened by *A Farewell to Arms.*

The novel engaged her strengths, her inner yearning for the truth about life's hardships and disappointments. She needed to get in touch with some hard core of deep feeling, to dig under the superficial froth of the media world of television. How can we be sensitive to others if we are afraid of pain? How can we form relationships or care about people if we paper over everything and trivialize our fears and hopes? Cola and cosmetics will not make us happy or serve as the bonding agent for relationships as the ads suggest. The trivial and simple will not only damage us and our relationships, but threaten our world, our species survival. We can laugh and chatter ourselves all the way to mass murder and nuclear destruction. All we have to do is shut down our affect systems with the help of Madison Avenue, or pretend we have done so.

1   David Lodge, *Out of the Shelter* (Harmondsworth: Penguin, 1970), p. 50.

2   Matthew Arnold, "Dover Beach," in *The Norton Anthology of English Literature*, Third Edition, Vol. 2, ed. M. H. Abrams, et al. (New York: Norton, 1974).

3   D. H. Lawrence, *Lady Chatterley's Lover* (Harmondsworth: Penguin, 1960), p. 219.

PART FOUR

Problems, Crises and Coping

CHAPTER TEN

Marriage and Union Dues

Marriage is an agreement to sleep next to an imperfect stranger. This contract requires a lot of trust, or if not trust, then courage, to put it mildly. So peculiar and unlikely is this idea that it bears looking into more closely. Why would an otherwise perfectly rational person forsake the tranquillity and freedom of private life, the pleasure of being responsible only for self, the freedom to get up and make french fries at 2:00 a.m. and then go thrash around in bed unrestrainedly; why, I say, would someone change all this for arguments about who burned the toast, where to spend Christmas, and why a birthday or anniversary has been forgotten?

The drive to mate, and most conveniently to mate for life, is a deep biological and biosocial urge. Mating for humans, as for other species, has its roots in our genetic program to reproduce ourselves. No matter what we may think are our motives, or how we explain our desire to ourselves, every time we are aroused and want to have sexual intercourse with a mate, we are encouraged by our genes, by the original program to reproduce. Our genetic design does not know we may be wearing a condom and acts as though coitus will always make more human beings. The gene cares nothing for individual death, only for species survival. So the drive to mate is built on powerful biological foundations.

Religious pressure to marry with the blessing of God and to stay married probably comes from an ancient belief that sex is connected with the fertility of everything and God favours fertility. Most religions like to think of sex as confined to the goal of reproduction, not as involving pleasure for its own sake. Reproduction should be confined to marriage. Sex should be confined to marriage, so let's get the kids married as soon as possible in case they make babies outside of marriage. Governments want people to marry to keep things tidy. Parents want grandchildren to carry on their genes, or, as they put it, the family name, but the family name is only the label for a line of genes. All these external pressures join with the internal pressure to marry and mate.

Human beings are more, however, than their reproductive drives. They like to talk. They have a complex language and with that language they communicate. Human beings must have feedback to know who they are; they need a response to see if they have been heard and if they have been understood. People *need* to communicate in order to share their experiences, what has happened to them, and they can do this by turning their experience into language. For this, they need a partner, preferably one who speaks the same language. A language so private that it defeats its own purpose is a sign of mental illness. The most human way of forming partnerships and of sharing thoughts and feelings is through language. People marry to achieve companionship and to have someone to talk to. But why, you may ask, is *marriage* necessary for this? The answer lies in trust. Marriage is a private agreement, but a public announcement of an agreement, to become a union, to move from "I" and "one" to "we." Marriage is a ceremony. People marry best where they trust most. To be heard, to be understood, to have feelings and thoughts respected and known, requires a great deal of trust, and, I should add, a great deal of work. When people join in this union, they agree to pay their dues, or pay the price. Trust requires honesty with the self as a prerequisite to honesty with the other. This is hard.

Friendships last longest if trust is reinforced and grows by continuous proof and demonstration. Trust is in my view the most basic cement of marriage. It is demonstrated, reinforced and nurtured through two forms of communication, touching (so sexual intimacy) and talking-listening. Being stroked and being heard depend on trust and in turn build trust.

Marriage then involves a tremendous amount of work and understanding. Where can you go to learn how to be married? What stands in the way of trust? Why is our true success rate in marriage not ninety-five percent? The answer is that people choose spouses by applying what they have learned in the past. If they go into this process without examining what they have learned in the past, they may choose someone out of a need, fear, fantasy, or modelling that controls them, rather than the other way round. Let's take an example. A young woman, Leanne, comes from a family where an abusive father reigned supreme, assaulted the mother and was usually (in Leanne's memory) either obnoxious or absent. Leanne's answer to the intense stress of the household, and to her own terror of the fighting and violence, was to turn away, literally turn her back on the conflict, and also turn away inside by a flight into fantasy. Where most young people have some fantasy romance of love and success, Leanne turned her fantasy into a program for her life. She would marry wealth, strength and caregiving—someone handsome, who adored her. Since her mate selection was the result of a fantasy view of the world, she was in for some shocks. Her husband was in fact a kind and gentle man, though somewhat domineering and opinionated. When he turned out to be human and fallible, Leanne took out a renewal of her lease on fantasy land and withdrew from him emotionally and often physically. She also became furious with him. It was not until she had been married many years that she and her husband sought therapy and she was ready to examine her past relations with her parents and the effect they had had on her. Had she been able to do this before marriage, even if she had chosen the same spouse she would have avoided some of the crisis and pain her later disappointment caused her.

The way we meet new experience is by using past experience to understand and organize everything we encounter. For a long time after I came to North America, whenever I heard police or factory sirens I would feel some of that panic that came when I heard air raid sirens during the war in England. Not until I had added these new sounds to my learned experience of sirens, extended my repertoire of siren sounds, was I free from this fear. Take another example. A young man, Tom, came to see me to deal with a problem. He was a homosexual, he said. To be a confessed homosexual is certainly not easy in our world. To make matters worse, his mother had left his father because she discovered she preferred being a lesbian. She lived with her lover, and the young man lived with the two women. He declared that his father hated and rejected him, would not talk to him and was ashamed of him. This was how the son viewed all that had happened. I asked how he knew his father felt this way. Through a series of conversations and pretend dialogues with his father, he was able to consider other possibilities. Incidents from the past were reviewed and new versions were applied. Finally Tom was able to call his father and began to visit him and talk. The past now came to look like this: The father felt diminished, a failure at his marriage. If he could not get his wife to love a man, him, then what use was he? He was afraid of being homosexual himself and could not offer his son any sympathy, support, or understanding because of his fear of understanding too much and his sense of having failed his son. The shame and embarrassment of the father on behalf of himself had been seen by Tom as directed at him. Tom was now able to understand his father anew, give his sympathy to his father and strike up a friendship and closeness for himself. He was able to feel better about his life. Self-pity and depression gave way to courage and hope. I call this rewriting the story. Everyone is a story, a collection of arranged experiences. People organize their past into a story. The bad news is that we tend to repeat the mistakes of our parents. The good news is that the story can be rewritten so as to better fit the management of new experiences.

In the 1950s a psychologist named George Kelly produced a highly elaborate and important theory he called "the psychology of personal constructs." By construct, Kelly referred to what I call story. People, he said, represent in their minds some version of experience in the form of a construct, and the sum of many such constructs forms the personality. These constructs are continually expanded and altered to accommodate new information, but the shape of the existing construct gives a shape to the incoming information. The constructs in the mind are like a screen. No matter what information comes in, it must pass through and so be shaped by the screen. The form of the new information is coded, coloured, interpreted by the existing construct program. A very crude example of this is the bigotry that stereotypes. A child may learn, for instance, that men with long hair are lazy, weird, hippy drug addicts. This view will provide the same profile for each new long-haired male who is encountered. Obviously, if constructs are so powerful in shaping new information, they can be extremely limiting, confining and even crippling. There may be many people, experiences, foods, places and so on that are lost to what Kelly calls impermeable constructs. There are far too many parts to this theory to discuss or present here, and the whole thing, with all its supporting research of the last thirty years, gets very complicated. All we really need to know now is that only careful and skillful reexamination of the existing construct or story can produce change that will free the individual from a version of the world that can become a prison.

Marriage can be a great opportunity to produce such changes. But all too often it is designed to reinforce existing problems. Marriage requires the adaptation of two stories to each other. A rigid story that will not be changed will try to impose itself on the spouse's story. "You must see it my way—my way or the doorway," is how one story comes to dominate the other. Take the marriage of Maud and Mac. Maud will have to be fitted to the existing story in the mind of Mac. If Mac cannot rewrite his story in a way that permits him to see how Maud sees, if he can't hear Maud's story for its own sake, Maud will become *Mac's version of Maud*. Maud will then give up her own version of herself, or else intense conflict will begin. This will lead to power struggles, blaming and alienation. Maud may accept Mac's version of herself because she married without any clear sense of who she was, what she wanted, or how she felt. She will try to be what Mac wants, even though this means giving up her power to Mac, being in a way in his control, his creature. The result of this is that resentment on both sides is inevitable.

Literature can be a powerful agent in the context of marriage. The reasons are clear. It is extremely difficult to get a clear picture of one's own marriage and almost impossible to know the truth about anyone else's. How many times have we said of our friends and acquaintances, "*They* are getting divorced? I thought they had the best marriage in the county," or "John always seemed like the perfect husband; I just can't see why Mary walked out on him!" Even to the therapist, appearances can be completely deceiving. I think we all want to fantasize and project blissful romance onto couples we know. I have seen a "perfect" young couple, handsome husband, pretty wife, five years married, no children, beautiful house and a dog, and I have said to myself, "How enviable must be their times together, sharing some music on weekends by the fire, making love from time to time, candles and spaghetti and a long-necked bottle of Chianti waiting by the winking crystal." In reality, they are wary of each other, awkward in their leisure time, avoiding closeness, trying to fill their hours with chores and repairs and arguing about whether to have children and how many and when. Literature shows us the reality, the complexity, the pitfalls and the survivals.

One of the commonest errors of belief in regard to marriage is the conviction that no matter what problems the partners bring with them, marriage will magically solve them all—that the mere act and fact of marriage will mean a clean start. But marriage is no magic solver of problems, and this is where fiction comes in. Attitudes strongly held are unlikely to be changed by a lecture or a textbook. It is necessary to feel the emotion of a story, to live through the simulation of fictive experience, before external material produces insight. *Also*, it is essential to read believing in the possibility that literature *can* speak to the reader about the reader's situation before the book can be heard. Before we can internalize the story and see its relevance to us, we must be able to know that it can be relevant. We need to trust our feelings. We need to permit ourselves the possibility of learning about our own lives from fiction. We need encouragement to see that the pleasure of fiction can be truly useful to us.

I gave a couple the novel *Diary of a Mad Housewife* to read. This is a valuable book for showing how normal it is to feel like you're going crazy. When a couple read the same novel they are able to focus on the same experience that is external to their own. Instead of each partner having to explain some aspect of his or her own life, each can talk about his or her own response to someone else's story, neatly and clearly laid out before them both. This enables them to be less defensive and confused, and clearer as to what they are discussing. They can confront a model problem that reflects theirs without confronting each other, because confronting each other keeps them locked into defended viewpoints.

Since reading is a *shared* experience, it can have the effect of bringing a couple closer. Reading the same story can be doing something together. The book becomes a shared reference point, a shared language, a way of referring to other experiences. Sometimes a story can show one spouse how the other feels more accurately than the husband or wife can show for him- or herself. Sometimes they quote the book at each other to show how it speaks for them. A person who is shy or scared of a spouse may find in a book a way of getting a message across.

The couple who read Sue Kaufman's novel were said to be having what in therapy jargon is called "communication problems." What this meant was that she was unable to explain what was bothering her, and he was too busy, successful and upbeat to be able to see that she could possibly be wanting or lacking anything. In *Diary*, the young woman's marriage is falling apart from sheer neglect. She feels trapped taking care of children, organizing social life, attending to her husband's needs. She feels *unknown*, unconsidered and unimportant. Whole parts of her mind are unexercised. Her creativity is unexpressed. Her thoughts and feelings are unheard. There seems to be no time for just sharing the self, expressing who she is, or saying what she feels about life, family and friends.

Her husband believes he is working hard for "them," for her, and so cannot pause long enough to earn the trust that would allow her to share her feelings. She is supposed to be grateful for his income and success. She seems strangely incapable of explaining herself. She takes to keeping a diary, and this saves her sanity but does not bring her closer to her spouse. I gave this novel to Betty and Sam. At first they seemed amazed that a therapist would ask them to read a novel. Then they found lots of excuses for putting it off. Finally they both read it. Her reaction was one of surprise. It was a good read, but what had it to do with them? The wife in the novel experiments with an extramarital affair, hoping that this will help with her depression and loneliness. She is not treated very well by her lover, but the experience does break open her silence and cause a healthy crisis in her marriage. Betty did not want to talk about her reading of the novel in couple therapy. She had a secret, and she was extremely afraid of Sam's jealousy and impatience. Moreover, she was afraid of my siding with her husband and condemning her, a male alliance against the fallen woman. In fact, she already felt condemned long before she had any reason to feel guilty. What the novel did, then, was to uncover for this woman a number of problems that would not go away just by not being discussed. This all came out in individual confessions made to me by Betty. The novel *exposed* her, she felt, embarrassed and revealed her before her husband. If she talked about her recognition of the woman's desperation, she would give away how unhappy she was and her temptations to infidelity, which scared her. At the same time, the story forced her to acknowledge the role of jealousy and secrecy in her marriage. When I saw Betty privately, a number of these feelings and fears were disclosed. The novel had proved to be a way of opening up areas that were very private and closed off—we had pried the lid off a number of scary feelings and discontents, not by challenging them directly, but by presenting a fictional situation for comparison. In fact, it did not matter much that the novel was not very close to the real-life situation. There were enough opportunities for comment and response that the story was able to make self-disclosure possible.

Sharing fiction is valuable in a marriage because it provides a channel of communication, of communication that is safe because it starts with the story of neither spouse. A story I like to give to couples is "Rope" by Katherine Anne Porter. This story captures perfectly the blame cycle that characterizes so much marital dialogue. Someone, one or the other spouse, taking turns, starts the attack. The one who feels attacked starts defending. Part of the defense is counterattack. In this story, the writer presents a dialogue that captures the aggrieved tones, the sarcasm and the frustration of both parties. A couple move to the country. They seem to have no car and no fridge. The story is from 1930, so my belief is that we are reading about the Great Depression. The nearest store is four miles away. He has returned from the store without her coffee. He has brought back a 25-yard coil of rope that was not on the list. The forgotten coffee and the unexpected rope are the triggers for the fascinating exchanges in this story. Here is an example:

> Her face changed at this, she reminded him he had forgot the coffee and had bought a worthless piece of rope. And when she thought of all the things they actually needed to make the place even decently fit to live in, well, she could cry, that was all. She looked so forlorn, so lost and despairing he couldn't believe it was only a piece of rope that was causing all the racket. What was the matter, for God's sake?
>
> Oh, would he please hush and go away, and stay away, if he could, for five minutes? By all means, yes, he would. He'd stay away indefinitely if she wished. Lord, yes, there was nothing he'd like better than to clear out and never come back. She couldn't for the life of her see what was holding him, then. It was a swell time. Here she was, stuck, miles from a railroad, with a half-empty house on her hands, and not a penny in her pocket, and everything on earth to do; it seemed the God-sent moment for him

to get out from under. She was surprised he hadn't stayed in town as it was until she had come out and done the work and got things straightened out. It was his usual trick.

It appeared to him that this was going a little far. Just a touch out of bounds, if she didn't mind his saying so. Why the hell had he stayed in town the summer before? To do a half-dozen extra jobs to get the money he had sent her. That was it. She knew perfectly well they couldn't have done it otherwise. She had agreed with him at the time. And that was the only time so help him he had ever left her to do anything by herself.

Oh, he could tell that to his great-grandmother. She had her notion of what had kept him in town. Considerably more than a notion, if he wanted to know. So, she was going to bring all that up again, was she? Well, she could just think what she pleased. He was tired of explaining. It may have looked funny but he had simply got hooked in, and what could he do? It was impossible to believe that she was going to take it seriously. Yes, yes, she knew how it was with a man: if he was left by himself a minute, some woman was certain to kidnap him. And naturally he couldn't hurt her feelings by refusing![1]

Forgetting the coffee is received by the wife as a statement from the husband to the effect, "I don't care about you and your desires." The rope is masculine self-indulgence. We can see a whole number of roles being played here. The martyr is played by both parties. Betrayed and neglected wife comes out. Henpecked husband makes an appearance. Long-suffering male vs. unreasonable female. They can't get past the accusations, the past, the defenses, the grievances stored up and repeated in a well-worn groove.

I gave this story to a couple, Al and Trudy, after they had played out scenes like this in front of me for about three weeks in a row and nothing else I had tried could stop them. Their first instinct was of course to identify with their own gender model, their counterpart in the story, and to blame the other party. I asked them to try to think of ways their counterparts might have behaved differently so as to produce different results. The husband said that "he" in the story never did apologize for forgetting her coffee. The wife wanted to know why "she" didn't walk with him and get her own coffee—she wondered at their old-fashioned role-bound ways. By talking about the "out there" rather than about themselves, they were able to start changing their own thinking. They were actually getting some practice in alternative ways of behaving as well as gaining insight into what they themselves typically did. Very quickly they began to talk about their own dialogues, and this meant they had moved out of purely reactive roles into being able to comment on the process. They were surprised to discover how defensive, afraid and insecure they were with each other.

Not all marriage issues are confined to marriage. Marriage is a partnership that requires candour, trust, negotiation. So do other partnerships. Stories that deal with teamwork, with coping with hardship, with saving and sacrificing may very well bring to the reader's mind connections with his own marriage. I assigned to a class of mature students a story by Stephen Crane, "The Open Boat," which describes the ordeal of a group of men in a lifeboat trying to survive a shipwreck at sea. My class, mostly women, responded very strongly to the story. To my surprise they related the behaviour of the boatmen to that of their families by talking of cooperation, of the need for working together to survive, of kindness, love and compassion as essential for a good family team. They spoke of dedication and determination in pursuing a goal. People, then, read from where they are, psychologically and emotionally. Readers take what they need from their reading. One male student told the class that the story helped him to realize the value of a recent experience—a group project that often required him to stay up all night in order to meet the common deadlines. Only by working together could he and the others reach the shore.

Jealousy is frequently at work in a marital partnership. Jealousy is a feeling, and the behaviour it carries with it is possessiveness. Now a certain amount of exclusivity is natural to a close partnership. In good marital relations individuals will want to protect their interests. When jealousy becomes a constant worry and fear, then conflict is bound to arise. Such a feeling has its origin in one basic outlook—a low opinion of self, a dependency, a need for approval from the other and a fear that this may be taken away. A jealous spouse feels inadequate in some way, replaceable, threatened by competition. Rather than examine the source of these feelings, the jealous partner seeks to manage the circumstances, to control the environment to make it safer. Literature, from the classics of antiquity to the pop lyrics of today, is filled with satiric portraits of the spouse, usually the husband, trying to keep his wife-treasure safe, by locking her up, by watching her or having her watched. "Every step you take, every move you make, I'll be watching you," goes the song. Not a very cheery way to conduct a relationship, is it?

The most vital ingredient in a good marriage is trust, trust with feelings, trust with sex, trust with money and so on. The strong, confident, emotionally independent spouse is able to encourage independence in the partner, and so reap the benefits of mutual love freely given rather than extracted by pressure. Jealousy can be a dark secret in the family, and as a secret can distort family relations for years. The jealous partner knows that admitting the jealousy is also to admit feeling second best, or to admit some worry about being

attractive, desirable, or pleasing enough. Often the jealousy is rooted in a version of past experience, even a premarital relationship.

A wonderful study of such secret jealousy and the pain it can
cause is the novel *Call it Sleep* by Henry Roth, a kind of minor
American classic. Many men experience in their jealousy doubts
about the paternity of their children, or of one child. This leads to a
great deal of family abuse. Both wife and child feel the brunt of a lot
of unexplained anger. *Call it Sleep* reveals with great sensitivity the
consequences of such a secret belief, how it poisons a relationship
and tortures the possessor of the belief. *Pygmalion* by Bernard Shaw
(best known now as the musical *My Fair Lady*) is based upon a classical tale that is very instructive. The artist brings to life a statue; she
is his creation. But once the statue becomes human everything gets
complicated, because being human means having a mind of one's
own. Love cannot be enforced.

Another writer who specializes in revealing the destructive
power of jealousy and secrecy is Nathaniel Hawthorne in *The Scarlet
Letter* and in other stories. Adultery has never been treated more
thoroughly in the context of religion and community attitudes than
in Hawthorne's *Scarlet Letter*. Hester Prynne, who believes herself single after many years of living alone, has an affair with the Puritan
minister and bears his child. The father refuses to acknowledge his
paternity. Her husband secretly returns and plots a horrible revenge.
Guilt, love, sexual passion, feminism and religious hypocrisy are all
examined in a classic tale of colonial days. People who are thinking
of committing adultery could do a lot worse than read this book.
There is no point in an abstract debate with oneself or another person about the rights and wrongs and costs and benefits of having a
love affair. A lonely, neglected, frustrated, or mistreated spouse may
easily be tempted by an attentive, considerate, admiring would-be
lover. It requires fiction to make the situation real, to put one right

into the picture. To imagine oneself facing the actual consequences of the problems and pleasures, one must read a story that reflects the issues in action; the reader must see people actually behaving, moving, talking, for the reality to strike home. Secret knowledge and deception can torture and drain the energy out of lovers. Guilt can be a poison that kills affection and compassion.

There is no limit to the demands of the possessive husband. If a wife thinks she can achieve happiness in marriage by unrestrained pleasingness, she is likely to end only with damage to herself. Hawthorne's wonderful story "The Birthmark" shows us how far men and women can go in this game of possession and control. I suppose Shakespeare's *Othello* is the most famous treatment of jealousy. It is a story of wife abuse that ends in murder. Jealousy is the tragic flaw in the otherwise noble hero.

Where can we find models, warnings, illustrations of our own dangerous beliefs and behaviours, if not in literature? All of literature grows out of human experience, the writer's experience and observation. It is rendered into story form for our benefit, a contribution to the general store of wisdom. Once we see that our reading can be related to our own lives, we have access to an enormous store of helping information.

How many of the thousands of premarital counselling groups that meet annually in North America use fiction as part of the process? Few or none, I'd be willing to bet. Yet what could be a more obvious source of case history, of example and warning, than stories of marriage? I have heard a most vigorous discussion by students, led by a young married couple, following a reading of Graham Greene's *Brighton Rock*. This novel raises a number of serious questions about sex, religion and marriage, not to mention the hunger for love and the power of loyalty even in the most unlikely circumstances. While young couples may be cautious about talking about themselves, or about violating romance by revealing negative feelings towards a spouse or fiancé, they can freely exchange views about a story out there that doesn't threaten. It's a start.

Another novel that deals effectively with jealousy and lust, in the setting of American material greed, is F. Scott Fitzgerald's *The Great Gatsby*. Although it was written about sixty years ago, this story raises questions that seem peculiarly appropriate to our free-enterprise, yuppie lifestyle. Gatsby, a man of infinite hope, devotes his life to winning the beautiful Daisy. To do so, he believes, he must acquire wealth, and in the pursuit of wealth he engages in some shady dealings. He dies in the attempt to win his lost love.

There are two ways to read a book like this, to read any book. One is as a foreign curiosity, an entertaining tale that has nothing to do with us. The other way is to ask ourselves if the novel connects to us in any way. Is my life being governed by a loss, or by the pursuit of some object or goal I cannot attain? Is it a quest that, however compelling it seems, causes me to compromise my principles? Do I have to impress, dazzle, become wealthy in order to be loved? How do I define success for my life? Married couples would do well to share a reading like this with a view to discussing some of these questions.

Marriages too often proceed as though questions of value, belief and morality can be left unexplored, as though the two partners do not have attitudes, feelings about what matters, what they care about most. Sometimes there is a kind of embarrassment about serious questions, questions of life values, goals, beliefs. In our culture many people treat themselves as robots, mechanical figures, cut off from feelings, caring, history and destiny. Sensitivity to questions of right and wrong, respect for our own feelings and those of our spouses, honesty about our compromises are important parts of our lives' meaning. Try to find those books you can connect with. Use your reading to raise your awareness of your own feelings and situation. Share your reading with your spouse. Reading will help you to raise some of the issues that you want and need to talk about and that can't be approached directly.

1   Katherine Anne Porter, "Rope," in *Flowering Judas and Other Stories* (New York: Modern Library, 1935).

CHAPTER ELEVEN

Separation, Divorce and Other Opportunities

W hen divorce and separation become inevitable, what can you do? I gave a talk some time ago to a group of people who either had recently been divorced or were in the process of separating. They conveyed to me the full range of emotions characteristic of this kind of loss. First, they want to deny that it can be happening, and they do this by clinging to the hope that it won't really happen. Their spouse will soon see the light, realize what she is missing and come home bearing gifts. They believe that if they can just find the right magic prescriptions they can change all this pain and produce happiness. Anger is a big part of what they feel, even bitterness. They are angry at a spouse who seems to have betrayed them, or who has failed to see their value, or who seems to have changed into someone quite different. Perhaps the rules have suddenly been altered, or new goals and desires have loomed to the fore in the marriage. They are hurt that things have not stayed the same. They are angry at themselves for failing, for having invested too much, or for being rejected.

This anger can spill over onto parents and children. Separated couples feel guilty for their children. They are scared about the future. They are frightened of increased economic stress. They are sad and depressed and lose confidence. What I had to say to this group was that divorce, when inevitable, is a great life opportunity, the chance of freedom and renewal, the possibility of real personal growth, like leaving home all over again. This cheerful message was at first rejected. It was an invitation to bravery and risk, independence and control. Many people wanted to cling to the past, bemoan their hard fate and stay with their loneliness and bitterness. One way to stay "married" is to refuse to be single in your mind. This is especially true for those who have given up the self in the service of marriage, who have married as a substitute for self-growth and independence. Many young people become extremely dependent on a spouse for status, money, affection, approval, work and role. Marriage can be a cop-out. The more power you have given away to another, the more necessary it is to cling to the "other" who is in control of your self-image and life role. To give up your own development by merging yourself in the marriage institution is to use marriage like a cult or the army.

Many young people marry without ever having left home, without having finished growing up, without having been alone, ever. They have no life experience as individuals, no experience of being challenged or tested, of discovering their own strengths or resourcefulness. Divorce, or at least separation, can be a priceless opportunity for backtracking and making up for this lost stage of development. Getting in touch with who *you* are, *you*, that is, separate from your spouse, how you feel, think, believe, dream, desire, is an essential life task. How can reading help in these goals? To begin with, novels and stories about being widowed, single, separated, or alone for any reason, can help you to normalize the situation. Novels like Judith Guest's *Ordinary People* and *Second Heaven* show us someone else's picture of the struggle to sort out what went wrong. From sharing these experiences in reading we can see that depression, sadness, anger and frustration are normal, not fatal, and perhaps even valuable.

There are advantages to moderate sadness and depression. These feelings slow us down, invite us to look inwards and get to know ourselves. We need the opportunity, to assess who we are and what we want and value. Painful feelings challenge us to honesty. What was missing in our marriage? How do we feel about our children? If, for want of a better term, we say we each have a soul, was the marriage good for our souls? Did we lie? Did we get abused, exploited? Did we allow ourselves to be used, intimidated, trapped or imprisoned?

Doris Lessing has written a very powerful story called "To Room Nineteen." It ends in a wife's suicide, but en route to that ending we see a perfectly controlled middle-class marriage go more and more sterile. Everything seems to be grounded in appearances, and no one seems to be *heard*. The couple seem to plan the life out of everything, and we witness the relentless withering away of a soul. It is possible, I think, to neglect the self, the essential genetic "I," to the point of self-destruction. A number of mature women students who read this story found in it a powerful warning. One of them wrote in an essay, "I wanted to get into the story and shake her (the heroine) and tell her to get hold of herself, to talk and demand a hearing." Another wrote to me,

> I guess I was just reading along, not feeling or thinking much of anything until we came to "Room 19." Suddenly, I was shocked and I realized that I was reading about myself, about what might have happened to me. I am divorced, for 6 years now, and not until I read this did I see what a narrow escape I had. I was being ground down. I don't feel guilty about leaving any more. I must never let that happen to me again.

Another student wrote, "This marriage was too successful, too perfectly middle-class, not painful enough. There was no struggle in it." Erica Jong's *Fear of Flying* and Nora Ephron's *Heartburn* surely owe their popularity to their ability to show the importance of self-respect and honesty. How many women have sacrificed personal development in a deadly trade-off for status, respectability, security and money?

If at First...

Why are people so hard on themselves? I suppose that marriage often feels like the end of life, the final goal. No sooner have we grown up, left home or left school, when bingo! we find a mate, amazingly, willing to marry us. Now the final crown of success has been achieved. From now on, we will live happily ever after; life is complete, happiness is assured and the fates, parents, teachers and friends must now be satisfied. When this does not happen, when we are not satisfied, when our life, society, or health demands a separation, or when our spouse departs, by choice or through accident, we blame ourselves.

Surprisingly, people who become single after being married feel *shame*. For some reason, being one after being two brings apology, failure, a sense of having let everyone down. There is, of course, a sense of loss, a change, a grief for the good things gone, of which there are always some. This is all understandable, and time, work, courage, thought, honesty are the antidotes that will ease the transition, aided by activity, friends, conversation and reading. Where divorce differs from the death of a loved one, is in the embarrassment, disappointment and self-condemnation that swamp the newly single. Not always, of course; sometimes there is a genuine relief and a sense of victory at escape. Frequently all these feelings exist together and are very confusing. Often, though, the end of marriage leads to a great sense of failure and to social withdrawal and fear. Frequently, the divorced person romanticizes and confuses the past and feels out of control, as though having "failed" to meet all the expectations of others and self. There is no hope of looking ahead, no strength to plan a future. There is also a sense of puzzlement; what went wrong, how did it happen?

Remember that marriage, sealed into history by The Wedding, has been elevated to the crowning achievement of life. After the speeches, the presents, the honeymoon, perhaps it is not surprising that individuals feel they have betrayed a multitude of expectations or have been deceived and rejected. And then there are the children, who love and need both parents and naturally hate change, insecurity and the loss of the "ideal" family. Children are often actually deceived by the great show of harmony put up by parents and feel very angry at what seems to them inexplicable and unexpected marriage dissolution.

Given all this it is hardly surprising that people once married should be very cautious about trying again and making the same mistakes again. We can only conclude that the desire to mate, for purposes of companionship, sex and affection, or the dreams of success and social redemption are too strong to be resisted. Since it is virtually impossible to know the truth about others' marriages, we will not find reliable models for success in observing people socially. The exception is one's parents' marriage, and the best that can be said about that is that they had you, or, in my case, me, and that makes us hardly detached observers. Appearances deceive. The hero of one moment is revealed as having feet of clay the next. The mystery of marriage can be penetrated from very few sources. An old Yiddish proverb says, "If you don't sleep under their bed, you can't know their affairs." There is myth, the bits and pieces we pick up from hearsay, proverbs, or sayings—for instance, "Marry in haste, repent at leisure." But such aids are mostly warnings, and who ever heard of lovers calling it off because of some ancient advice?

As for television and movies, who can trust them? Only fiction gives us a whole tradition of stories based on real-life experience and then turned into a view, a version, of the world. Dickens' novels, for example, abound in carefully and vividly drawn portraits of marriage. Some of these are built out of observations, are the composites of impressions from watching others, and some are built out of lived experience. These include the Pickwicks' and David Copperfield's efforts at marriage. Most writers have taught us something to add to our knowledge of the range of possible marriages—the expedient, the convenient, the arranged, the sadistic, the happy—and of the whole range of conflict, betrayal and misunderstanding that we find in life. Most of Thomas Hardy, for instance, is about marriage. So is the work of George Eliot, Jane Austen, the Brontës, and so is much of Shakespeare, and so on. Marriage is, after all, the most interesting of human arrangements, even if, or because, it remains largely a mystery. To see how our own marriage works or might work, we must read about others'. This is how we will extend the range of our marital knowledge and experience, for we cannot live through many marriages just to find out, not even if we are Hollywood marriage marathoners.

Divorce has become much easier and is an option for many people in unhappy marriages. Once, divorce was only for the rich— one of the subjects explored in detail in Dickens' *Hard Times*, if you are interested. Poor people did not even think of divorce. Besides the economic barrier, there were religious and social taboos on divorce, so strong that it never even occurred to most people to think of this option to unhappy union. You make your bed and you lie upon it, in both senses. Marriage in the past may have been for better or worse, but it was certainly for ever. I can remember a saying from my childhood, "When hunger comes in at the door, loves flies out the window"; but I can't remember a single case of divorce among any of my relatives or family's friends. Not until a cousin went to the U.S. and remarried not once but twice, did the concept enter family conversation. He was regarded as a lunatic fringe character, corrupted by the outlandish customs of America, where anything was possible, including divorce, murder, cowboys and Indians, gangs on the waterfront and Jane Russell, as we had seen from the movies. Everything in America was larger and more sensational.

Now that divorce is commonplace, many children have the experience of more than one set of parents. Plenty of writers have been through the pain and confusion of ending one marriage and starting another, and they show us that we are not alone. I have been reading many wonderful stories about divorce, separation, remarriage and stepparenting. Let's look at one example of the last. Stepparenting comes about through marriage, not necessarily through divorce. In Robert K. Smith's *Jane's House* we have a powerful portrait of what it is like stepping into a deceased wife's shoes by moving into her house, bed, kitchen and role. A fellow student of mine when I was in training as a therapist told me she had remarried in precisely these circumstances. Everyone in her new family was supposed to love her, but nobody seemed to, and she felt she was being compared unfavourably to the previous wife-mom, "Jane," all the time. Not until she read *Jane's House*, she said, did she realize that what she was experiencing was not only normal and well recognized, but survivable and capable of being changed. She felt less alone and more comfortable from seeing herself, from being understood, in the book and in her reading experience of it. My friend told me, "It was a great relief to read that book, a revelation. I felt as though I had found a reason, an explanation, maybe I wasn't going crazy after all." A number of other novels, like Nancy Thayer's *Stepping*, like Alice Munro's *Who Do You Think You Are?* and *Something I've Been Meaning to Tell You*, and like James Carrol's *Fault Lines*, treat this subject. A variety of stories by many writers—Bobbie Ann

Mason, Audrey Thomas, Alice Walker, Raymond Carver, Sandra Birdsell, Doris Lessing, Mavis Gallant, Ethel Wilson and others— show us how much interest and commentary there is in modern fiction about contemporary dilemmas. You can sort through this reading to help you to figure out where you fit in, what you feel, what you want and what you can do about it. If you persist in thinking of yourself as peculiar and isolated you will remain locked in confusion and pain. You can put your situation into perspective by reading. You can find that others have experienced similar feelings and problems. You can rejoin the human race.

CHAPTER TWELVE

Everyone Loses Some of the Time

D ivorce, the end of a marriage, whether desired or not, is a form of loss. It is natural, therefore, that it should bear some resemblance to the experience of grief. Losses take time to get over. You cannot be preached out of your feelings. You cannot go around the grief, make an end run and put it aside. The only way through the valley of the shadow is down the middle. This is hard, and it is natural to want to avoid the reality of pain. There is a time during grief when reading may be impossible. Reading that portrays loss may just be too hard to bear at certain times, or reading that is distracting may be too hard to concentrate on. There is a time for just experiencing feelings, for thinking, for being alone, for being in contact with loving survivors who try to share your grief. Perhaps at such times the only helpful reading is the soothing acceptance expressed in Ecclesiastes. Remember, reading is work; it requires thought, energy and concentration. It does provoke thoughts, memories and associations that may be intolerable at certain times. People need a period during which to cling to their grief, to those feelings that are their link with the lost object of love. If you feel you have lost part of yourself, you can feel hurt, angry, deprived, or rejected.

There are many kinds of loss, and I want to deal with a variety of them, but the hardest is surely the death of a beloved close spouse in a well-established, mutually respectful relationship. There comes a time when it is appropriate to rejoin the human community, when a little distance from pain has made it possible to accept the loss in a larger perspective, as part of a shared experience, a human pattern. This is the reason for the success of grief groups, gatherings of people who are in the same emotional condition, who can understand and support one another and help each member feel less alone. For this reason, reading about death and loss is most beneficial in a group context where the responses to the reading can be part of the shared experience. The best book I know on grief and survival is James Agee's *A Death in the Family*. This is a rather long and "literary" novel that is best read slowly and in parts, with some record-keeping of revelations and responses that can be shared with others who are reading the book. The goal of such reading is to broaden one's perspective, to be less alone, to sense an emergence from the isolating pain of personal loss. No one can, of course, know your particular pain, your own exact memories and fears and what it means to you personally, day to day, to be without your special, unique companion. But you can find out that, while the details are yours, a similar pain, similar feelings and a similar deprivation are known to others. It is important not to be left with a feeling of unique victimization by loss. Here is a poem by Emily Dickinson, for instance, that expresses for all of us the horror of that numbness that comes with surviving a great loss:

> After great pain, a formal feeling
>   comes—
> The Nerves sit ceremonious, like
>   Tombs—
> The stiff Heart questions was it
>   He, that bore,
> And Yesterday, or Centuries
>   before?

The Feet, mechanical, go
    round—
Of Ground, or Air, or
    Ought—
A Wooden way
Regardless grown,
A Quartz contentment, like a
    stone—
This is the Hour of Lead—
Remembered, if outlived,
As Freezing persons, recollect
    the Snow—
First—Chill—then Stupor—then
    the letting go—[1]

Read this aloud to yourself. Don't worry about meanings of individual words and phrases, get the feeling-sense of the whole thing. The poet captures and conveys with great accuracy the aching numbness of one stage of grief. It is valuable to everybody to know that such feelings have been recognized and expressed in memorable fashion, put into the language-control of poetry. And it's important for people in grief to use the power of literature for expression of their own unexpressed feelings. People who are gifted with this power to give memorable expression to feelings are a resource to the species. They assist us in our coping, in our surviving. Most of us find it very difficult to express ourselves, and so we need the specialists, the novelists and poets, to help us.

A useful and affective novel for children, *Beat the Turtle Drum* by Constance C. Greene conveys very well the sense of numbness, unreality and unbelievability at the death of a close family member, in this case a sibling. The pain of sibling loss can be devastating, and in the midst of parental grief and family trauma the child's pain and bewilderment may get overlooked. One of the most famous books about childhood grief is *A Taste of Blackberries* by Doris Buchanan Smith, which deals with the loss of a friend. Literature is a valuable way to recognize and acknowledge this pain; it provides a means of releasing and getting access to grief feelings. Parents would be well advised to use this kind of resource to assist them in helping their children. Teachers and school counsellors need to be especially aware of and sensitive to the situation of a grieving student. They can devise a reading program that constitutes the basis of a working through of grief.

The ending to Hemingway's *A Farewell to Arms* presents one of the most famous deaths in literature and the end of a perfect romance. The surviving lover, Henry, conveys to us strongly the numbness, despair and emptiness I have been discussing. When I was newly married for the first time and read *A Farewell to Arms* in graduate school, I was disturbed and a bit scared by the ending and tended to make light of it to make myself feel more comfortable. To put down Hemingway's ending, where Catherine and the baby die and Henry walks out of the hospital and into the rain, I would tell the story I remembered from Richard Gordon's *Doctor in the House*, a comic account of medical school in England. The student has final exams and is asked to do a forceps delivery on a dummy baby and mother. He attaches the forceps to the baby's head and pulls. Nothing happens. He puts one knee on the mother, braces his other foot against the chair and pulls with all his might. The baby is yanked free, student and forceps flying backwards across the room. The examiner picks up the forceps, walks over to the dazed student lying in the corner of the room and says, "Now hit the father over the head with this and you'll have killed the whole bloody family." Or something like that. In fact, *A Farewell to Arms* was important in giving expression to a fear of loss that was really there in me and that would have remained unacknowledged, repressed, and so have turned into one more anxiety.

A very remarkable story of loss and grief is Henry James' "The Beast in the Jungle." The hero, blind to the love that sits under his very nose and failing to see that his female friend and confidante *is* his destiny (so self-absorbed is he), finally loses her when she dies. As he attends and thinks at the graveside, he is visited by a revelation of the truth, of what he has lost without ever having experienced. He sees another grieving man at another graveside ravaged by a sorrow that the speaker cannot at first understand.

> What had the man *had*, to make him by the loss of it so bleed and yet live?
>
> Something—and this reached him with a pang—that he, John Marcher, hadn't; the proof of which was precisely John Marcher's arid end. No passion had ever touched him, for this was what passion meant; he had survived and maundered and pined, but where had been *his* deep ravage? The extraordinary thing we speak of was the sudden rush of the result of this question. The sight that had just met his eyes named to him, as in letters of quick flame, something he had utterly, insanely missed, and what he had missed made these things a train of fire, made them mark themselves in an anguish of inward throbs. He had seen outside of his life, not learned it within, the way a woman was mourned when she had been loved for herself: such was the force of his conviction of the meaning of the stranger's face, which still flared for him as a smoky torch. It hadn't come to him, the knowledge, on the wings of experience; it had brushed him,

jostled him, upset him, with the disrespect of chance,
the insolence of accident. Now that the illumination had
begun, however, it blazed to the zenith, and what he
presently stood there gazing at was the sounded void of
his life. He gazed, he drew breath, in pain; he turned
in his dismay, and, turning, he had before him in sharper
incision than ever the open page of his story. The name
on the table smote him as the passage of his neighbour
had done, and what it said to him, full in the face, was
that she was what he had missed.[2]

This seems to me shockingly powerful as an explanation of
loss, not the loss of someone loved, but the loss of opportunity to
love. The loss of a loved one may be inevitable, but the courage to
love before it is too late is something we can work for. While we are
on the subject of unexpressed emotion, I should say something
about the physiological consequences of emotion. Many diseases are
thought to have some link with emotional discomfort. To put this in
the most modest way possible, it seems likely that emotional distress, especially long-term, can be a factor in disease or sickness or
injury. I am not speaking of imagined symptoms but of observable
damage, ulcers, cancers, migraines, dizziness, high blood pressure,
anorexia and other eating disorders, and many other problems.
Much of this kind of physical result is currently attributed to something vaguely called "stress." This discomfort, conflict, tension and
sense of pressure, panic, or being one way or another out of control,
leads to some body response. Anger, frustration, sadness, self-condemnation and so on can be turned on the self. Suicide, a murder of
the self, is sometimes the consequence of a frustrated, successfully
inhibited desire to murder somebody else, or of an anger at part of
the self that causes problems or is thought to do so. Unacknowledged

anger does not disappear just because it is denied. The body knows what the mind refuses to admit. There is a price for going around tensed up, fists clenched, shoulders hunched, neck and face muscles taut, breathing contracted—all to keep anger or hurt in, unexpressed. Reading can be an important source of emotional expression and a mirror for exposing to the reader feelings, situations, or ideas that need to be recognized and thus brought into conscious control. Remember that what is not known cannot be managed.

I gave a story by Sandra Birdsell, "The Wednesday Circle," to a client, Linda, who I thought would enjoy it because the setting and background were very similar to Linda's own, and we were discussing her adolescence—the girl in the story is thirteen. Linda was a tense person, not very forthcoming, who had problems sleeping as well as some loss of appetite. She was twenty-eight. In all the five weeks we had met we had never discussed sexual abuse. The girl in the story has to fetch eggs from a neighbour farmer who sexually harasses and fondles her, keeping her from telling by threats and shame. This becomes a torment to her, makes her nauseated, sleepless and disturbed about many things. Linda read the story, and after I had asked her a few questions about her liking it, just when I was about to drop it, she blurted out, "That happened to me, you know." In the discussion that followed I learned that in a baby-sitting job when she was thirteen Linda had been abused by the father of the child she was to care for, either when he drove her home or when he came home early on some excuse. For fifteen years Linda had tolerated emotions and symptoms that were making her sick. Her recovery began when she could accept her own victimization by talking about it. This became possible for her when she could read about another child, treated compassionately by an author who recognized that such things happen and victims are not to blame. I do not know if Linda would ever have talked to me about her experience had she not read the story.

As I said before, there are many kinds of losses we can grieve for. Death is only one form of loss, but others, loss of a job, a house, a limb, money, or a skill, can be the source of large-scale pain and grief. Some losses require normalizing responses, adjustment, understanding and acceptance. All such losses also produce many common responses in the sufferer. There is the feeling of anger, the "why me?" victim feeling, a sense of diminishment, of being less, and with it a feeling of fear, of failure, of anxiety about the future. There is the sense that having been hurt we should withdraw, sulk, cut out and not try to go another round. If we can get past this, gird our loins and enter the fray of life again, we join the ranks of survivors. A little later on I have more to say about the literature of survival. For now, it should be clear that times of loss, or times following loss, require that we come to see that our suffering is not exclusive to us, that pain makes us part of the species. A major movement today for achieving this is the establishment of groups, where people with some common need or situation share their stories and convey a sense of support, trust and community in suffering. Groups for rape victims, incest victims, single parents and people with disabilities can all be very effective. There is hardly a human circumstance of suffering for which, at least in cities, one cannot find or form a group.

One of the surprising things about such groups is how underused the aid of literature is in them. Experience shows that fiction and poetry are very effective in permitting disclosure, the sharing of feelings and experiences that are otherwise very difficult to voice in a group. Not only is it embarrassing to talk about painful experiences in front of others, experiences that may have been kept secret for years; it is often very hard to find the language in which to express deeply felt but also vaguely felt emotions. There are passages in Margaret Laurence's *The Diviners*, for instance, that are excellent for calling forth responses. Here is an example:

"Forasmuch as it hath pleased Almighty God to take unto himself the soul of our brother here departed, we therefore commit his body to the ground—"

The words are murmured with a kindly awkwardness by the young unknown minister whose brother Christie Logan manifestly was not, although this is by no means the minister's fault. Perhaps he even wonders who Christie was, and perhaps, if Morag could bring herself to express the years, he might even like to know. But it is not possible, not now, not here.

Then the minister and the pallbearers (all unknown, persuaded by Hector to serve) depart. Only Morag and Hector Jonas remain, and one other.

Scotty Grant is not as old as Morag has imagined him. He is in fact a good-looking man in his early sixties, with the red-tanned neck and arms of someone who has spent most of his life as a farmer, battling the land which he has now sold, or, hopefully but not likely, turned over to his sons. He wears a blue open-necked workshirt and unpressed grey trousers. Just as well—kilts in this context would make it into a farce. Maybe it is going to be that, anyway. Would Christie have laughed?

"You sure you want me to do this?" Scotty asks, uncertainly.

Morag glares at him, angry because as yet unable to grieve. But she must not take it out on him.

"Yes, Mr. Grant—please."

He swings the pipes up, and there is the low mutter of the drones. Then he begins, pacing the hillside as he plays. And Morag sees, with the strength of conviction, that this is Christie's true burial.

*And Piper Gunn, he was a great tall man, with the voice of
drums and the heart of a child, and the gall of a thousand, and
the strength of conviction.*

The piper plays "The Flowers of the Forest," the long-
ago pibroch, the lament for the dead, over Christie Logan's
grave. And only now is Morag released into her mourning.[3]

When a story heightens your awareness, it puts you in touch
with feelings and thoughts that had not been connected before. Such
connections are real and important to the reader and should be wel-
comed and examined. An example occurred to me recently. I had
been counselling a young woman, Edith, who was in great conflict
between her desire to please her father, who disapproved of her
career choice, and her desire to please herself. I suppose she did not
want to lose her father, lose his affection and respect. Like most of
us, she had been brought up trying to please her parents. There
comes a time when we must end our childhood, and sometimes this
is very difficult. Edith read Constance Beresford-Howe's *The Book of
Eve*, where the heroine, in her sixties, walks out of her marriage and
chooses freedom and poverty. Edith had not thought of herself as
old, as ever being old, and when she put the loss of her father's
approval against the loss of her life choices, when she saw herself as
old and alone and not having done what she wanted, a great relief
swept over her at having done what she wanted to do for herself. Her
father would have to love her with her choices or not at all. Edith
found approval and support in the book, which on the face of it had
nothing to do with her present situation. By putting her dilemma in
a whole-life perspective, she could see the stages of her growth and
what was necessary to her outlook in the present.

Many people have had to make painful choices that involve
losses. Many have had to give up languages and leave the countries

where they grew up in order to seek safety or freedom in strange and often inhospitable lands. Canada and the U.S. are countries of immigrants. Many others have had to leave homes and marriages and jobs to save themselves, sometimes to save their lives, or their sanity. Morley Torgov's *The Abramsky Variations* is an excellent and easily readable tale of an immigrant's struggle to survive and of his son's and grandson's lives in his new country, Canada. This book is particularly useful for children of immigrants, who often fail to understand the hardships their grandparents endured. The once famous generation gap is particularly wide when children grow up in a culture different from that of their forebears. It helps to read about the trials and tribulations of one's parents so that some of that gap can be closed by an understanding, not of the facts but of the feelings, by the actual sense of what it was like that fiction provides through its dialogue, its description and its inner, mental reporting.

Some time ago, I was the guest on a Canadian Broadcasting Corporation radio phone-in show. We invited people to call and talk about books or poems that had made a difference to their lives, helped in some way at a particular time. There were three, among many calls, that had to do with losses and language. One woman called to tell us that after her father died she felt very bad that she had not said "I love you" to him. Then she came across this little poem she attributed to a Lawrence Craig Green:

People so seldom say
I love you, and then it's
either too late or love goes,
so when I tell you I love
you, it doesn't mean I know
you'll never go, only that
I wish you didn't have to.

This did a number of things for her, I believe. Since it fitted her mood and regret so aptly, it showed her that the need to express love verbally was well recognized and that she was not pining about nothing. It gave words to her that she could share with her family without talking directly to them about her own feelings, so that the poem could "stand in" for her. Because she could use the poem to change a behaviour, the experience of regret and frustration was not wasted; she could make efforts to teach her own children and could prevent the same regrets from being passed on to them. She phoned in to our program to share her joy and gratitude, I think, for the words that had been a timely help.

We also heard from a writer, Nella Benson, who wanted to share a fan letter from a reader in the U.S. The letter was an expression of gratitude from a prison inmate who had found great solace and food for thought in Benson's novel *Amaranth*. Benson explained that the book had been written as therapy to assist her in coming to terms with the death of her son. Now of course a death or serious loss of any kind always demands that we look back. People who survive always ask themselves if there was anything they might have done to prevent the disaster. They remember all the left-undone or unsaid things. They blame themselves. They blame the departed for not being more careful or whatever. They pore over good times and bad to try to arrange the story in a shape that makes sense. Though it seems a surprising parallel, a prisoner who has been sentenced to five years in jail for armed robbery might very well go through a similar process or review of the past. "I have lost my freedom," he might reason, "and my wife and family—at least for five years. I have lost my reputation, my job, my self-esteem. What led to this? Where did I go wrong? What was my life like before I did this crime? How can I reconstruct my life after this ordeal?" So the prisoner wrote to Benson to thank her for her novel. She told us that of many fan letters this one meant most to her—she had reached out with her novel to someone in pain and loneliness with a message that touched his heart. Such are the uses of fiction.

A third call was from a man in Detroit, Michigan, who felt that he must share an experience in reading that, even as he talked about it, seemed to bemuse and intrigue him. I could almost visualize him shaking his head in surprise. He told us that many years ago he had been really down on his luck. He had no job, work was hard to find, and he hinted at marital stress also. He read, during this very depressing time, a novel called *The Luck of Ginger Coffey* (it's by Brian Moore) about an immigrant from Ireland to Canada who has a very hard time getting along or surviving. Our phone caller suggested that this novel helped him to survive, showed him he was not alone, gave him hope that his lot would and could improve, as did Coffey's. By being amusing and ironic while at the same time describing the reader's situation and feelings, the novel was able to distance him a little from his sense of despair and help him to step out of it sufficiently to have hope. Undoubtedly, this altered thinking, which removed him slightly from being a helpless victim, empowered him to change his situation. You are more likely to lose if you feel like a loser, a victim, a target, or a bad boy or girl. As I say, this caller sounded bemused that a novel could have helped him through his dark time, though he insisted that it had. In fact I think that my presence on the radio program, encouraging people to read for their lives, gave him permission for the first time to admit openly, and even to believe, the important role a work of fiction had played in helping him through a difficult period of his life.

I want to mention two other guesses about this man and his phone call. I wish now I had asked him about both. I bet that he had not told this story about the novel to anyone before, and also that he realized the power of his reading experience only in hindsight. It takes time, in many cases, for reading to work its full magic, and time for us to put its effect into place in our history. This is partly why research in this area is very difficult. The full impact of reading is often slow because reading enters into changes in thinking and feeling over time. And more time must pass for the changed way of seeing things to produce results. In other words, experience takes time to happen, and only experience will show us the changes that interact with and result from an altered "I" acting on the world.

One more word on grief. When I was a graduate student, we studied this poem:

Bells for John Whiteside's Daughter

There was such speed in her little body,
And such lightness in her footfall,
It is no wonder that her brown study
Astonishes us all.

Her wars were bruited in our high window.
We looked among orchard trees and beyond,
Where she took arms against her shadow,
Or harried unto the pond

The lazy geese, like a snow cloud
Dripping their snow on the green grass,
Tricking and stopping, sleepy and proud,
Who cried in goose, Alas,

For the tireless heart within the little
Lady with rod that made them rise
From their noon apple-dreams, and scuttle
Goose-fashion under the skies!

But now go the bells, and we are ready;
In one house we are sternly stopped
To say we are vexed at her brown study,
Lying so primly propped.[4]

At the time, I did not understand it very well. It was explained to me
by a fellow student, a young man who had good reason to understand it. He had lost a three-year-old daughter to meningitis. I
remember his telling me, in answer to my question, that the only
theory around as to the origin of his daughter's disease was that she
might have eaten some snow that had infected her. My shocked con-
dolences were a form of sharing his grief, and I, who had no children, was able for a brief few minutes to draw close to my peer
through the agency of the poem. I don't know if my colleague would
ever have told me his personal story had it not been for our studying
together John Crowe Ransom's lyric. Now that I have had children of
my own, I wonder at the strength of a grieving parent to read such a
poem, let alone discuss it. And yet it is the stricken ones who have
the strength, who have already seen the worst and who have the
need to explore, feel, share and own their loss. Literature is enabling,
giving permission to speak and face the unspeakable, giving sound
and picture to the groan, the inarticulate cry and gasp of pain.

It seems obscene to speak of the uses of death, or to imagine
that one can ever be prepared for such terrible losses as I have just
described. Maybe we can be inoculated against panic at the dentist's
office, but surely not against the pain of losing a loved one, a piece
of ourselves, a child, a spouse, a limb. Those in grief do, must, I
think, for a time feel inconsolable. For those of us who have time to
think, prepare, order our view of the world, there are some useful
lessons to be learned from the grief of others. J. Z. Young, a famous
British brain surgeon, says of death in the book he wrote in retire-

ment: "Death is a part of the program of life. And this should not be considered an absurd, paradoxical, or pessimistic view. We are all familiar with programmed death for other organisms—from annual plants to mayflies. We know that it is appropriate for them to die at the right time."⁵

Death comes to everyone, sooner or later, whether our own or someone else's comes first. There is some point, I think, in confronting our worst fears, if not because it will lessen the pain and terror of actual grief, then because it relieves our present anxiety, increases our compassion for others, keeps us in touch with the cycle of seasons, with our membership in a mortal species, and deepens our pleasure and seriousness in our life and relationships while we have them. When my mother died, I discovered in the classroom that I could not read John Donne's magnificent devotion aloud, and simply stopped. Now I can see that this and other literature worked to prevent me from evading and discounting my pain. Literature enabled me to talk about the death of my mother with an older and beloved colleague, Geoff Durrant, a man who understood both the literature and my emptiness. I owe literature a lot. I never underestimate its power. I am no longer even surprised by its surprises. John Donne was in no doubt about the connection between story and life:

> All *mankinde* is of one *Author*, and is one *volume*; when one
> Man dies, one *Chapter* is not *torne* out of the *booke*, but
> *translated* into a better *language*; and every *Chapter* must be
> so *translated*; God emploies several translators; some peeces
> are translated by *age*, some by *sicknesse*, some by *warre*,
> some by *justice*; but Gods hand is in every *translation*; and
> his hand shall binde up all our scattered leaves againe,
> for that *Librarie* where every *booke* shall lie open to one
> another: As therefore the *Bell* that rings to a Sermon,

calls not upon the Preacher onely, but upon the
Congregation to come; so this Bell calls us all: but how
much more mee, who am brought so neere the *doore* by
this *sicknesse*.[6]

1   Emily Dickinson, "J. 341," in *The American Tradition in Literature*, Vol. 2, ed. Sculley Bradley, et al. (New York: Random House, 1981).

2   Henry James, "The Beast in the Jungle," in *Story*, ed. Boyd Litzinger and Joyce Carol Oates (Lexington: D.C. Heath, 1985).

3   Margaret Laurence, *The Diviners* (Toronto: McClelland and Stewart, 1974), pp. 328-29.

4   John Crowe Ransom, "Bells for John Whiteside's Daughter," in *The American Tradition in Literature*, Vol.2.

5   J. Z. Young, *Programs of the Brain* (Oxford: Oxford University Press, 1978), p. 28.

6   John Donne, "XVII. Meditation," in *The Complete Poetry and Selected Prose of John Donne*, ed. Charles M. Coffin (New York: Modern Library, 1952).

PART FIVE

Reading in Our Time

CHAPTER THIRTEEN

Pushups or Pushovers: It's All in Your Mind

We can give up on our minds and, by passively absorbing the simplest messages, hand ourselves over to someone else, or we can insist on getting more information and examining it critically. Has anybody noticed that the first thing you do to establish totalitarian government, after you have killed or imprisoned the opposition, is to control all reading materials, shut down all but government presses and screen all publications to ensure their conformity? And has anyone noticed that this control over words includes censorship of fiction and poetry? Why, you may ask, should this be necessary? Isn't fiction only make-believe? No one could possibly take it seriously, and as for poetry, well, who reads poetry on Wall Street? Don't be fooled: fiction changes minds.

Some people think that Harriet Beecher Stowe's *Uncle Tom's Cabin* started the American Civil War. Nobody denies that it was a significant factor in changing consciousness about slavery. Plato, in his dialogue on the ideal state, *The Republic*, calls for a ban on poetry. In Russia, Boris Pasternak's novel on the revolution, *Doctor Zhivago*, was banned for decades. In Britain, Lawrence's *Lady Chatterley's Lover* was banned for obscenity because it violated the code of silence around sexual matters (and incidentally attacked the aristocracy). In Victorian England, the novels of Charles Dickens, Mrs. Gaskell, Charles Kingsley, Charlotte M. Yonge and George Eliot were basic to changing the plight of women and improving working conditions. In fact, the novels of the prime minister, Benjamin Disraeli, were more influential than his legislation, in that they prepared minds for social change.

The first Public Education Act in England maintained that in a democracy where people are to vote, they must be able to read. But what if they can read only what the government decides they should read? Ah, but that can't happen here, we say; this is a democracy, governments don't censor free thought. On the other hand, they don't do much to guarantee free expression, either. Let's look at this problem more closely. In the so-called free market, what gets published is dependent on the judgement of publishers. Publishers include the people who own newspapers, the book publishers and the magazine people. The same problems apply to them all—they are in this business to make money. In the free market system, publishers want to sell lots of books. This means that, as big publishers gobble up little publishers, only those books of mass appeal are of interest to them. Offending books (that might represent important though different viewpoints) are shunned or dropped from lists, and other books are manufactured for the great middle mass of opinion. Although the press appears to be free, it is self-regulating according to market demands. Readers don't always get what they need; they get what they are given, and they are informed and educated by what they are given.

Mental activity is uncomfortable, especially if it is unusual. The simple idea is less effort than the complex. We all know from experience how hard we have had to think to understand and study some things. Those who deal with mass everything have no special interest in education, in enlightening and stretching the minds of a population. Theirs is not a public service goal, theirs is a profit goal. And a profit goal means not rocking the mental boat. The undisturbed mind continues to absorb the familiar. The familiar puts us to sleep. Being asleep, we can gradually lose our will, our freedom to be different, our creativity. While we are asleep, our environment can be freely destroyed, our fellow human beings abused without our caring much, our creativity, feeling, excitement for life itself drained away. We can easily be induced to drowse our lives away and all without a shot being fired. It would be a serious mistake to believe that our freedom depends on free elections and a government-controlled military and so-called freedom of the press. A population can be controlled by careful screening of the kind and quantity of information it receives. Literature is the primary source of complex information, because it combines masses of observed data, details of the observable world, with emotional language that makes the information believable and memorable. In fact, a dictatorship might very well permit a textbook called, say, *The Pros and Cons of Free Love* or of *Capitalism* or of *Communism*, a book of abstract discourse, complete with statistical tables, graphs, charts and foot-notes, but the same government would ban a novel that tells a gripping story, engages the emotions of the reader and paints an appealing picture of free love, capitalism, or communism. This has been the fate of many novels.

Many novels have been written about the dangers of control by a policy of information suppression and planned ignorance, about the tyrannies of religious simple-mindedness or unbridled technology and machine worship. In Orwell's *Nineteen Eighty-Four*, the total control of population is rooted in control of information: all media is government media; language is being redesigned to purge it of ambiguities and emotional overtones; and history is being replaced by new versions daily. Terror is merely the anesthetic to hold the patient still while the surgery takes place. *Individual identity is replaced by state identity.* Everyone believes the same things. Behaviour is managed by slogans—state jingles replace thought, wisdom and tradition. Individual thinking is forbidden. People are robotized and so made obedient and submissive. Allegiance is shifted from self, family and group to the state, in blind, unquestioning devotion. Once we start on the path to conformity, not thinking, not questioning, not discussing, not inquiring, not caring, not feeling, not hurting, not forming personal relationships, then I see no reason why we should not continue along that path to Orwell's state, to anti-Utopia, to death.

Populations can be controlled without torture and without terror, or at least without the kind of terror that involves police brutality and midnight disappearances. People can be drugged and put to sleep with pleasure. Aldous Huxley in *Brave New World* shows us a state of citizens robotized and sedated with pleasure, distracted from all pain and puzzlement and served by other worker clones made in laboratories. Here, sameness has become a planned way of life, and even biology has been programmed to eliminate diversity. This is a society in which literature has been eliminated, since it provokes thought and a range of feelings, and in which movies and other entertainments are designed to produce thoughtless and only pleasurable sensation. The same is true of sex, which has become one more mind-blanking pleasure, uncomplicated by reproduction, culture, relationship, or longterm goals of any kind. Huxley teaches us that pleasure can turn us into robots as efficiently as industry or the thought police. It does not make much difference, from a cosmic or species point of view, whether the population is an unthinking, unhappy, uncreative, uniform blob because of state terror or because of state stroking. The results are the same. Notice that in both states the literature has been removed.

So too has literature been removed in Ray Bradbury's version of a mindless society, *Fahrenheit 451*. In this vision of things to come, books are illegal and are removed and burned by the fire department. People failing to turn in libraries of their own are liable to the death penalty. What has replaced them is wall-to-wall soap opera TV, which takes over and replaces the independent lives of viewers and substitutes the program's own life instead. In one representative case, as I've mentioned, this leads to madness and suicide.

One of the most convincing versions of the end result of contemporary trends is Kurt Vonnegut's *Player Piano*. The title is a reference to a machine that eliminates the need for the pianist—an emblem of what happens to an America that makes labour redundant and leaves most people without work in a machine society. The result is an angry, despairing and useless population. People who invent clever gadgets and widgets make themselves obsolete.

All of these books are warnings. People who do not read and do not demand a wide range of material to read, especially fiction, give up access to essential information about their world, about their relation to it and to themselves, and about how others think and feel.

YOUR WORLD

Fiction is a primary source of information. Because we think of novels and stories as entertainment, a source of pleasure, we tend to forget how much we learn as we amuse ourselves. We accumulate pictures and facts about places we may never visit. Other places, houses, villages, towns, countries, customs, dress and furnishings become part of our awareness. We can leaf through a thousand *National Geographic* magazines and remember virtually nothing, because it is not processed by us as *story*. Writers give us the colour, the texture, the taste, smell and sound of places. Reading at our own pace we use language to organize and store these impressions into our existing construct of the world and so to expand that construct. Our reading can become an internalized reference system to larger worlds than our physical experience permits. By reading we overcome the limits of space and time-barriers to our learning. Stories are compressed information, packaged in such a way that we can store it easily.

Recently, in a bibliotherapy workshop, I ran an experiment that dramatically illustrated some of the differences between film and reading. The film I chose was a forty-minute National Film Board version of a short story by Alistair MacLeod, "In the Fall." It is an excellent film, beautifully acted and visually pleasing, very faithful to the story, its events and characters. Many viewers are deeply affected by it. The story tells of a poor Nova Scotia family and their pain at having to sacrifice an old horse that is a friend of the father's from the days when they worked in the mines together. The mother is a prime mover in forcing this decision on the family. She raises a few chickens for a little profit and food, and near the end of the story, after the horse is driven away in a truck to the slaughterhouse, the little boy expresses his outrage in a dramatic way, as recalled by the narrator, his older brother. First we saw the film; then I read this passage aloud:

> It is only then that I realize that David is no longer with me, but even as the question comes to the surface so also does its answer and I run toward the squawking of the chicken-house.
>
> Within the building it is difficult to see and difficult to breathe and difficult to believe that so small a boy could wreak such havoc in so short a time. The air is thick with myriad dust particles from the disturbed floor, and bits of straw and tiny white scarlet-flecked feathers eddy and dip and swirl. The frightened capons, many of them already bloodied and mangled, attempt short and ungainly flights, often colliding with each other in mid-air. Their overfed bodies are too heavy for their weak and unused wings and they are barely able to get off the floor and flounder for a few feet before thumping down to dusty crippled landings.

They are screaming with terror and their screams seem as unnatural as their flights, as if they had been terribly miscast in the most unsuitable of roles. Many of them are already lifeless and crumpled and dustied and bloodied on the floor, like sad, grey, wadded newspapers that had been used to wipe up blood. The sheen of their feathers forever gone.

In the midst of it all David moves like a small blood-spattered dervish swinging his axe in all directions and almost unknowingly, as if he were blindfolded. Dust has settled on the dampness of his face and the tears make tiny trails through its greyness, like lonely little rivers that have really nothing to water. A single tiny feather is plastered to his forehead and he is coughing and sobbing, both at the same time.

When my father appears beside me in the doorway he seems to notice for the first time that he is not alone. With a final exhausted heave he throws the axe at my father. . . . He has had very little strength with which to throw the axe and it clatters uselessly off the wall and comes to rest against my father's boot, wet and bloodied with feathers and bits of flesh still clinging to its blade.

I am tremendously sorry for the capons, now so ruined and so useless, and for my mother and for all the time and work she has put into them for all of us. But I do not know what to do and I know not what to say.[1]

The camera captured at a glance the blood-spattered boy in the hen-house, the face of the child, the shock of his brother and parents. The audience physically experienced a sense of shock, almost a nausea, and a degree of catharsis, a breaking of the tension that the movie had built up to—a relief and sadness that this violence released. This segment of the film took about a minute. The reading that followed revealed some interesting things. My audience was surprised that hearing the story piece could be so powerful and informative, when put beside a vivid filming of the same episode.

For one thing, reading slows the whole process down, makes it more manageable and digestible and less shocking. The language also seems to produce more detachment by making comparisons that we have to work out in our brains. Yet at the same time there is a greater intimacy in the reading. This part of the film is almost silent, except for the terrified squawk of the chickens (sacrificed for art—the birds could not have been artificial), but the story has a voice—the voice of the eldest son—and it is his own, unique voice that speaks to us personally, trustingly and generously, sharing his inmost thoughts and painful memories, touching not only our hearts, but because of the *language*, our understanding. The experience of the film hardly leaves us time or room to think—it shows us everything or at least all it can show. The language demands that we *think our way to feeling*, however fast our reading seems.

The reading did one more thing that I had never thought of before as special to the power of language. You know the way a camera can focus, zoom to close-up, scan the horizon. This is of course a crude copy of the function of the membranes of the human eye. Well, language can call upon all the resources of the body's own ability, while the film is limited by the camera. It would be dizzying, tiring, nauseating to watch for more than a few seconds on film what the reader can do by the hour. Language invites us to focus on a tiny microspeck, a face, a distant ship at sea, graffiti on a factory wall, a limping chicken, a thousand images and sensory impressions, millisecond by millisecond, hour by hour, without ill effect and as exercise to our minds. *Story can bypass the eye to produce visual effects.* This makes possible multiple visual feats without discomfort. No wonder devoted readers are certain that reading stories is the best entertainment the species has yet come up with. It is an extension of who we are as mentally active organisms. So we have learned two important things just now about reading:

1. Since language originates in sound, every written story has a voice we can hear as we read, and join with if we like the sound of it. If you read any story aloud and listen very carefully, you will hear below your own voice the voice of the writer coming through, borrowing your sound equipment.

2. Writing enlists the full physiological model of the reader, who is able to see, hear, taste, smell and touch, *as well as* move, while reading at rest. This is achieved because all these powers *originate in the brain* and reading language gives access to them directly as *mental representation.*

Imagine That!

The reading of fiction (and poetry) will give you more densely packed, easily remembered, pleasurably received information than any other activity. But it will do something else as well, something you need in order to be fully human, that is, in order to achieve your potential as a creative, in-control manager of your life. It will exercise and improve your imagination. This is how it works. The language you read as fiction specializes in calling into action your senses—you can see pictures and hear sounds. In order *to supply* the text with these pictures, sound effects, smells and so on, you must raid your memory store, since only you, from your own store, can supply *your* reading. You thus exercise your memory. Literature helps you to exercise your memory because your memory is keyed to feelings associated with memory and literature specializes in calling forth feelings. The best-remembered events, people and places have feelings strongly associated with them.

So now you are reading along, your memory humming away like a happy, well-powered databank supplying all the information you need to activate the language you are processing. Not quite! Since you are not reading, or reviewing, an exact replica of your own life (which would be interesting only for a limited time—you would be imprisoned in one story), you must adapt to new information, you will get only an approximate fit of your material to the writer's material. *The calling into play of what you already know to make sense of what you don't know is the power of imagination.*

Every time we put things together that don't normally go together (don't "normally," because we have not put them together before), we are using imagination. Once a pattern is familiar, then the hard work (and the pleasure and stimulation) is over and we can rely merely on memory. Imagination is the mental process involved in problem solving. Children are using it when they pile blocks up or figure out how to hold seven toys at once and open the door. Cleaning your teeth does not require imagination until you go on a wilderness canoe trip and discover you've forgotten your toothbrush. Without imagination we could not invent, prevent, or supply content. The best practice for the imagination is to read fiction and poetry. That is because you must use your imaginative power almost all of the time to make sense of what you are reading. If you read a lot, one of the many incalculable benefits is this mental exercise. It's work, but it's fun work and it's good for you.

Here is pan of a poem by Ralph Gustafson that illustrates very obviously the putting together of unlinked images that jerks our minds into activity:

Come, let us take the air
And stop the bus and pay the fare,

Drink sweetly of city streets
And dream of love on upper seats.

Summer has broken on this town
Has blossomed gold on concrete lawn

Broken gold in lovers' veins,
Smashed the million windowpanes.

And when the summer sun is set,
On the sidewalk we shall sit

In kitchen chairs and listen to
The radio that sings for you

And you, my love, shall watch with me
The uptown strip of galaxy.[2]

And here is a passage from Dickens' *Bleak House* that sets the scene
for the novel, which will convey a picture of a society in a moral fog.
Notice how reading this forces you to scan and zoom and focus visually, calling up scenes and details in your mind. Pay attention to the
mental mechanics of your reading, in this experiment.

Fog everywhere. Fog up the river, where it flows
among green aits [little islands] and meadows; fog down
the river, where it rolls defiled among the tiers of ship-
ping, and the waterside pollutions of a great (and dirty)
city. Fog on the Essex marshes, fog on the Kentish heights.
Fog creeping into the cabooses of collier-brigs; fog lying out
on the yards, and hovering in the rigging of great ships; fog

drooping on the gunwales of barges and small boats. Fog in the eyes and throats of ancient Greenwich pensioners, wheezing by the firesides of their wards; fog in the stem and bowl of the afternoon pipe of the wrathful skipper, down in his close cabin; fog cruelly pinching the toes and fingers of his shivering little prentice boy on deck. Chance people on the bridges peeping over the parapets into a nether sky of fog, with fog all around them, as if they were up in a balloon, and hanging in the misty clouds.[3]

LANGUAGE POWER

Metaphor is the language power of transformation, the turning of one thing magically into another by shifting brain imagery. So, for instance, in the Gustafson poem, "drink sweetly of city streets" uses the idea of drinking by mouth and transfers it to drinking in with the eyes and other senses. At the same time, to make this possible, the streets must become drinkable, from solid to a pleasant liquid the body can absorb. While this is literally impossible, we accept the idea as a way of describing experience that makes it seem like it is possible—in other words, we use language to make sense of body-mind experiences, felt experience. This felt experience actually does move the world around—solids feel like liquids and vice versa, eyes caress, disappointment tastes bitter and so on. The language that helps us to explain and place these experiences is called metaphoric language. Poets (and novelists) are people peculiarly gifted in making language work in this way. They examine their own experience minutely and find the language to rename their experience and render it into a transferable form. We may have had a similar experience, but until we recognize the language for it, we don't register it in conscious memory. *From reading we learn language.*

Metaphor does one other important thing. It collapses time. Language works in sequences. Syntax requires that words come in a certain order to make sense. Metaphor acts like a double exposure or a montage—it produces two images simultaneously so that each is seen in terms of the other. Here is an example. This is a stanza from a poem by Avi Boxer expressing loneliness for an absent lover:

I water empty flowerpots
bandage rosebush stumps
and sever rotting limbs
from the elm
sighing over my skylight.[4]

Metaphor blends two things and so makes two things happen at once; here, "sever rotting limbs" blends images of disease and amputation (forgetting) with images of horticulture. Clusters of images do even more; we feel the implied comparison of the dying elm and the sighing poet under the shaded skylight, for instance.

Language teaches us its many tricks, devices and miracles as we engage in the very act of reading and making sense of it. When we do so, we receive two important benefits:

1. We can use what we read to unravel the mystery of our own lives and feelings.

2. We acquire language power to use in our own communication.

By using metaphor and imagery in our own language, we gain a hearing, enliven our communication, bring life to language that becomes dead and worn out by familiarity. Fiction and poetry give us renewed language to assist us in expressing ourselves effectively. To be effective is to be heard, to be noticed, to make change. Abstract language does not call forth the reader's image-making power. We need metaphor to come alive.

1   Alistair MacLeod, "In the Fall," in *The Lost Salt Gift of Blood* (Toronto: McClelland & Stewart, 1987).

2   Ralph Gustafson, "City Song," in *Love Where the Nights Are Long*, sel. Irving Layton (Toronto: McClelland & Stewart, 1962).

3   Charles Dickens, *Bleak House* (London: Oxford University Press, 1948), p. 1.

4   Avi Boxer, "Letter in Late September," in *Love Where the Nights Are Long*.

CHAPTER FOURTEEN

Grow Old Along with Yourself

Dishonour not the aged, for you shall be one of them.

Nowadays, more of us are getting older—the elderly are forming an ever-larger percentage of the population. There are
two ways to approach aging. One is to ignore it, to pretend
we will never grow old, to put off thinking about it forever. In this
approach, literature has nothing to say. The other possibility is to prepare for old age by planning for it, talking about it and reading about
it. Anxiety about the loss of power over body and mind and about the
drawing closer to inevitable death—these fears can be greatly
reduced by the use of literature as a means of confronting reality.

People in our society live longer than they used to, and more
people do so with more resources. Pensions are now commonplace,
and most working people can look forward to many years of retirement with a lot of leisure time on their hands. On the other hand,
older people, the senior generation of their families, do not have an
honoured role, a respected place assigned to them by virtue of their
age. We do not sit at the feet of the elderly. We do not feel privileged
by their presence in our homes. We worship youth, athletics, physical power and energy, noise. Old people try to stay young in desperation. Mental activity, wisdom, experience and the knowledge that
comes with living through history rank low on the scale of what we
value. We worship the new and innovative, not the tried and true.

In such a climate, long life can be a blessing or a curse, depending on our awareness and our ability to accept the reality of our situa-

tions. My conclusion is that the young, those who have not yet reached sixty or thereabouts, would do well to read about aging. The young elderly, those sixty to seventy-five, and the advanced elderly, those over seventy-five, would be better off reading about what interests and amuses them, which may or may not be other elderly people.

Reading for old age can be a very useful form of preparation. Just as children must prepare for adolescence, and youth for leaving home and marrying, and young marrieds for career and parenting, so we all need to come to terms with our individual aging processes. Aging has a bad name for many reasons, all of them cultural. In the cosmetic Disney world of fantasy-youth-instant pleasure worship, age is an intruder. The elderly may rock, but they don't rock and roll. Old people have either made it or they haven't, economically, sexually, socially, and if they haven't, they're not going to. Youth is all promise, all panting possibility. Commercial North America loves massaging possibility, dangling golden carrots, teasing with promise, dragging rouged herrings stuffed with dreams across the path of life. Isn't this the culture that invented "petting," the great adolescent trade-off for the great fulfillment to come? We can flirt with the future, wear makeup and tight jeans, and work to pay off our Corvettes and condos while we dream of power, playmates and beaches. The elderly have no part in that world, except perhaps regret at its passing or at its having deceived them. King Lear's fool says he wishes the king had grown wise before he grew old. Is there anything sadder than seeing the elderly desperately pretending to be youthful, trying to lie about their ages, having surgery, dyeing hair and coating faces in cosmetic masks in order to deny the reality of their own season? My favourite poem about aging is Shakespeare's timeless sonnet, which accepts age with dignity, sadness, and gratitude for love, a love that is not withheld or withdrawn in the face of death:

That time of year thou mayst in me behold
When yellow leaves, or none, or few, do hang
Upon those boughs which shake against the cold,
Bare ruin'd choirs, where late the sweet birds sang.
In me thou see'st the twilight of such day
As after sunset fadeth in the west;
Which by and by black night doth take away,
Death's second self, that seals up all in rest.
In me thou see'st the glowing of such fire,
That on the ashes of his youth doth lie,
As the death-bed whereon it must expire,
Consum'd with that which it was nourish'd by.
    This thou perceiv'st, which makes thy love more strong,
    To love that well which thou must leave ere long.[1]

There is a quiet courage and beauty about this view that I honour. The poet writes a love poem that respects both himself and his beloved. There is a great comfort in reading the life stages, all of them, as part of the rhythm of life, in seeing one's aging as connected to the earth's cycles of birth, death and renewal. For the elderly, the spring still comes, the leaves still green and the birds still sing every year. Not until all sight, sound, smell and texture have gone, until pain is too great to bear or joy can be taken in nothing, are we ready to say that the time is right for dying. In our culture we too often write off the elderly prematurely and fail to celebrate their experience, to share our joys with them and to make a place for their beauty, for the grandeur of greyness and wrinkles, for the calm of slowness. Wordsworth puts it like this, in his ode to immortality:

What though the radiance which was once so bright
Be now forever taken from my sight,

Though nothing can bring back the hour
Of splendor in the grass, of glory in the flower
    We will grieve not, rather find
    Strength in what remains behind;
    In the primal sympathy
    Which having been must ever be;
    In the soothing thoughts that spring
    Out of human suffering;
    In the faith that looks through death,
In years that bring the philosophic mind.[2]

I take the destruction of land, the pollution of water and air, the loss of wildlife, personally. I am the loser. My life is impoverished and blighted by such monstrous and wanton waste. Our native North American relatives are right to teach us that relentless killing of trees, poisoning of birds and fishes, raping of land is a blight of our own persons. All of this comes from alienation, a failure to see our connections to all life forms. Our rejection and embarrassment at aging is part and parcel of our contempt for ourselves, for everything but money and power, the gods of Western society.

Preparing for aging is, then, an opportunity for assessing what matters, what we value, what we wish to have done. There are many life tasks to accomplish in this process, and literature can help us greatly to gain perspective, make plans and find a place in the order of life. Literature can help us to take control of our destiny and be active in our thinking and feeling. One of the gratifying results of sharing literature of aging with students whose ages range from nineteen to sixty-five is seeing their surprise, pleasure and enlightenment as they gain insight from reading into how the elderly feel and think about themselves. First they see how others feel, and then they see how they feel about their own aging, what they want to have happen and what they need to do. For instance, here is a poem we share that surprises readers with its revelation about the inner person; it is a voice that is not often heard and that cries out for respect for what we cannot always see and therefore too often ignore:

A crabbit old woman wrote this

What do you see, nurses, what do you see?
   Are you thinking, when you look at me—
A crabbit old woman, not very wise,
   Uncertain of habit, with far-away eyes,
Who dribbles her food and makes no reply
   When you say in a loud voice—"I do wish you'd try."
Who seems not to notice the things that you do
   And forever is losing a stocking or shoe,
Who unresisting or not, lets you do as you will
   With bathing and feeding, the long day to fill.
Is that what you're thinking, is that what you see?
   Then open your eyes, nurse, you're not looking at me.
I'll tell you who I am as I sit here so still;
   As I rise at your bidding, as I eat at your will.

I'm a small child of ten with a father and mother,
   Brothers and sisters, who love one another,
A young girl of sixteen with wings on her feet,
   Dreaming that soon now a lover she'll meet;
A bride soon at twenty—my heart gives a leap,
   Remembering the vows that I promised to keep;
At twenty-five now I have young of my own
   Who need me to build a secure happy home;
A woman of thirty, my young ones grow fast,
   Bound to each other with ties that should last;

At forty, my young sons have grown and are gone,
> But my man's beside me to see I don't mourn;

At fifty once more babies play round my knee,
> Again we know children, my loved one and me.

Dark days are upon me, my husband is dead,
> I look at the future, I shudder with dread,

For my young are all rearing young of their own,
> And I think of the years and the love that I've known.

I'm an old woman now and nature is cruel—
> 'Tis her jest to make old age look like a fool.

The body is crumbled, grace and vigor depart,
> There is now a stone where I once had a heart.

But inside this old carcass a young girl still dwells,
> And now and again my battered heart swells.

I remember the joys, I remember the pain
> And I'm loving and living life over again,

I think of the years all too few—gone too fast.
> And accept the stark fact that nothing can last—

So open your eyes, nurses, open and see
> Not a crabbit old woman, look closer—see ME.[3]

Many readers of this poem are shocked at what it says about care-givers. It tells us that stereotyping is commonplace and that exter-nals and appearances are taken as all there is. Those who do not protest are assumed to have no thoughts or feelings. Those who do protest are "crabbit," trouble-makers, difficult patients. We have heard of racism, sexism, and anti-Semitism; now we have ageism, a lumping of all the elderly together as burdensome, grumpy, senile, useless and smelly. Literature is essential for giving a voice to those who are not articulate or powerful, who have no medium for expressing their needs. There is no Ministry of Aging, no political party of the elderly. Who will speak the unheard thoughts and feelings of the quiet ones? Stories give us what we need to hear.

People often say to me, I wish I had read this, or had known of this, earlier, when my mother (or father or grandparent) was alive, so that I could have read it to her or with her, or so that I could have known what I wanted to ask or say. Recently I had my own similar experience. There is a wonderfully tender and strong story by Tillie Olsen called "Tell Me a Riddle," now the basis for an excellent film of the same title. I read the story and was deeply affected by it. Thinking and talking about its effect on me some time later I was struck by memories of my own grandparents and by how little I knew of them. I remember my mother's mother as someone very stern, silent and domineering, like a frightening queen on a throne in her dingy basement apartment, the mother of ten or eleven children, one of them my mother. She came from Russia, and I thought of her after reading Olsen's short story. I thought of the immense courage our immigrant ancestors must have had to overcome terrible obstacles in running from oppression and slavery to raise their children, you, maybe, and me, in relative freedom and security. I thought of the memories, surely many of them terrifying, that my grandmother must have had stored to disturb her nights and cause her constant fear and anxiety for her children, memories many of which she must have passed on to them, and I grieved for the loss of those stories, my family inheritance. I mourned for my unknown, unheard grandparents and honoured them in my heart for the lives of their children and my children. Because of "Tell Me a Riddle" and its tale of an elderly refugee couple nearing the end of their days, I have rethought my family's origins and what they mean to me. I have learned greater respect for and sensitivity to all refugees from oppression and starvation, and I have learned that family stories must be shared and passed on, in words, photographs and songs. We take our strengths as well as our weaknesses from the past.

Elder abuse is becoming an openly discussed social issue. It is powerfully presented in many stories, two of which I use often. One is May Sarton's powerful little novel, *As We Are Now*. It tells the story of a woman, a retired teacher, placed prematurely in a private nursing home for the convenience of her surviving family. The place is run by a resentful and insensitive family as a means of making money. They seem to me untrained and uneducated, and they have almost certainly not read books like the one they exist in. The inmates of this place are virtual prisoners, and any rebellion is quelled by medication, often administered without the patient's knowledge. There are plenty of lessons here to warn us about what to avoid, but there are also many questions forced into the reader's mind about how to cope and survive in such a setting. In spite of my description, the novel is not depressing to read because the story is of a dramatic and dynamic struggle between the heroine and her jailors, a story of courage and hope.

The other story is a short one called "Dancing Bear" by Guy Vanderhaeghe. It shows us an old man attended in his own home by a sadistic woman hired by the man's son. A telling comparison is made between the old man's helpless situation and that of an old dancing bear he recalls from his childhood, a bear which the man, when a child, saw tormented and abused by its human master. The great beast is reduced to pathetic suffering, cringing and beaten, a ring through its nose. I can't help but think there is a connection between our toleration of such treatment for animals and the episodes of sadism in our treatment of the human beings placed in our care.

These stories have two benefits for readers. One is that they sensitize us to the needs of others, increase our own level of awareness as to how we treat and care for others. We don't want to be like the so-called caregivers in the stories. They are more like prison wardens or torturers, hardened of heart, deaf to the pleas and blind to the looks of those who suffer humiliation and indignity at their hands. Sensitizing is necessary to the future of caregiving; it will enable those who will run institutions, or who will make a living managing the elderly, to empathize with their dependants.

The other benefit of such reading is that it encourages us to recognize that we might some day be in a position to receive treatment of this kind ourselves. What, the reader asks, will happen to me? Will I end up in an ugly, uncaring institution, eating awful, scant food, without privacy, without respect, deprived of appropriate recreation, conversation and stimulation? Such questioning, I have found, leads readers to think carefully about what plans they wish to make for themselves, even to make some plans, contracts with family, savings and money arrangements, to protect them against spending their declining years in a hostile, unpleasant setting. This is a form of inoculation against future suffering. It is also a way of liberating the reader from present anxiety about the future, anxiety that may have been latent and unrecognized until the reading and the thought or discussion attendant upon the reading. This abreaction, reaction against elements of the story, is very helpful in clarifying what matters to us, what we do want and care about.

I have been writing about reading in preparation for old age; I want to turn now to reading in old age. The issues of concern to the elderly go far beyond those of power, economics, housing and care. Just as there are special needs and tasks for each stage of human growth and development, so there are tasks appropriate to being old, needs that must be understood and respected in a humane and civilized society. These needs and tasks are carefully revealed in deeply affecting ways in a variety of literature.

What will it be like, to be old? The recognition that people are individuals is the antidote to stereotyping. Some people are aged before they are old; others are sprightly and active at ninety. I heard of one grandfather of a student, married for the third time, driving his own car and still working his own farm at ninety-one. Jackrabbit Johannsen was still skiing through the woods at a fair old clip when he turned ninety-six. For most of us, however, it is likely that age will slow us down. We will lose some vigour and we will suffer some sensory deficits. Except in a few sad cases, we won't lose our long-term memory, and we will experience the need to sort out some story of our life. Truths and secrets long suppressed will seek the light of day in our consciousness with ever more urgency. This is called the life review process. There are many good models of this in literature. The best, I believe, is *All Passion Spent*, a beautifully sensitive portrait of a woman in her nineties by Vita Sackville-West. The wife of a former prime minister, the heroine of this novel is released by his death from a long lifetime of service, keeping up appearances, and social obligations. Finally, in her last year, she does what *she* wants, and much of this time is devoted to seclusion, peaceful reminiscing, and assessing her own history. She wants to examine how her life happened, what it meant, how much was her own will, what she missed and what she achieved. And for the first time in her life she chooses her own friends.

It is curious, but no accident, that all my illustrations are about women by women authors. Women have for so long seen themselves as attached to men, as handing over their selves to men—what they do, where they live, who their friends are, what they think—that it is not surprising in our more liberated time to find women writing about freedom, even though this freedom can come only in old age. Margaret Laurence's *The Stone Angel* tells us the story of a warm, proud, strong old woman reviewing her life and showing the reader in the process the anguish of having been too proud to reveal true feelings, the cost of holding on to grievances and hurts. Life is not over until it is over, of course, so this book is important, for if family matters have not been put right, by confessing or confronting; if hurts, needs and desires remain unexpressed, then the frustration and pain do not go away. For the sake of the living as well as the dying, peace and honesty are required. The courage of the elderly is in setting matters right. "Irina" by Mavis Gallant is likewise a story of an old woman freed by widowhood who takes to pleasing herself. There is a wonderful calm and control about this story that suggests the peace that comes with being in harmony with oneself.

The Book of Eve by Constance Beresford-Howe shows us a woman leaving husband and home at sixty-five to be alone, facing the challenges of coping for and by herself. I have recommended this book to many people, mostly women, and it almost always helps them to see the pleasures and possibilities of independence. One client, Maria, had left a marriage of twenty years, a comfortable home and social respectability and had gone with one of two teenage children to live in a small apartment and start life over as a single woman again. Her decision was made out of desperation. It is possible to be lonelier in a dead marriage than by oneself. But to know that one is dying inside, to be quietly going mad like the woman in Sue Kaufman's Diary of a Mad Housewife or Penelope Mortimer's The Pumpkin Eater or Linda Lauren's Honesty, is not so easy to explain to spouse, friends and relatives. Maria was tormented by guilt, by the sense that it was not right to do what she wanted, to run away and be free. Her background celebrated selflessness and duty, social service and sacrifice. Literature, especially The Book of Eve, helped her to feel justified, understood and empathized with by another woman. The knowledge that the world accepted the book as one person's story, a plausible story, made her story possible.

Gradually she grew stronger and accepted her own decision as right for her, after she had taken it without fully understanding what had driven her to it. Reading was part of her personal growing process. She was able, with the help of this story, to read her past with clearer understanding.

Aging makes heavy demands that I can only describe as spiritual. What I mean by this is that the knowledge of the reality of death and final reckonings and last stages challenges much of the teaching that has guided and determined life decisions and events in our younger days. When we can believe that a long life stretches before us, we can put off, discount, or rationalize matters of the heart or soul. We can avoid major questions of our own being and identify them as not urgent. We can drift along on the current of values and goals learned from parents, church and school. For many, old age is the most challenging time. Not only do retirement and leisure take away the distraction of work and the sense of being usefully busy, but age itself is cause for reassessment. We want to leave things tidy, we want to be renowned and remembered as we truly are, so we are faced with looking at who that is. We must seek and find some wisdom before we can leave it to our children, and that wisdom requires self-knowledge. Reading shows us the record of what others have seen and thought about self, life, values and relations—matters too weighty for the busyness of the middle years. In my experience no piece of writing is more useful in preparing for aging, as many students have told me, than Cicero's ancient essay on that subject. Pretending to explain to younger men, Cicero writes lucidly about the fears of being old and the compensations for being old. He tells us that all of life is of a piece, that we are preparing for aging and death all our lives, if we will but know it. I have been told by many that their attitudes to the elderly and to their own aging have been permanently changed by Cicero. Here is an example:

When I reflect on the subject, I find that the reasons why old age is regarded as unhappy are four: one, it withdraws us from active employments; another, it impairs physical vigor; the third, it deprives us of nearly all sensual pleasures; and four, it is the verge of death. Let us see, if you please, how much force and justice there is in these several reasons....

"Old age withdraws us from active employments." You mean, do you not, those that involve youth and vigor? Are there no old men's employments which are carried on by the intellect even when the body is feeble?...There is nothing, then, in the argument that old age is devoid of useful activity. To say that is like saying that a steersman sitting quietly in the stern and holding the tiller contributes nothing to sailing the ship, for others climb the masts, run up and down the gangways, man the pumps. He may not be doing what younger men do, but what he does is better and more important. Large affairs are not performed by muscle, speed, nimbleness, but by reflection, character, judgment. In age these qualities are not diminished but augmented.[4]

Perhaps all of this, what I have been saying, is more neatly expressed in more graspable form by Charles Dickens than by anyone else. *A Christmas Carol* is not usually thought of as a story on aging, but look at what it can tell us. Old Scrooge has been a model of business. He has made himself rich, devoted himself to profit and greed. Scrooge goes through a life review, looks at his present condition, sees ahead to his death and decides to rewrite his life story, changing its inevitable conclusion. It is not too late for Scrooge to look into his own heart, his losses and his world. We, too, can look at every

Christmas past, at the quality of our present life, and in the face of death do what we must to be true to the gift of life. Scrooge also shows us that the power of future-thinking is powerful indeed. Scrooge is forced to see three stories, but not until he looks into a possible future can he change his mind. In old age he will need people, love, honesty. He does not want to be remembered with contempt and hatred. He is forced to review his life and think about his death in order to affect the quality of his present life. Scrooge is reborn as after a bad dream, to find that he has the power to change his life, that it is not too late.

1   William Shakespeare, "Sonnet LXXIII," in *The Complete Works of William Shakespeare*, ed. W. J. Craig (London: Oxford University Press, 1919).

2   William Wordsworth, "Ode: Intimations of Immortality," in *The Norton Anthology Of English Literature*, Third Edition, Vol.2, ed. M. H. Abrams, et al. (New York: Norton, 1974).

3   Dr. Benjamin Schlesinger, University of Toronto Professor of Social Work, came across this anonymous poem while teaching at a summer institute in St. Francis Xavier University, Antigonish, Nova Scotia. Reprinted from the Vancouver Family Institute's "Transition" (Summer, 1981).

4   Cicero, "On Old Age," in *The Basic Works of Cicero*, ed. Moses Hadas (New York: Modern Library, 1951).

CHAPTER FIFTEEN

Not Funny at the Time!

I have been writing about what happens to most people who manage to get born: growing up, getting married, growing old and dying. For many of us, even most perhaps, there are less predictable events and situations that occur and form crises we are challenged to overcome. Can literature help?

READING FOR WELLNESS

Here is part of a letter sent to me by a fellow student from my therapy training years:

> Ten years ago my daughter was in Toronto's Hospital for Sick Children for five weeks with cancer. She was eight. We were told she might only live two months, or that she might get better. She underwent a battery of tests, a biopsy, and finally, painful, sickening chemotherapy. I felt like I was living in hell. And yet I coped.
>
> In retrospect I have some insight into the mechanism that made that possible. Everything is relative. A particular experience is perceived very differently depending with what you compare it. If I had compared my experience to that of my neighbours and friends, it might have been unbearable. If I compared it instead to that of a family from South America, who was coping with what we were, plus the problems of being so far away from home, our problems became bearable.

There were many opportunities at Sick Kids to make comparisons with situations that looked worse than what we were facing. At least our daughter had a chance, slim though it was. Others faced certain death. If our daughter got better, her life would be normal. Others faced a lifetime of painful struggle with a problem that would never go away. With comparisons like these, I could even feel lucky that the situation was not worse.

This method of coping was carried through to my reading material. I did not consciously choose books for this purpose. It was only years later that I realized how the reading I had been drawn to during that terrible time had been an extension of the method of coping I had found in the hospital environment. People thought my choices of *Roots* and *Armageddon* were strange, even depressing. They would have chosen for me something more upbeat to cheer me up, but by reading about people who I thought were suffering more than I was, I found it possible to cope with the horror in my own life.

I do not know how I knew those books were what I needed. Somehow, though, I found them.

The remarkable thing about reading in such situations is not only that people manage to find what they need, though they do seem to have an uncanny knack for doing that, but even more *that they find what they need in what they read*. What strikes one reader as significant or memorable in a story may be quite different from what another reader takes from the same book. The key factor is the state of mind, the mood or need, that is brought to the reading. One of the books that stands out in my memory from adolescence must have served a similar function to that described in my fellow student's letter. I was a chronic asthmatic as a child and spent many a school day at home in bed struggling to breathe and reading. My asthma improved but was to stay with me in some form all my life. The book I happened upon was *The Plague and I* by Betty MacDonald, who had written a more famous book called *The Egg and I*, a funny story about chicken farming that I think was made into a film. The plague was tuberculosis, and the book, along with the disease, has faded from most memories, but not from mine. I devoured it and can still remember some scenes vividly. For one thing, it was about a respiratory disease, and I had one of those. For another, she was much worse off than I, and underwent gruesome procedures that horrified me and made me grateful I only had asthma. For another, she got better, so I learned people could recover from disease, and that gave me hope. Most of all, I remember that her sanitarium was somewhere in the mountains, Switzerland I think, and I revelled in her convalescence, breathed with her the cool, dry, clean air as she sat on the balcony in the sun, while I lay wheezing in foggy, damp London.

About a year ago, a colleague of mine gave me *As We Are Now* by May Sarton. As I've mentioned, it presents a portrait of an old woman in a grim nursing home. Now my friend Isobel is not old and is vigorously pursuing her career, but the book she gave me had been given to her when she was in hospital with a back injury that rendered her helpless, totally dependent on others and feeling dispirited and frightened of her unaccustomed weakness. She recalled looking at her breakfast tray, unreachable at the end of the bed where some unthinking nurse had left it, and watching her egg and sausage congeal into inedibility, while frustration brought tears to her eyes. Reading May Sarton's little book did two things for Isobel. First, it awakened her understanding of the suffering of others who are helpless, through sickness or age, and it moved her deeply, since she was vulnerable to its portrait, temporarily placed in circumstances very similar to those of the central character of the novel. Instead of being a disgruntled and sad visitor to a strange world of suffering, she became, through her reading part of it, fully sensitive to what it meant. She was reading about her own condition, and so was able to gain some larger and compassionate perspective on it, a compassion that would include herself and help her understand the frustration of such a situation. Second, she was able to feel, at the same time, an immense relief and gratitude that she could get better and leave the hospital and take care of herself again.

For this particular reader, it was a profound and surprising reading experience, one that fundamentally altered her perspective on some things, and knowing of my interest in the reading process, she passed on a copy of the book to me because she wanted to share her experience. She has also given me permission to share it with you. I think there are millions of readers who have had deeply significant experiences from reading, but who somehow cannot share them or explain them. There is sometimes a shyness or embarrassment at the idea that "merely" reading has produced such powerful responses and insights. Not so for Sandra Martin, who claimed in a column for *Empress* magazine that her providing reading for a friend in post-surgery helped the friend get well quickly:

> Since there was little I could do to ease her physical situation, I thought I'd relieve some of the frustrations and ennui of her month-long convalescence. So instead of sending a cauldron of chicken soup or having her three kids for a sleepover, I arrived on her doorstep with a package of comfort books.

The author goes on to explain that "comfort books" are not classics, but books that are immensely readable and relevant, that "belong to specific eras and places." The three books she chose for her friend—Bernice Rubens' *A Five Year Sentence*, William Trevor's *Fools of Fortune* and Jane Gardam's *Crusoe's Daughter*—have in common lively and believable characters and relationships that one can recognize as possible and near enough to one's ordinary concerns to be engaging. Oddly enough, these three books all reveal a kind of life-affirming struggle and hopefulness. Martin concludes her column with an unreserved claim for the healing power of reading: "Only yesterday, scarcely two weeks out of hospital, she walked from her house to mine to return them and to offer me in exchange A. N. Wilson's appropriately titled book *The Healing Art*....Her doctor is amazed at her recovery. I'm not, and neither is she."[1]

As a matter of fact, *The Healing Art* is a fascinating story of two cancer patients and their comparative fortunes. It contains a savage swipe at the British medical system, which suffers from chronic government underfunding, and portrays the courage of two women who undergo surgery for breast cancer. I think this is a good novel for those who fear and have experience of cancer, especially the kind described therein. We always wonder what we would do in such situations, how we would respond, plan and cope. These women do cope and do reassess their lives and values as a result of very frightening experiences. We learn from the cases of others. Just recently I read Bobbie Ann Mason's novel, *Spence & Lila*, which centres on a family coping with the mother's mastectomy. It is a tour de force of ordinary life and I recommend it. These books ought to be part of the program of every group formed to help women and their families cope with cancer and post-surgical trauma.

Reading for sickness requires certain commonsense rules. For one thing, books to be held in bed should be small enough to manage comfortably and easy to read, so that we do not add to existing frustrations. The subject matter depends of course on the reader and the situation, yet there is no need to be hypersensitive or nervous about choosing books. In all the cases I have cited, one criterion of book selection was that the giver had read the book, had enjoyed it and wanted to share it. As I said before, the reader takes what she needs, and rejects what is too uncomfortable anyway. Sometimes, facing difficult aspects of our own situation is part of the healing process. Suppose that anger, fear, anxiety, frustration and so on can contribute to the sickness and interfere with wellness. I think it very likely that, in addition to the helpful cognitive value of reading—that is, using imagination and so mentally escaping the boredom and discomfort of sickness, and being able to see new ways of understanding one's situation—there are direct biochemical results also. Pleasure, interest and excitement are powerful emotions requiring the release of neurochemicals that affect mood and attitude. We change ways of feeling by realizing other feelings. Healing may occur by an alteration in feeling processes as well as thinking processes. Laughter, sadness, empathy and excitement have significant effects on body function and condition and may successfully interfere with stressors that are contributing to negative and self-destructive emotions. Depressed people, for instance, tend to be inactive, and inactivity is bad for bodies. Not only can anxiety be produced by stress, but feelings of helplessness and suppressed emotion lead to a variety of harmful behaviours, including smoking, drinking and eating disorders. Reading has an important role to play in breaking up and changing patterns of viewing the world and the reader's place in it.

WARS WE DIDN'T DECLARE

Not only criminals go to prison. Good people, courageous people fighting cruelty and oppression and injustice, can easily find themselves the target of the authorities they oppose. Could it happen to us? Of course it could. We have enough history to show us some horrible surprises and changes in social affairs. People who have lived through wars, revolutions and military coups did not always know what was coming. The less surprised we are in such situations, the better. The better informed we are, the more likely we are to prevent social horror. The more we say it can't happen here, the likelier it is to happen. Sleeping dogs don't protect. If we find ourselves in prison, or being tortured, how will we survive?

Jacobo Timerman was an editor of a newspaper in Argentina. I have already quoted from his gripping autobiographical story, *Prisoner Without a Name, Cell Without a Number*. The military dictatorship did not like his opposition and pro-democratic stand, so they jailed him and began a program of systematic torture to get him to confess to being the tool of conspirators who were dangerous to the state. Timerman's advice to readers on how to survive torture shocked me. To be confronted by the cold-blooded challenge that I, the protected, secure reader, might one day unpredictably find myself in jail being tortured gave me a lot to think about. So I tried to practice in my mind how it would feel to follow Timerman's counsel. The trouble is that one never knows, of course, one's own strengths and weaknesses, but I know this story will always come to mind as a point of reference. Also, Timerman's story, and many others, strengthens my resolve to be very attentive to losses of freedom, to control by any power alliance, government or private. I think I feel after reading his book a tiny bit less helpless and anxious about surviving horrors like his, not only because I have some immunization through my reading, but because this courageous man of deep convictions and humanity had the will to survive. I would feel less alone and less unique. His book models the survival of the humble hero.

There are many stories of simple and amazing courage, as well as ingenuity, in defeating the forces of power and evil. Len Deighton's *The Ipcress File*, for example, shows us a man who resists relentless torture and brainwashing by putting himself secretly through so much pain from a festering sore he creates in his hand that he produces an interfering pain distracting enough to block the hypnotic program of mind altering. Orwell's *Nineteen Eighty-Four* is another example of warning and bravery. The dangers of complete totalitarianism are graphically outlined in this picture of the world dominated by totally controlling police states that demand body and soul submission. The value of such books is that they give us images and language with which to protect ourselves. I grew up—after 1948—with "Big Brother is watching you," and I have no doubt that my paranoid sensitivity to authoritarian control has much to do with my identification with Orwell's story of oppression. I remember hours of discussion with my sixteen-year-old friends as to how we would defeat the hideous powers of O'Brien and what devices might help us to evade the total invasion of our privacy, an issue very much on the minds of adolescents. We were also forced to confront our own deepest phobias by the model of Room 101, the torture chamber where you must face your worst fear—in Winston's case, rats, confined to a cage into which his head is inserted. I have no doubt that this was therapeutic for my friends and me, as we discussed what horror awaited each of us in our own Room 101. Another book that shows the courage needed to survive in war is Laurens Van Der Post's *The Seed and the Sower*. It tells the story of prisoners of war in Japan and how humanity can prevail over hardship and ideology. One woman I know who read this novel told me it had the effect on her of individualizing males and showing her a kindness and tenderness in men that she had not believed in before.

A novel that conveys some of the same spirit of survival and compassion under conditions of great hardship and suffering is Nevil Shute's *A Town like Alice*, and here it is women who are shown as war victims, as they are also in Alberto Moravia's *Two Women*. *The Diary of*

Anne Frank is perhaps one of the most powerful stories to grow out of war. It manages to convey the incredible strength of the human impulse for normal growth, love and development under conditions of unimaginable fear, deprivation and anxiety. I named one of my daughters Anna after Anne Frank. When she read the book as a teenager, she was deeply affected by it. I think it showed her, as she empathized with, identified with and grieved for the young diarist, that her own confusion and troubles in growing up were universal, and that if Anne could try to sort out her feelings and love her family in such circumstances, then she herself could certainly do so. This book has had similar responses from countless readers, who find support in and draw courage from the story of Anne, who died in a Nazi death camp without ever having given up her faith in humanity. For me *The Diary of Anne Frank* is a very important book for a quite different reason. Since I am the father of daughters myself, reading it, absorbing the charm of its young female adolescence, rouses in me more intense anger than anything I have ever read. This story focuses all my speechless outrage that ordinary, decent people should be, have been, subjected to such suffering, humiliation and death because of their being Jewish. The realization that under Nazi rule the mere fact of being born into the world of Jewish parents was a guarantee of pain and death is most poignantly conveyed by the very normalcy of Anne Frank's feelings and their contrast with her situation.

Of course there are many shocking accounts and stories of the Holocaust and the camps. A short story that is highly effective, and that breaks through the detachment from history of many of my students, is Cynthia Ozick's "The Shawl." For many readers, this story shatters their intellectual and rational reserve, shakes their self-protective idea that the hideous experiences of others can be generalized into statistics. Pain can dehumanize us. Effective fiction causes us to experience empathy and shock at the pain of individuals, for fiction always gets at the universal through the particular. William Styron's *Sophie's Choice* is a remarkable story about the struggle to survive extreme pain and trauma. I always think of a dear friend of mine in connection with this book. She was Polish and a Holocaust survivor who had lost all her family in death camps. She talked little of her ordeals and was a kind, helpful friend to me in graduate school. She married my roommate. I will never forget hearing of her suicide many years later in New York, where she and I had once visited the Frick Collection together and strolled along Fifth Avenue. She died before *Sophie's Choice* was published. I wish we had been able to talk about such things together, thirty years ago, when I did not know, graduate student in English though I was, the power of fiction to open up the scarred and festering wounds of the heart for healing examination. The more we know of human experience of war, of how hurt our fellow human beings can be, the more we understand, the better able we are to join with them in compassion, love and support. And the more we can say "no" to oppression, tyranny and cruelty.

The Ivory Leg is the Hook

In Herman Melville's *Moby Dick*, Captain Ahab devotes his life to revenge. He thinks of nothing but "white whale," and even has an artificial leg made of whalebone, just in case he should forget for a moment the connection between his loss and its cause. On his travels he meets up with another victim of the whale, Captain Boomer, who has likewise lost a limb, in his case an arm, to the same white whale. Boomer's response to his affliction is quite different. For one thing, he wants to avoid the whale henceforth, and for another, he is grateful to have escaped so lightly. He makes nothing of his loss and says his hook is so convenient he is thinking of replacing his remaining hand with a second one. This story has always seemed to me a very neat summation of the two extremes on the scale of response to physical affliction. The mindset about disability determines the life.

Terry is forty-three now. I am telling his story with his permission. I met him a few years ago, when he attended a class of mine. In 1963 Terry was living up north. He was seventeen, strong, full of the energy, hope and ambition of youth. One summer day he dived off a dock into Lake Temiskaming, and slipped; a shallow dive became a deep dive, and the accident, which happened in seconds, made Terry into a quadriplegic. He spent the next twenty years in hospital, and when he finally wheeled himself out of there and into university he grabbed at the chance, he told me, to study English. I asked him what reading literature had meant and still means to him. Here is a summary of what he told me.

During all those years in a chronic care ward, Terry had a lot of time on his hands so was able to read a lot. He had always been keen on literature, so it was natural that he should turn to the world of novels and poetry to pass his time. Now, however, reading took on a special value for him. For one thing, since he was physically limited and blocked in his view by the walls of the institution, his world had become very small, and literature helped to expand that world and let him see beyond its narrow confines. He read "the classics," as he put it—the Romantic poets, Shakespeare and much fiction. Furthermore, he told me, Keats and Wordsworth showed him a world of value and feeling, of sympathy and delight with nature, that he could not feel but wanted to feel—a level of spiritual or sensual satisfaction he could aim for. He quoted Wordsworth's lines,

> To me the meanest flower that blows can give
> Thoughts that do often lie too deep for tears.[2]

Terry wanted to get to that place, beyond tears, where he could experience the wonder of a connection to things outside himself, where he could come fully alive in his mind, where he was not injured. Some of this was escape, he explained, escape from his present constraints, his immediate environment. But the escape was important because it showed him another world he could believe in, perhaps even get to, a world of fields and trees and flowers that he had lost for a while.

Among the novels that mattered to Terry, two seemed to stand out. One was *Lady Chatterley's Lover*, which I have mentioned before. In this novel, Lord Chatterley is confined to a wheelchair, and is also afflicted with sexual impotence. Terry saw in this portrayal a negative image of himself that he resented. He regards this use of a paraplegic as an exploitation furthering the myth that the physically impaired are helpless and asexual. The value of his response was that it raised questions for him about how he saw himself and how others saw him. Was he paranoid? Was he afflicted with self-pity? Did he have to tolerate being stereotyped and classed with a group as though he had no individuality? These questions were new for Terry, though, as I pointed out to him, blacks and Jews and women have grown up asking them and seeing challenging images in literature.

The other book that seems really important to Terry is Virginia Woolf's *To the Lighthouse*, a pioneering work of feminist fiction that explores the power of the inner life, the distance that exists between outward mechanical actions, gestures, speech and chores, and the felt life that is experienced mostly in silence. This book validates and gives a voice to that life, in a way Terry found deeply significant. He responded to the book's sensitivity and drew strength from its recognition that his inner life, his thoughts and feelings, counted, and that not all human experience should be measured in track and field medals, not even in those won in the wheelchair Olympics. Human beings are much more than legs and arms; when brains can't make these work, they pour more energy into other things. Terry has helped me to understand this, and I am grateful. He is writing his own story, and I hope the world will one day get to read it.

Attitude largely determines the satisfactions that life has to offer people with disabilities. Some disabilities are worse than others, so generalizing is difficult. All suffering is relative. It is hard to imagine a more frustrating life situation than that described in Brian Clark's *Whose Life Is It, Anyway?* In that story, an active, healthy, attractive sculptor, full of life, in love, and successful in every way, becomes quadriplegic as the result of a car accident. He can do nothing for himself and is totally dependent on others for basic services. He is, in effect, just a head, a brain left intact but unable to call upon the body for any feeling or satisfaction. He wants to die, and establishing his right to do so is the drama of the story.

For those with less severe disabilities, it is essential that there be opportunity to explore in detail the possibilities of control, life management, achievement and usefulness, satisfaction and pleasure, in the face of significant physical impairments, restraint and discomfort. Mental power can grow and flourish in the face of physical limitation. Spiritual and emotional and sensory satisfaction are possible. The difficulty of achieving such satisfaction must not, however, be underestimated. Coming to terms with the reality of the situation is the most difficult and sensitive part of the process, for without understanding what the limitations of handicaps are, people with handicaps cannot have the possibilities of achievement opened to them. Literature can be immensely helpful; it can explore and explain their personal responses, make opportunities for them to feel and to question their feelings without having to undergo the confrontation of one-on-one therapeutic challenge. Stories and descriptions can articulate the unspeakable, for them as for everyone. The reader who has a disability can control the speed and intensity of his response and match it to the emotional energy and readiness he has available. And remember, the experience of reader control is in this case a demonstration in practice that the reader is not helpless; the reading process itself invites mental action and activity and feeds back a positive sense of accomplishment.

Handicaps come in many forms, some physical, some emotional, some social, some economic. The reader who has a handicap will quickly recognize the extent to which prisoners of conscience are handicapped. Women have often been profoundly handicapped, and Margaret Atwood's *The Handmaid's Tale* warns us of a return to the enslavement of women, which she sees in the wave of the right-wing Christian fundamentalism that seems to be a peculiarity of our time. A particular skin colour can be a crippling handicap that keeps people in poverty, prison, ghettos and ignorance, as we see in South Africa and even closer to home. Readers with handicaps will make the comparison and extend their kinship to millions of others whose circumstances constitute a challenge as well as a limitation. Through fiction, their world can be greatly expanded.

1   Sandra Martin, "Novel Solace," *Empress*, April, 1987, pp. 7-8.

2   William Wordsworth, "Ode: Intimations of Immortality," in *The Norton Anthology of English Literature*, Third Edition, Vol.2, ed. M. B. Abrams, et al. (New York: Norton, 1974).

CHAPTER SIXTEEN

Subjects, Objects and Rejects

The Library of Congress reader survey (1978) shows that women read more than men. In the U.S., women read everything more than men. No one has satisfactorily explained why this should be so. My own research in Canada shows a similar finding for fiction.[1] In addition, not only do women read more than men, but they are more aware of the value of fiction to them at various points in their lives. University teachers of English across Canada will tell you that their classes are dominated by women— which probably means among other things that women did better in English in school than their male counterparts.

If this were the eighteenth century we could explain the finding socially. Women, in the early days of novel writing 250 years ago, were assumed to be the primary consumers of fiction. They did not have access to worldly occupations in commerce and industry; they did not have access to universities, medicine, church and government as professions. They stayed at home. If they became governesses, they read as part of their education. So what was regarded as the light and trivial amusement of fiction reading belonged mostly to women, whose light and frothy minds "useless" fiction well suited.

I guess it doesn't take much imagination to see that the worlds of entertainment created by printed fiction were a godsend to women of past eras. In a society where movies and TV were not an option, reading became a means of adventuring (rather than escaping—a put-down word) into realms of information and experience denied women in the roles permitted to them. Travel, romance, danger, meeting new people were possible through fiction, when not possible in their real lives. So many were the restraints on women that the world was a prison, an extension of the rules governing behaviour at home. By means of fiction, through stories whose writers were conscious that their main audience was female, women overcame depression, and sometimes even madness. One cannot help but wonder how many "female disorders" and "complaints," as sicknesses in women used to be called, were owing to the craziness of a sexism that took away large areas of control and freedom.

In the nineteenth century things got worse, if anything. Women were much more generally employed and abused as workers, servants and labourers, as were their male counterparts and even their children, but that did not free women from intense pressures and rules governing speech, dress, behaviour and movement. Today, my female students are amazed at what they read about such times in fiction, amazed and outraged. For instance, when they read of a group of men sitting around and discussing women and Lady Constance Chatterley in her presence, while she sits silently by like a household object, these students become almost speechless with indignation. The heroine of Henry James' *The Portrait of a Lady* is described as being a utensil to be hung decoratively on the wall, and Dombey's wife in Dickens' *Dombey and Son* is acquired as a "bosom to hang jewels upon."

My mother was a great reader, and no doubt turned me into one. Like so many of her contemporaries in the twentieth century, she found the world a fearful place and the rules governing her behaviour strong as iron bands. I can see now what I did not see while she was alive, that fiction gave her active and lively imagination a way of surviving much hardship, loneliness and fear. She was an avid reader of newspapers also, and these put her through bouts of excruciating daily anxiety; fiction, on the other hand, made her calm and happy. Thank God for libraries!

All this is well and good for the past, where we can see very clearly the function of fiction in the lives of women. Yet today women remain the more enthusiastic readers. Women seem to have learned (perhaps because of their reduced social opportunities they have recognized their need) that reading can help them to cope with and understand their roles, relationships and problems. The connection between women and literature is long and profound. Women writers have been prominent since the early days of printed fiction, and their names rank high among the "greats" and among the most productive. Jane Austen, the Brontës, George Eliot are only the tip of the iceberg. Hundreds of lesser lights shine through history. Today many of the best-read and most prolific writers are women. Considering how difficult it has been for women to achieve such prominence in many other fields, we must wonder at this special connection between women and literature, in the reading and writing of which nothing seems to have thwarted them. And nothing has probably done more to liberate women, to give them a sense of themselves as human, valid, important, intelligent, influential and abused, than literature. Stories have the power to reflect back to them affirmative and compassionate images of themselves, when men and institutions present only unyielding, stony surfaces reflecting nothing but contempt.

For millions of women, reading still functions as a primary source of life information and emotional exercise. In 1984, I listened with great interest to a radio program of the Canadian Broadcasting Corporation on popular romance literature, the luridly covered paperbacks that sell in the millions around the world.[2] There are people, women mostly, who devour these novels and in fact become knowledgeable and even expert on them. They learn to choose them carefully, have their favourite authors and can, in some cases, read several a week. One such reader is Darlene Sanchez, who gave this explanation of what she finds in such reading:

> I find that when I pick up a romance, I'm involved in somebody else's life. And for the time that I'm reading it, I am in a distant place, I am involved in somebody else's problems. I'm involved in their passion, their conflict, their total emotional levels, I'm involved in that. And I can sympathize with them and I can cry with them, and I can do what I want with them. And when I close the book, I'm finished, and I can walk away without really feeling any emotional ties to that. And then I take a look at my husband and I say well, you know, he's not so bad. He's like that guy, he's better, he's worse, he's—you know, it just depends on the frame of mind you were in before you read the book, then when you come out of it you say he's not that bad, we can work things out. He's all right. But they tend to make you feel very emotional, very loving, very tender. You feel like things are okay, they'll work out in the long run if you just work hard enough at them. Because if these two people who seem like they're never going to get together can get together, then your little problems along the way are going to work out, no problem. (p.4)

Using feeling as information, Darlene brings new shapes from fiction to apply to the patterns of her own relations, which are locked into one pattern. She is free to see things slightly differently, to rethink and reexamine her life. She is using models and she is experiencing emotions that may be blocked off by the needs of every day or the unreceptivity of her spouse, children, friends, or parents. You don't cry and feel and express with some people, or with most people, or, for some readers, with anybody. That does not mean it's unimportant to feel and experience the range of emotion you are capable of. Most readers of fiction would have a hard time expressing themselves in terms of the intellectual argument and debate of feminism, abortion, daycare vs. home care. But intellect and abstract ideas are only a little piece of what makes up human minds. The emotions and their pathways take up a large part of the brain and its activities. It is from fiction and its emotional language that readers can learn to see how they feel about things, for a story can clarify by its use of narrative devices a situation that can never otherwise be fully apprehended, never otherwise be grasped by the whole mind.

Darlene tells us, "I for one am a housewife, and I don't think I'm a bored housewife sitting around all day with nothing to do." (p.4) The common view is that women who read pulp romances as a habit are escapists. I've got nothing against escape; what else is a package tour to Mexico or a cruise to the Virgin Islands? In fact, I have met only two escapist readers in my life. One was a man who read himself away from his marriage and family. He hid in reading, would not deal with family problems, avoided his wife and, when not working, lost himself in books. The other was a woman in her thirties, a librarian who worked behind the scenes with books all day and then became a recluse in evenings and on weekends, avoiding people and living inside stories. This bothered her parents, who consulted a counselor, though the woman did not see a problem herself. As I say, escapists are rare. Carolyn Nichols, senior editor of Loveswept Romances, surveyed the readers of her series:

> As I've gotten to know them, travelling around the
> country, learned something about their lives, it really
> supported some theories that I had about who they were,

and certainly supported some data I had seen in surveys, namely that these women are not at all escapists, but rather people who are intensely involved in their communities—in terms of the school system or local crime problem, clean up committees—all kinds of things. Often they work too, and they have families. They're not escaping from anything when they read the romances, but rather they are gravitating to the kind of entertainment that's really compatible with their world view which is solution oriented, positive, optimistic, upbeat. (p.5)

Strangely enough, the contempt so often heaped upon romance readers by the literary elite is not directed at the gigantic industry and readership of detective fiction, which has been a largely male-dominated production. I can't but wonder if snobbery does not depend on who has the power. With a few outstanding exceptions, detective fiction until very recently was not written by women; it was not about women, and it presented all or most of the macho male stereotypes, including the soft porn images of women as sexual prizes, essentially gullible, beautiful and disposable. The satisfaction of detective fiction resides in problem solving. In the midst of confusion and dilemma, we may read about success, mental mastery over chaos and deceit, justice brought about by brain power and charm, and endings that tie all the ends up. Our suspense is a prelude to resolution, and because crime usually does not require us to identify with itself (most of us are timid, law-abiding citizens), we can participate confidently and not be deeply moved. We need to flirt with the other side of ourselves, the repressed side that is tempted to fraud, theft, revenge and terrorism, to taking wild risks, to breaking rules. Reading is our safety valve; in the end, our having flirted with crime restores us to the safety of the right side, the side that teaches "crime does not pay."

The women who enjoy romance are enjoying the same ficti-tious experiences that give expression to the forbidden and the desired. The inner world of the imagination is not satisfied with PTA meetings and church suppers. Mental health will not be served by pretending that the need for passion, excitement, adventure and novelty does not exist in the human heart. Only bionic brains, sci-fi hulks, are free from such needs. Here is what Star Helmer, vice pres-ident of Harlequin, said about her books:

I think that romances provide a certain emotional stimulation. As with any good fiction, if you can make the reader feel the character's sense of regret, sadness, joy, laughter, tears—whatever the emotion is, if the author can make that come alive, then you're going to have a stimulating book. For example, the example of good repartee. Good repartee is something that people generally talk about why they like romances, if they're getting into specifics. Most people when they're angry and they're in an argument do not have the witty, precise comebacks. You usually think about it two days later and say, oh, you know, why didn't I think of it? But the heroine is right there. And she's got it all and you go—right, I want to be like that. And in a way, that's success too. I was listening to a woman from Long Island talk about why she liked romances—Carol. Carol said, "I am a very boring person. I have very nice neighbours, but they're boring. I have a lovely husband, but let's face it, he's boring. Meanwhile, inside, I'm intelligent, sensitive, sensuous and brilliant. And that's why I like reading these romances, because I know I'm just like these heroines." (p.6)

We have to face the fact that in spite of significant changes in the roles of women they still read more than men. More than half of romance readers work outside the home. They must be finding something important in this fiction that assists them in coping with their emotional and mental needs, needs that can never be satisfied by one mate, one place, one or two roles and one life. As with other fiction, much can be learned from romance. Janice Radway, who has done much research on readers of romance, tells us,

> ...a lot of people scorn this [Romance as educator] and say that this is ridiculous, you can't learn from a romance. But in fact, the women believe that romance writers spend an enormous amount of time doing research, and this is the case. They go to libraries, they use archives, they use documents, and they situate the romance in a historical period, in a foreign country or whatever. The women turn to romances then because it's a way of learning about the outside world. (p.15)

I don't know what Emily Dickinson, a nineteenth-century American poet, would have said about popular romances, but here is what she wrote about reading, the democratization of reading that has led to romances:

A Book
There is no Frigate like a book
To take us Lands away
Nor any Coursers like a Page
Of prancing Poetry—
This Travel may the poorest take
Without offence or Toll—

How frugal is the Chariot
That bears the Human soul.[3]

As I said before, women read other things besides romances, and English classes in universities are dominated by women. In my counselling practice, I find that women are almost invariably more inclined to read than men. Reading can be extremely valuable in normalizing and explaining damaging experience that has been suppressed and not talked about. Take the case of sexual abuse. Though men are sometimes the victims, sexual abuse remains a women's issue because of its frequency among women. So common is the occurrence of sexual abuse among them, that dealing with its consequences has been a regular and normal part of everyday marriage and family therapy. The experience of childhood sexual assault almost always brings a sense of profound betrayal, shame, disgust with self, blame of self, fear, mistrust of males and also a great deal of anger. Any combination of these feelings produces damaged self-esteem, a sense of despair and injustice and a feeling of isolation. Since the victim is living with secret self-dislike, it is necessary to verbalize the outrage as part of recognizing the brutal betrayal of trust, especially in cases of incest. Victims find a community from reading. I have probably used Charlotte Vale Allen's book *Daddy's Girl* more often than any other with clients. The results are usually dramatic. Reading of the long and painful imprisonment in sexual slavery of this despairing child enables others to recognize their own innocence, their victimization. Their anger at the child Charlotte's treatment liberates their own long-repressed anger and directs it where it belongs, at the parents who have violated a sacred and biological trust to protect and nurture. The great detail of the story helps readers to call up their own past. As a reader told me just recently, "I was able to recall the wallpaper in the bedroom."

Remember that part of this reading experience is the knowledge that others, everywhere, are reading the same thing, reading your (the reader's) experience and feeling emotions like yours. Without having to endure personal, public exposure, the reader takes comfort and strength from being vindicated, explained, justified by published writing. Reading breaks down barriers.

No book I know of has been more widely read and personally useful to women than *Anne of Green Gables*. The success of this novel is astonishing. Somehow, the redheaded, talkative, fanciful and ever-rebounding orphan Anne has tapped the heartstrings of countless female readers around the world. In her they see hope, they see courage, they see their own intelligence speaking up for itself and refusing to be ignored. Anne gives voice to an unspoken sense of resentment and outcastness that women feel for any number of reasons. One client says, "I was the youngest of five girls and then came my brother, who could do no wrong." Another says, "I was the last child of four and the only girl—I was not important." Anne was supposed to have been a boy and got sent by mistake to Green Gables. How did that make her feel? And how many female readers feel that therein lies the story of their lives? How often I have heard, "I should have been a boy." No matter what the affliction, loneliness, secret pain, it seems that readers can find an echo of it in Anne's story and can secretly cheer for her and so cheer for themselves. I know one severely abused incest victim who suffered at home as a sexual stand-in for her mother from childhood to her mid-teens, and who told me that Anne (she read all the Anne books many times) was her life raft and that without those books she thinks she would have died of despair and heartbreak. Montgomery seems to touch some key, tap some wellspring of solace for females struggling to grow up in the face of untold hardship. Who can tell how many lives she has saved by her writing?

Women are naturally angry at being subjected to centuries of abuse. Assault, insult, rape are still commonplace in our society. Undoubtedly, with the disappearance of many Victorian taboos on the speaking and publishing of such matters, fiction has become perhaps the single most powerful agent in raising into consciousness and teaching female viewpoints, experiences and sensibilities. A writer whom many feminists dislike, D. H. Lawrence, did much to pave the way for modern feminists, first by writing *Lady Chatterley's Lover* and breaking open censorship with it, and second by giving women great prominence in his widely-read fiction-fiction read by men. Today we are beginning to recognize that the treatment of women has produced many special problems, and these are elegantly exposed and revealed in literature. Women and aging have been receiving much attention. As I've discussed, many wonderful portraits of elderly women serve to inoculate young women against future hardship and exploitation. For instance, Elizabeth Taylor's *Mrs. Palfrey at the Claremont* shows us how vulnerable is a surviving widow who has all her life been dependent on a controlling husband. Once she is alone, Mrs. Palfrey finds managing money, making living arrangements, dealing with people and generally trying to cope with worldly matters extremely difficult, frustratingly difficult. Turned into literature, this portrait is usefully challenging to readers, who nowadays feel that such helplessness is unnecessary. "I won't let that happen to me" is a common response. As I've mentioned, stories like "Irina" by Mavis Gallant and *The Book of Eve* by Constance Beresford-Howe enable readers to identify with images of their future selves. How do I want my life to develop and end? How will I want to age? "Must I wait a whole lifetime and my husband's death"—this from an unmarried twenty-year-old—"until I can be free to do what I want, live where I want, decorate a room as I want?"

Graham Greene's *Travels with my Aunt* presents a picture of an extraordinary old woman who breaks all the rules, lives dangerously and scorns the safe and secure world from which she extracts her nephew, a retired banker. This is a wonderful story for stirring up readers and giving them plenty to think about, especially for causing them to question how much they are satisfied with their own lives. One of the most interesting results of female readers' reading about older women is the challenge they feel to review their present circumstances. When I was an undergraduate I shared a huge room in an old house owned by the lady downstairs, who ran a hairdressing salon. I remember noticing her, on the fringes of my mind, as attractive, energetic, outgoing and single. She used to pass on to me rather racy novels, no doubt daring for their time. As a student of English Literature, snob that I was, I paid no attention to these, seeing that they did not compare to Scott, Thackeray, Dickens and Hardy. Besides, the woman was ancient, thirty years old if she was a day, and if there was a message in her attempt to share her reading I did not receive it. Oh, how right it is, that youth is wasted on the young! I think of this woman now, as I write about women, because I am sure she would have loved Aunt Augusta in Greene's novel. In her she would have found confirmation for the jolly, independent and freewheeling life I am sure simmered on the first floor, and from which, innocent that I was, I excluded myself.

There are many stories that record the defeats and triumphs of women. Today the challenges for women are different, but if anything, more complicated than ever. Women are faced with many possible choices, none of which is easy. If they choose careers they must fit them into a program that may include marriage and childbearing, while they compete in male-dominated organizations and suffer all the normal discouragements that a career can entail. Men have for the most part not found the worlds of commerce, industry, or the professions easy to navigate. If women stay at home they risk the stigma of seeming unambitious and unproductive and the possibility of being unprepared for widowhood. This is a time of transition, and we have not yet adopted attitudes and set up institutions that can respond supportively and practically to women's equality. In the current situation the reading of fiction can be enormously helpful. Women writing for women can assist their readers with models, examples, explanations of ideas, situations, problems and solutions, with sympathy and with many kinds of useful information about the way the world works.

I think for instance of a wonderful book by Rosemary Daniell called *Fatal Flowers*, which tells the story of a woman's growing up in the American South and how she is taught to regard herself as a charming prize for a man, a flower with no will of its own, staying pretty to be picked when the occasion is right. I gave this novel to a woman who, it seemed to me, regarded herself like this. The only praise she ever received, she said, was when she was bathed and groomed and paraded for her father to approve her looks. Male approval for her looks was the goal of her life. Reading *Fatal Flowers* helped her to believe that her story, or at least that part of it, was a product of culture, that she was part of a whole social program and not an isolated individual "freak" who was somehow to blame for being so vulnerable to and dependent on males.

I do not know what could be as effective as reading in helping individuals to overcome the sense of weirdness that renders them helpless with guilt and embarrassment. If I tell someone that being a victim is not her fault I may be regarded as being nice, as practicing a trick of therapy, or as giving one person's opinion—and not an objective opinion at that, since I have a stake in my client's wellbeing. Print is a powerful source of authority. It seems to be objective-that is, it is not aimed personally at the client-reader, is not her story per se. Printed stories reveal larger worlds and lay out what happens clearly, in language that is designed by an accomplished writer. And print stays put, acquires a kind of fixedness, so you can refer to it, quote it, reread it, and rely on it as one unalterable version. You can carry it around with you, share it in its exact words and store it. My words, like other conversation, make some impression perhaps, but the impression is not preserved, may be hard to recall, does not acquire visibility and so loses "objectness." The comfort of the book is its "thereness," on the shelf or in the library, to prove its existence, to prove that I did indeed read it in those very words.

Women today, then, need the network of support, insight and information that can be known, felt and thought through fiction. Just as though the human need calls forth what is necessary to satisfy it, so we find a great surge of wonderful contemporary writing useful to women. Margaret Atwood, Bobbie Ann Mason, Alice Walker, Alice Munro, Sandra Birdsell, Tillie Olsen, Mavis Gallant, Margaret Laurence, Ann Beattie, Joyce Carol Oates, Doris Lessing, Anne Tyler, Grace Paley—these are just a few of the writers who produced short stories and novels that assist women in managing their worlds. Find what you like and need among these and others and then read for yourself with the aid of the questionnaires at the back of this book.

Put Down or Shut Up

If women have been treated like a "minority," so have actual minorities. Here, for instance, is what one man, Len, told me about his homosexuality: "I'm not bothered or bugged by being homosexual— I feel normal. The problem is my relatives and friends don't, or won't, understand. I can't tell my father, he'll hit the roof. It's kinda lonely for me. It's others who think I'm a freak." This young man did not want to become part of a gay community or cruise gay bars. His sex drive was not very strong, so he felt no urgency about that, but he did want sympathetic, open and honest friendship and affection, like everyone else. He needed permission and acceptance from some wider context, some form of social approval and understanding. He could hardly find this in the small, conservative Ontario town where he lived and worked. It seemed to me that fiction would give a view of a larger world that could embrace and console Len as he struggled for an acceptance he could not find locally.

To suggest useful readings to Len required some awareness that his situation was not basically different from that of many others who were not homosexual, but who had good reason to feel as though they were—I searched for the term—misfits. There is a whole misfit literature, the most famous example being "The Ugly Duckling"—a story with a bit of a sellout ending, that suggests only those who find themselves in with the wrong species become victims of prejudice. I always wonder how Andersen would cope with a swan that was, say, black, or had only one leg or a short neck. I remember witnessing an extraordinarily touching scene in Kew Gardens, when two small children of a visiting black family knelt by a pond and grinned and squealed with delight at a black swan among all the white ones; only it held their interest, and from this majestic, black, different bird they could hardly be torn away. The swans were of course not bigoted, and the black bird appeared to be totally integrated.

I wanted Len, with the help of misfit literature, to see that he had a kinship with many others who from time to time run afoul of their social customs or practices or beliefs. I asked him to read Hawthorne's *The Scarlet Letter* and keep a record of his responses to it. Where one reader, also a man, had seen the book as focused on hypocrisy and deceptive appearances, a story of public dishonesty and private shame, Len found it a painful story of loneliness and courage in the face of persecution. He was upset and indignant at the treatment of the heroine. I asked him to read Shirley Jackson's short story "The Lottery," where an innocent woman gets stoned to death as part of an annual ritual that lasts long after anyone knows the reason for it. I suggested Judy Blume's story *Blubber*, about school persecution of a misfit, and finally I began to suggest some homosexual literature.

There are two "classic" novels of homosexuality that everyone would do well to read and that should be part of the reading list for general education. Both are gripping, intriguing, lively stories of struggle. One is *Maurice* by E. M. Forster, written in 1913-14 and so controversial and original that it had to await publication until 1971. The other is *The Well of Loneliness* by Radclyffe Hall, the pioneer story of the anguish of being a lesbian. Both these books are important landmarks of literature. In them we see the torment of people learning to come to terms with being different in a profound way, in their very core—the social stigma is intense. The pain of loneliness and secrecy is shown from the inside. Since the cause of the homosexual's being odd, different and not "normal" must be kept a secret, and he must suffer embarrassment and practice concealment as he grows into adolescence and adulthood, reading can be an important source of reassurance. It can show that there is a sub-group normalcy, a minority that can make him less alone. "I know how you feel"—when it is believable—is one of the most reassuring sentences we can ever hear. This is what books, poems, can say to us, again and again. The other day, after we had read a poem by Alden Nowlan on the sexual fantasies of a middle-aged man shopping in the supermarket, a student told me she found reading about someone else's fantasies reassuring—it made her feel "it's not just me." I like that way of summing up some of the satisfaction literature gives—the "it's not just me" relief.

The "people of the Book," that's what Mohammed called Jews, among others. It interests me that Jews, given their history, should have produced such a huge volume of literature. Like women, Jews must have found in literature the means for expression, communication and solace. Since public and social life have been until recently inhospitable to Jews, writing has provided a voice and an audience that would otherwise not have come together. Writing creates bonds that leap time and space, which otherwise make for the isolation of minorities. Overcoming isolation is a necessary survival strategy for groups excluded from influence. Ghettos are not only enforced by circumstances, but reinforced by the needs of those who join, needs for common values, language, history, religion and status in the face of the larger, hostile world. *Literature forms communities.* It functions as a secular liturgy, the sacred documents of a group of believers, as in the case of Dickens lovers, for instance, who form Dickens Societies—likewise with Jane Austen Clubs, James Joyce Societies, and a host of others.

Perhaps the power of literature as a support system for minority members is best summarized by a personal story. Not long ago, some parents of Jewish children who attend our local high school launched a much-publicized attack on the inclusion in the curriculum of Shakespeare's *The Merchant of Venice.* The play centres on the persecution and revenge (thwarted in the last act) of the Jewish moneylender (today's banker) Shylock. One or two children at the school, as I remember, complained that they had been subjected to insult after the play had been introduced in the classroom. This struck a deep chord of memory in me. My experience of the play in school in England was completely different. To start with, the context in which I lived at school was one of chronic prejudice. My daily life might include anything from casual racist insult to physical attack. Indeed, the only other Jew in this boys-only school in London, England, often stood back to back with me while we fought off assaults from our classmates during "playtime," the dreaded break period of morning and afternoon. You must understand that this situation was more or less a total mystery to me. I knew that as a Jew I was odd and different and would suffer persecution, but the reasons were not available. I can remember no satisfactory discussion of any kind with parents, teachers, rabbi, or social worker. School counsellors were an uninvented breed. My mind and soul cried out at the injustice of this system, the complicity and silence of the world. I was lonely, frightened, angry and frustrated. Then we came to study *The Merchant of Venice*. We read the play as a classroom drama, taking parts. Can you guess what role the teacher assigned to me? Right, Shylock! I suppose it is necessary to explain that I loved Shakespeare anyway, loved literature, was the most avid reader in the class and endured the rest of school for English periods. Now I wonder, looking back, was that teacher a racist or a psychology genius to put me in the role of the Jew-villain of the play? You see, of course, that that was my role in the school anyway, class scapegoat. Before I read this play, however, I had no voice to cry out against the injustice, no tradition or history of Jewish literature to call upon for explanation or support. I had no language to break through the boneheads of my persecutors. *No one understood me!* And then, into my mouth were placed these words, with which I could respond to my roughneck peers:

> I am a Jew. Hath not a Jew eyes? hath not a Jew
> hands, organs, dimensions, senses, affections, passions?
> fed with the same food, hurt with the same weapons,
> subject to the same diseases, healed by the same means,
> warmed and cooled by the same winter and summer, as
> a Christian is? If you prick us, do we not bleed? If you
> tickle us, do we not laugh? If you poison us, do we not
> die? and if you wrong us, shall we not revenge? If we
> are like you in the rest, we will resemble you in that. If a
> Jew wrong a Christian, what is his humility? Revenge.

If a Christian wrong a Jew, what should his sufferance
be by Christian example? Why, revenge. The villainy
you teach me I will execute, and it shall go hard but I
will better the instruction.[4]

Never did boy recite more passionately and pointedly these
lines. What did I care that Shylock is defeated, insulted, reviled,
gloated over? What did I care that the Christians in the play deceive
the court and each other to arrive at their fragile victory? For all I
knew, Shakespeare may have been an ahead-of-his-time liberationist,
for women and Jews, or a male chauvinist anti-Semite. What I did
know was that he had given me a voice, understood exactly the outraged feeling of injustice and frustration that waited to howl forth
from within me. The great poet had empowered me with language,
and shown my links to others who had felt the weight of exile and
cruelty across the ages. Shylock offers to lend money to Antonio as a
gesture of goodwill, a no-interest loan. He is scorned and rejected; so
be it. I was one with Shylock facing his tormentors, the hypocrites
who preach to him of the quality of mercy in the final act. Neither
of us was getting much mercy from our Christian neighbours.
Shakespeare's language was a great gift that explained to me, in a
nutshell, the power literature has for minority readers.

If you feel alone, not understood, not empowered to be heard,
or not able to explain what it feels like to be in your situation, there
is literature that will explain you and give you the voice, the model,
through which you can be validated. As new situations arise, new
voices will arise to explain and create their versions, in the service of
voiceless readers. Recently the Parliament of Canada passed a bill
granting Japanese Canadians an apology and compensation for their
internment and loss of property during World War II. In the course of
the parliamentary debate, one party leader, Edward Broadbent, read,

with tears in his eyes, a passage from Joy Kogawa's novel *Obasan*, which deals with that Japanese-Canadian experience. This novel played an important part in shaping the Canadian conscience on this matter, as it evolved towards righting a wrong. No one can ever measure such a process, how fiction works to influence and change public policy or a nation's outlook or feeling, and the reason lies in the complexity of the process. Fiction does not act alone to produce change. It is part of all the information that accumulates in human minds. As story gives shape to events of the past, it gradually influences the way we think, gives form to our vague feelings and brings them into consciousness. Our passion for research and measuring should not blind us to the reality that many powerful shaping influences—parents, school, mentors, friends, sickness and accident, and, yes, poetry and fiction—though none of these can be measured, deeply influence who we are and the way we think and feel. Other heroes than Shylock have spoken to me powerfully—in Bernard Shaw's *Saint Joan*, in Philip Roth's *The Professor of Desire*; the child hero in Henry Roth's *Call it Sleep*, Grey Owl, Hamlet, Hester Prynne in Hawthorne's *The Scarlet Letter*, Nicholas Nickleby in Dickens' novel of that name—all speak to me in an intensely personal way and help to shape me. You can find help in literature and you can take what you need back with you into your daily life. The treasure-trove of fiction and poetry is inexhaustible, self-renewing and belongs to all those who can read.

1   Joseph Gold and Fred Gloade, "Affective Reading and Its Life Applications," in *The Arts in Psychotherapy*, 15 (1988), 235-44.

2   Claire E. Harrison, "Love at First Sight," CBC *Ideas*, Oct. 16-30, 1984. Further references to this transcript will be given in the text by page number.

3   Emily Dickinson, "A Book," in *The Poems of Emily Dickinson*, ed. Thomas H. Johnson (Cambridge, Mass.: Belknap Press, 1958).

4   William Shakespeare, *The Merchant of Venice*, III.i, in *The Complete Works* (Harmondsworth: Penguin, 1969).

CHAPTER SEVENTEEN

Once upon a time—
In School

Everyone knows that children love stories and poems. Parents and teachers find the rhythms of poetry, the suspense and drama of story, the words of song surefire methods for gaining attention and conveying important information. Children long to learn to read if they see adults reading and if adults read to them. If the reader has the key to turning the black, squiggly marks on the pages of a book into the magic of story, the magic of people, places and events that can be seen and experienced inside the listener, then the listener wants that power too. Children at a certain age are eager, willing, even impatient, to work hard to learn the wizardry of reading, so that they will not be dependent on someone else's time and inclination for the pleasure of story. Story enjoyment is a joy for children. How is it then that so many adults I meet claim to have been put off reading in school? I asked a group of university students this question the other day. One said, "Children don't have to take something called *English*."

If this is the problem we should look closely at what it means. If literature is a really important human resource, how can we accept a situation that tolerates the loss of this resource to millions of people? With the coming of literacy in the late 1900s, there also came public education and public libraries. After the First World War, there began to emerge in universities departments of English. When working people began to demand the ability to read, they did not do so in order to read fiction. First working men, then women, wanted religious tracts, political information, arguments like those of Tom Paine, whose writings are credited with no small part in the American Revolution. Gradually, however, social and political criticism and commentary found their way into fiction. Novels like Charles Dickens' *Bleak House* satirized aspects of law, *Oliver Twist* condemned the workhouse system and *Hard Times* ridiculed certain developments in education. These are just three of hundreds of examples. Fiction proved to be enormously popular as a way of informing readers about their world and entertaining them at the same time. Novels were issued in parts, installments, like serial magazines, and so were affordable. This method of publication reinforced the readers' feeling that they lived through the ongoing drama of other people's lives, which became the readers' own. You will recognize the origins of TV soap opera serials here. Fiction was at first not considered serious enough (or too corrupting, too distracting and enticing) to be encouraged—the churches were against it.

When universities made literature part of their curriculum, they had to turn it into something very serious and professional in order to justify its inclusion. They did this by following the usual pattern for creating exclusive, elite clubs or cults. They discouraged the notion that reading was fun. They invented a secret language for talking about literature that you could learn only if you were admitted to the cult. They studied only works that had stood the test of time, they arranged for works to stand the test of time by studying them, and they particularly favoured literature that was difficult to read. They instituted tests that would decide if participants had earned the right to claim any knowledge of literature. In other words, they created an "expertise" of reading; they cornered the market in "understanding" literature, and they made reading seem very complicated.

To be fair, the plus side of this has been to keep "the classics" alive and in print. For many readers, the university has been the place where they learned to appreciate the riches of past literature, hard reading, that might otherwise have been lost to generations. The problem has been the cost: a split between professional readers of "good" literature and unauthorized readers of popular literature.

The trouble with judgements of "good" and "great" in literature is that we fall in love with our own verdicts—they become self-reinforcing. Shakespeare is the outstanding example of a writer who has achieved almost divine status, but even Shakespeare has flaws, as Samuel Johnson points out in a passage designed to help us to keep in touch with reality:

> Yet it must be at last confessed, that as we owe every thing to him [Shakespeare], he owes something to us; that, if much of his praise is paid by perception and judgement, much is likewise given by custom and veneration. We fix our eyes upon his graces, and turn them from his deformities, and endure in him what we should in another loath or despise.[1]

Teachers do in schools what professors do in universities. Having learned what is "good" literature, and how to be serious and professional about it, they naturally carry their attitudes with them into the classroom. At a certain point in the progression of the curriculum they divide learning into subject areas. These are compartments that shut off the materials of the subject—novels in English, flowers in Botany, frogs in Biology, sex in Health Science and so on—and ensure that the materials don't slip into other people's compartments, like ticket holders in the blues sneaking into the red seats at half-time. Until very recently, English classes in secondary schools studied literature and language just as their teachers in university did. Students were required to read a few books very intensively. They examined *Hamlet, Great Expectations,* or *Huckleberry Finn* from every angle, memorizing events, characters, symbols, plot, structure, history and meaning, chapter by chapter, scene by scene. This was not meant to be fun. It was meant to be work. The teacher was the authority who knew the one "right" answer, which the student had to "psyche out." The works had been selected by the authorities—embodied in the teacher—and so were of unquestioned value, importance and durability. Teachers did not seem to be very good listeners, not really interested and respectful listeners to students. Students who were very brave might venture to say something, if they felt they could say what the teacher wanted to hear.

The problem with this setup is that for those who were not good at the process of psyching out the right answer, or for those who came to regard reading as hard work, reading outside of the classroom became unattractive. Watching TV is not hard work. Reading is a process that for learners makes no distinction between kinds of reading. If school is the place where reading is learned, and if that activity becomes unpleasant, then all reading will become unpleasant—or unattainable. If eating and mealtimes are unpleasant enough for children, they will lose enthusiasm for food—the joy of eating will be lost to them.

There are signs today of a movement toward what has come to be known as reader-response. The theory goes like this: The text is a code, a kind of message-in-waiting, a potential experience. To activate it requires a reading. The reader activates the story or poem by using her own special experiences and language to make sense of the thing read. This means that each reader has a unique reading of the story, no matter how slightly hers differs from every other reading. There is no one, absolute, fixed meaning to the story. I like this change in direction because it is truer to the actual experience of reading.[2] My own memories and associations, the ones that come to my mind while I'm reading, my own feelings, are what matter to me and what I have to offer to other readers.

I recently conducted a little classroom experiment to demonstrate to students the validity and pleasure of a reader-response approach to literature. I chose as our subject a story by Honoré de Balzac, "A Passion in the Desert." This is a story within a story, told by an old soldier, who reminisces to an acquaintance about how he was lost in the desert and how he struck up a close relationship with a panther. I asked a group of readers to volunteer their impressions, their most important conclusions about the story, based on their own responses to it. One said it was about the changes of love. I put this on the board. The second said it was about loss and made her feel very sad. This too went on the board. Another said it was about bonding between creatures, even human and animal, and how love could occur anywhere. Another said it was about trust and the need for it in order for love to survive. Another said that love saved the man's life. All these were added to the list. Finally, I offered my own—that for me the story is about how story is made and how it functions in human life. I asked the group to look at all the answers on the blackboard and tell me which was the right one. There was a pause—silence. Having been trained that there is only one right answer, their first instinct was to try to guess which answer I liked best. Finally, one brave soul, sensing my scheme and realizing that her peers could not be more right or wrong than she herself, since all the comments were simply personal convictions, volunteered that they were all right. I pressed the point. Surely my reading must be the most right, the best and true, for was I not, after all, the professor? They laughed, seeing through my little game, as I had intended and hoped they would. The wonder of the text, the story, the poem, is its infinite subtlety to fit the receiving, decoding mind. The reader looks inside himself to find feelings and memories to make sense of the literature, and in doing so produces a special blend of meaning.

To impose a single, authoritative meaning on the text is to turn reading into a rote learning process and to deny the reader the value and importance of the experience as personal. To insist on a hunt for one true meaning is to depersonalize reading. And it is the process of depersonalizing education that leads to boredom, hostility and dropping out. The latest idea to come from school boards, as I read in the local newspaper recently, is not to reexamine curricula and methods to keep students in school, but *to seek greater legal powers to force them to stay*. Don't improve the product, just *force* people to buy it. Students who seek relevance in their education are in need of information and experience for the whole person, for a whole life. Young people don't drop out of school because they are not learning a job skill, but because they cannot see that what they learn has any connection to their own life and needs, their needs as whole thinking, feeling, coping persons in a context of family and society. The nearer students get to the end of high school, the more academic and objectified and the less relevant their studies become. This is not because the "subjects" are not important; it is because they are presented without sufficient reference to the power and function of the observer, or reader, for the student to alter the thing observed.

During their training, teachers could help everyone by memorizing and understanding these rules:

Rule I.   The whatness of the material studied is changed by the howness of the study process.

Rule II.   Reading is not a "subject"—it is a human perceptual strategy, a behaviour.

Rule III.   a) Information is a component in a system that includes the student.

b) Information is changed as perception changes.

Rule IV.   The teacher's experience is not the students' experience.

Rule V.   Testing and grading students is measuring their ability to adapt to the teacher's system.

Corollary: A student can get A's in many subjects and never have expressed an original thought, developed an innate talent, or experienced pleasure and excitement with the course.

Rule VI.   Students are feeling, thinking, coping, growing, individual organisms. They have something to say that is their own.

Rule VII.   Students are not good or bad—they are responding to context.

What are the implications of Rules I and II for literature and reading in schools?

GOALS

The primary purpose in offering reading in school is to provide opportunity for students to experience pleasure and control. This requires giving them a greater quantity of reading, more choices in reading and more encouragement of their personal response. Education has often diminished the pleasure of reading. This is intolerable. It is a situation that can be changed only by giving more power to the reader. Reading response must be democratized. Individual responses must be respected. The prevailing method of detached examination of texts with a view to interpretation means too little gets read. This method is remote from the actual experience of reading.

THEORY

Students do not know how they read, and they have a right to know what we know about how it works and what their books are doing when they read. They will read more attentively and enthusiastically when they know the purpose and benefits of reading. In order to know these, they must first be taught some of the fundamentals of language, the history of writing, the origins of story, and the importance of story-making in managing human affairs.

GRADING

Reading should be removed from the curriculum as a "subject." Literature should be a foundation process for every grade and every area of learning. The encouragement of reading requires the separation of this process from the curriculum of "subjects." Remember that reading is the development of a mental process for managing all other material, life experience and relationships. Reading literature need not be graded. Only by having freedom from being tested can students be permitted to enjoy and experience the process without having to join in the game of pleasing the teacher that accompanies the "subject" now. Literature can be attached to every other subject, and English teachers can participate in all other subjects. Literature can be used to teach history, ecology, politics, law, art, philosophy, problem solving, writing, psychology, science, sexuality, family studies, sport, geography and economics.

METHOD

Teachers must overcome the tendency to be right about meaning in reading. If they will open up to hear their students' responses they will learn a lot, free themselves from frustration and stress and avoid making discouraging judgements about wrong interpretations. Learn to listen. Change your mind. Learn to over-listen, hearing the voice, intention, experience behind the words. Think about what is heard and ask other students what they hear.

Students can keep a reading-response journal that runs from the time they can write until they leave high school. If they can't write, they can keep pictorial records or audio tapes. Such a journal is feedback to the student that proves he has a voice, a response, feelings and thoughts. It is good writing practice. It is a way of being heard. It proves to the teacher that reading is happening. It does not have to be graded. It can be shared with others. It is a record of personal growth.

Put reading and literature first, ahead of yourself, above the system. In large classes students can be encouraged to share responses with peers in small groups. This is extremely effective for spreading ideas, for feeling heard and listened to, for sharing enthusiasms.

Students should be encouraged to add to reading lists, to share books found on their own that peers might enjoy. Books that have proved helpful to one student might be helpful to others.

SUMMARY

Reading is too important and too basic to be left in a "subject" slot. The power, pleasure and usefulness of literature last a lifetime; literature continues to be a primary source of information and experience. Those who understand the value and usefulness of fiction and poetry must be the ones to work on behalf of their students and their children and the have-nots of reading. Nowadays I hear the politicians who determine educational policy crying loudly for education as job training, for a work force narrowly specialized in high-tech competition and the management of machinery. If they do not understand the value of reading, how can they know what they deprive others of? We must aim for a quality of life that involves the whole person, the person who ages, raises families, grieves for losses, dreams of adventure, relates to friends and prepares for death. The loss of reading will be a species loss. It is the same kind of ignorance that leads to indifference to beauty and want of empathy for others, and ecological destruction of the planet.

The magic, beauty and solace of our natural world, our woods, streams and fields, our food and light and air, celebrated by our poets and writers, will be lost to those who do not learn how to see them and feel them. Literature can help us. Writers teach us how to see and feel about our world. That world is being squandered by the greed and ignorance of the bunkered productivity worshippers. The masters of expedience in corporate boardrooms, in governments, or in the Pentagon are not functionally illiterate. They just don't know how to read. Unless we change our educational bias, we will produce more and more "educated" technocrats, well equipped to destroy our planet and ignorant of the nature of the loss.

1   Samuel Johnson, "Preface to Shakespeare," in *Criticism: The Major Statements*, ed. Charles Kaplan (New York: St. Martin's Press, 1986).

2   Joseph Gold, "The Function of Fiction: A Biological Model," in *Novel*, Winter/Spring, 1988. This paper was presented in April, 1987 at the conference on "Why the Novel Matters" held at Brown University, Providence, Rhode Island.

PART SIX

The End of the Beginning

CHAPTER EIGHTEEN

Conclusion

*It's amazing, you know, sometimes I look at a word and suddenly
I realize I can read it! People must think I'm crazy when I grin
at a word but it's better than having people think you're crazy because
you can't read. Now I go to the library. One day I hope I can pick
up a whole book and just read it, just like that.*

A student in a literacy class

THE THREE L'S

Literacy; Leisure; Libraries. Let's start with the first "L." It should be clear by now that the uses of reading are profound. The benefits, practical results, applications and peculiar pleasures cannot be duplicated from other sources. Obviously, being able to read is essential for quite ordinary tasks. People must read signs, forms, letters, instructions, labels on household products, medicines, foods. These are fairly basic survival readings. The other day two workers came to install a new chimney at my house. The chimney kit included instructions. By reading them, the workers put up the chimney. Had they not been able to read, they would have been out of that job, and probably most others.

Beyond survival in a print society on a day-to-day basis, there is the need to feel like a participant in the social affairs of the state, and therefore truly a citizen. Newspapers, magazines, election material, vacation material, advertising and fund-raising literature, books on history and geography, reference books, dictionaries, encyclopedias, business material—all of these provide the next level of reading for what seem like perfectly ordinary coping and surviving strategies to those of us who take reading for granted. For those who can't read, the world of these revelations is a closed place, an impenetrable mystery. Imagine if you can the frustration, humiliation and struggle, the lack of privilege and degree of disadvantage, for those who are illiterate.

Yet these are only the more trivial achievements of language. There are still the sublime pleasures that literature conveys as it connects us to larger worlds, other minds and our own feelings and biographies. The functionally illiterate, as they are called, do not even know, cannot imagine, the immense range of human information denied to them. Perhaps they have in some cases been read to. Perhaps they know the pleasure of story. But think of their dependence, their inability to find what they need and to follow an interest or enjoy an experience at their own will. To be illiterate and wander through a library must be a genuine torture to those who have even a tiny glimpse of the mind-opening worlds of literature.

Discussions of the horrors of illiteracy hardly mention such elevated concepts as personal growth, personal relations and the pleasures of the imagination—let's say spiritual life. We have, even in our most laudatory descriptions of the benefits of reading, consistently underrated its importance. After food, warmth and shelter/safety, what comes next? Story, of course. Story contains the link between the "I" and the rest out there. Story is the organizing system for putting experience into code, so that we can store it, exchange it and reproduce it. The story of someone else's experience is an augmentation to my own experience, a feedforward component for managing my own life. What are the attitudes to literature that we often hear? One common theme is that you don't need it, you won't find it important to your basic requirements, getting in the crops, making babies, catching fish, paying bills. The view of human beings implied by this attitude is one of mechanical slavery. Robots don't need literature. Slaves are not encouraged to read and write, for obvious reasons. I say that story is essential to normal human functioning. You can have story without reading. But remember that in a literate society like ours, which has lost an oral, word-of-mouth tradition of stories, folklore, storytellers and storytelling occasions, if we take away literacy, take away books, discourage story acquisition from reading, we produce a more profoundly deprived people than were our early preliterate ancestors, who could not read and write, but who had a reservoir of heard stories. There has, of course, been a resurgence of storytelling by professional storytellers in recent years, but listening to such people is still a long way from being an ordinary, routine part of our lives.

The reductionist view of reading says that literature is decorative and frivolous and not necessary for survival—a view that is erroneous, ugly and arrogant. The other popular view of reading that leads to inequity and underprivilege is the elitist view, that reading is only for those whose aims are higher education, professional careers, university training. Because this view sees literature as a frill, it can deprive those who don't aspire to higher education of the benefits of a love of literature. This keeping of literature for the otherwise well-educated, which grows out of a failure to see the benefits of literature and language as profound and universal, as the major goal of education, creates permanent class divisions and an underprivileged mass of semiliterate, semiarticulate dependants.

The benefits of reading are derived without much pain or sacrifice. As a leisure activity, reading gives exercise to the mind without taxing body muscles, heart, or lungs very much. By and large, reading is not dangerous to your health. Reading is a quiet activity—and if you were to spend too much time reading you would lose muscle tone and general physical fitness. Reading does burn up calories, but not as many as cycling for the same length of time. When the body needs to be quiet, however, the mind need not be passive. Let's talk about leisure for a while.

Leisure

Leisure time is time with no enforced activity, no activity necessitated by some pressure, in other words, no work. Work is compelled activity—earning money to live on, repairing a roof to keep the rain out, digging a grave, fixing the drains, or building a fire to call for help after your shipwreck on a desert island. Leisure is freedom from such pressure, time when you can choose to do what you feel like. So reading for a course requirement is not leisure reading, but picking up your favourite novel and reading it in the bath, as a friend of mine does, is leisure. People who don't have to work are said to lead lives of leisure.

People use leisure time for either active or passive pursuits. Watching a sport, especially watching it on television, is passive. Physical inactivity is a serious threat to the health of a modern industrial population. Undoubtedly, more and more labour saving leads to more and more inactivity. People who do not have to walk, run, scrub floors or clothes, push lawnmowers, plant food, get up to tune a radio or television set, move the hand to brush teeth, prepare food and so on, are in danger of physical decay. They must join health spas, or jog, or force themselves to some other form of exercise in order to stay alive and well. We can see this kind of development and stress clearly, but it is not so easy to see that not having to think about menus, prepare food, walk and run and swim, not having to do such things as these, means we do not have to think. If we can see how our leisure time is rendered passive, we will begin to grasp the danger to ourselves, our culture and our political freedom. Even reading is made simple for us by predigested summaries of books—Classic Comics, Coles Notes, *Reader's Digest*.

The end of such a trend could be a population of vegetables controlled and organized by a few literate technocrats and executives who have retained some grasp on how things work and who can still think, talk, write and read. The kind of world we are creating requires us to be more mentally alert and sophisticated *while at the same time encouraging us to be more passive and inactive.* We need to be more on our toes to cope with changing systems, while we are tempted to be more on our bums by the hypnotizing effects of mind-numbing entertainment and machinery that replaces us. The structures of the past are breaking up and reforming into new, unfamiliar patterns. Our moral, religious, dietary, geographical, environmental, sexual and familial beliefs and customs are yielding to new arrangements and possibilities. No amount of fundamentalist or right-wing yearning for the past will stop this evolution. For our personal and familial and social well-being, we must be well informed, alert, thoughtful, imaginative, responsive, adaptable, flexible and compassionate.

I am both amazed and depressed to hear and read *daily* the silliness of our leaders, who tell us that we must be *educated to compete,* to get our share of *world markets,* to out-invent the Japanese. We are not to be educated, notice, for our personal, emotional and physical well-being; not to be educated to improve the life quality of citizens, to be part of a more gentle, happy, harmonious social group, to make our lives more joyous, loving, pleasurable, beautiful and meaningful. No! We are to go to school in order to make ever smaller radios and calculators, though they are already so small that only a myopic trained cockroach could operate them without effort. We must have programs that will render us cashless—and so more passive and dependent; robots that will iron our hankies and make our toast; cars that will drive themselves—while we watch shopping catalogues on TV, I suppose. We must compete for all this, dedicate our lives to the goals of competition, consumerism and greed. When will this madness end? It will end when the great consuming mass of wage earners like you and me realize that we have been conned, realize that the great literacy movement of the nineteenth century was meant to make people free and powerful, not passive readers of advertisements. Literacy is relative; we can read more or less. But if we read less it may be worse than not reading at all, for we put ourselves more into the power of those who decide what we will read and for what purpose. A little literacy may simply make us more manageable.

To be free, to be mentally stimulated, to escape the limits of our own settings, environments, influences, we need to read fiction in large doses and fully consciously. Since literature is mental and emotional exercise, what better time to read than when we have most leisure—in retirement. As our bodies become less active and vigorous, our minds can become more so. Once we overcome the idea that reading is a waste of time, we can be free to explore our own thoughts and feelings with the help of books. We can develop greater understanding of relationships; we can travel in our minds and train ourselves to look at detail. Stories can give us ways to arrange what we see and experience, can give us the material for conversation, can help us to make contact with our grandchildren by reading to them. We can pass on the gift of literacy, the love of reading. The struggle to keep reading alive is a struggle for our own independence, feelings and control.

Why do so many people like to read at night, end their day with a book they enjoy? Each of us is a story. We pile up experience, events, conversations, sights and sounds, but we do it hourly, daily, weekly, month in, month out, in a kind of jumble. Most of us are not writers, novelists, story-makers, and we are not very good, certainly not very well trained, at organizing our material into an understandable narrative. So our daily lives are like a collection of random notes, jumbled together in a shoe box, not placed in a sequence that makes any kind of sense. Things happen to us, not us to them. We do not impose order on experience. Novelists are people who do that. They take their experience and they weave it into a tapestry where others, readers, can see the pattern and take pleasure in the harmony and order of the whole. By reading story we can feel the peace of sense, and by sharing this we get the feeling of sense, the model that making sense is possible.

A great deal of dreaming is an attempt by our minds to make sense of information that is chaos as it happens to us. We do not have time, do not make time, to examine the meaning or significance to our lives of various experiences. When we sleep, we review or highlight what requires our attention, sometimes to our surprise; for what we thought unimportant or what we chose to ignore returns in our dreams, demanding our attention. We make stories in our dreams; there we are all writers, of amazing skill. So people read at night to slow down and exchange the chaos of their day for the beauty of ordered language that welcomes the reader into a world of shared experience managed confidently by the writer—*a world that does not ask us to give up our own individual world, but enables us to use and organize our own experience in the process of deciphering someone else's.* When we read, we do not truly escape—there is no escape from ourselves; there is relief from our chaos; *we reorganize and regenerate.*

Most of us work at tasks that require little or no thought, not much feeling and hardly any compassion or understanding. Indeed, the contrary is true: most workers must avoid thought and feeling to get the job done. Whether in factories, offices, driving, construction, cleaning, repairing, inputting, whatever it is, the talents and life skills of most people are not challenged. For people who must in some way automate themselves, it becomes very important to read.

Fiction is the best way to keep alive feeling, idea and imagination. The people who are to be seen reading fiction in the subway on the way to or from work are using a coping strategy. They are awakening parts of themselves that will wither and die from disuse. They are experiencing interest, emotion and thought. They are storing up images and people to use and consult and enjoy while they perform the mechanical tasks that prevent reading. *The stories they internalize are programs for rearranging their own thoughts in adaptive ways.* Most of these people, and I have heard many of them on radio interviews, apologize for their reading, discount the activity as merely passing time, as an alternative to staring into space, or reading again and again the subway advertisements. Readers have not been trained to evaluate the significance of what they read to their own survival, and they do not have the language to explain the relevance and importance of reading. Even more, the importance of what people read is personal, and they are reluctant to expose their own feelings and pleasure, their emotions, in public.

I have the impression that because reading is not celebrated in our world, in our society, readers often feel embarrassed at what seems like an old-fashioned activity, as though being literate is kinky, subversive. In a society that worships money and what is called productivity—and these are the true gods of our society—one must apologize for seeking emotional and spiritual well-being. These are desperate times, for we may become fully automated and live in physical comfort for a hundred years, yet want to die of boredom, ugliness and spiritual decay. If we think in terms of human history, if we can imagine our species as a part of nature, growing, changing, interacting with our environment, then perhaps we can see writers and fiction as a natural phenomenon, a by-product of human development, an adaptation to fulfil a need. As the need grows greater, so the production of a necessary tool emerges. In the same way that telegraph and radio, or writing itself, emerged as a consequence of travel, commerce and discovery, so the production of fiction has increased enormously, and necessarily. The time has come to turn to fiction seriously as a resource for helping us to cope with the age of industrial technology, an era that threatens us with gradually encroaching dehumanization. Medieval religion or nineteenth-century economics will not stem this process. Coping with it will require a number of rehumanizing strategies, many of which are already emerging. Reading literature is among the most effective of such strategies, and the time has come to recognize formally the role of fiction in the management of personal responses to change.

LIBRARIES

The third "L." Libraries were an outcome of the growth of literacy, of the demand for reading material by a population without the means to buy and own books. For centuries after print made books widely available, only the wealthiest families could assemble personal libraries, which often consisted of gorgeous leather-bound volumes with gold leaf lettering on their spines. Today, most people who can read own at least a few books. With the rise of book prices, however, and more especially with the huge number of novels and anthologies of stories flourishing about us, we must turn more and more to our libraries. Before I talk about libraries, and about and to librarians, I want to say one word on used books.

Used books have in recent years taken on a new value and interest by virtue of the fact that new books have become very expensive. Because the number of new books has increased dramatically, and because publishers are turning more and more to mass markets, books that have had a small but passing success, or a small but loyal following, have been allowed to drop out of print. The number of out-of-print books has increased as the number of new books has grown. The longer a book remains out of print the scarcer it becomes, until it is called a "collector's item." Such books have increased greatly in value and constitute an excellent investment. This is especially true of first editions, the first print run of a book that is likely to be popular and go through many printings, especially if it is destined to become a modern classic. Examples are the novels of Hemingway, Faulkner, Steinbeck, Thomas Wolfe and Scott Fitzgerald. Writers of this stature will have first editions that will now be very valuable—and very hard to find. However, there are used book stores in all kinds of unlikely and unbusy small towns and villages, and if you can wade through the mass of worthless *Reader's Digests* in Goodwill stores, you might just find the odd "first." Take a list of first edition dates of your favourite books and go looking for fun—and maybe profit.

Contemporary writers who are likely to become very valuable in the future are more findable and affordable, like Margaret Atwood, Mordecai Richler, William Styron, John Updike and so on. By finding modern first editions you get a hardcover prized possession for the same price as a new paperback. Browsing through used book stores can be very tiring and dusty. So make a list of particular items that interest you and keep it with you. For people who like reading this can be a thrilling hobby, and you will be surprised how quickly you become knowledgeable. People who run used book stores love books. Talk to them. They like to talk about books and are full of knowledge, and you will find a fellow spirit with whom to share enthusiasms. A good example of such hardcover prizes are the early Stephen King books, published under the name of Bachmann, which, if you can find one for $10, may very well fetch you twenty or thirty times that price in return.

There are books which you will borrow from the library or a friend and which will mean something very special to you. In those cases try to find a used hardcover copy of the book. Many people have said that books are friends, and it is good to have your special friends about you, on call, so to speak, when you need them. A good example is detective fiction. It comes and goes out of print with great rapidity. I recently read *The Old Dick* by L. A. Morse, borrowed long-distance from a library in Ottawa. I enjoyed it so much I wanted it by me, so I phoned around, found a good used paperback copy and scooted downtown to pay my $2.00 and pick it up. I felt very good driving it home, as it sat in the passenger seat like a recovered child, who has been lost in the shopping mall.

Aside from our special friend books and those we have been given as gifts, which sometimes carry special meaning, most of our reading will be done from public libraries. Libraries must be the most underrated institutions in our society. I marvel when I think of the priceless services that libraries offer to every citizen, and I deplore the struggle librarians are having to squeeze essential funds from governments. When I was a child and I discovered the local library at the North Circular Roundabout on the Cambridge Road in North London (that's a real place!), I entered an enchanted world, a universe filled with treasures that could never be exhausted. Walking along the stacks and pulling out books was like running my hands through boxes of jewels. I was suddenly rich, richer than Long John Silver in *Treasure Island*, richer than all those crooks in movies who open suitcases filled with packets of hundred-dollar bills. I adored the librarian, small, redheaded and ancient (she was probably twenty-five), who showed me books, and suggested books, and frowned when I became addicted to the writing of H. E. Bates. Libraries are strongholds of democracy, fortresses for self-education and the best free entertainment in the world.

Yet libraries today are underachievers. Librarians today still tend to be people who love books but are timid of people. Things have improved, of course: librarians are well trained, extremely knowledgeable, immensely helpful, and skillful at a dazzling variety of tasks. They must learn, however, to be more public. They must promote reading, politicize on their own behalf, sell themselves and their immense resource of reading. Librarians must beware of becoming instruments of technology, agents of productivity indirectly, and even directly, serving the goals of the marketing society, searching databases for small businesses and looking up facts for people trying to win prizes on radio stations. The library must serve readers first and keep alive the great tradition of reading for pleasure and personal growth.

Libraries are in a position to assist people with reading for all the life issues I have discussed. Because they know books and love books, librarians can offer special collections pulled together to focus on special issues like marriage and divorce, aging and dying, coping with illness, immigration, employment and growing up. They can advertise special weeks when the library resources are devoted to such a promotion, produce readings of books aloud, display collections, discuss books with borrowers by being especially prepared. Certain libraries have done a lot already with children's programs, bookmobiles and public displays. But there's much more to be done, and now is the time to do it. The library can be a natural centre for book lovers' clubs, making space and leadership available for those who love to read and exchange views on their reading. *Librarians must enlist their clientele in the battle for funding.* If you care about your library, dear reader, whom have you told about it, whom have you written? The things we take for granted are the things we lose. Write to your M.P. or congressman, write to your chief of local libraries, and tell them why reading matters to you and that you want books not bombs. If you, reader, are a librarian, stop apologizing for your role and become aggressive in defense of fiction. Can public libraries disappear? You bet they can, washed away in the reactionary tide of marketing madness, or privatized!

It is not easy to make the quiet case for reading against the screams for productivity and immediate results, for applied-research-only, the howls for censorship, the black-and-white boneheadedness of right-wing expediency. Libraries can be lost as part of the loss of clean air and water, freedom of thought, public broadcasting, time for contemplation and spiritual growth, the loss of compassion, patience and sensitivity. The rule of law and order means no diversity of view, no dissent and no time for poetry, grace, birdsong, or love. Nineteen-eighty-four is not over, so don't breathe easy yet! Is reading Flora Thompson's *Lark Rise to Candleford* or Shakespeare's *A Midsummer Night's Dream* productive, socially useful, or employment efficient? By the time you start to explain the value system within which to frame your answer, the technocrats are yawning and gathering books for the bonfire, prior to signing a development deal for a banking tower where the library used to be. In the 60s Joni Mitchell lamented the cutting down of trees to put up a parking lot. "Don't it always seem to go that you don't know what you've got till it's gone," she sang. The same may be sung of libraries, after they've gone.

There are three steps you can take to protect yourselves. First, demand literacy in the school system and funding for school and public libraries. Movie clips and media kits are no substitute for reading. Insist that your children learn not only to read but to enjoy reading, and that they read a lot. The engagement with books can be taught, if you demand it. If necessary, do it yourself.

Second, set aside a part of your budget for personal library building—it's good insurance just in case the worst happens. Read Bradbury's *Fahrenheit 451* and you'll see what I mean. Make a will and in it leave your library to your children, preferably to one child to keep the library intact, the child who likes to read most, if you have one. Insure your library against fire.

Third, support your local library by borrowing books, suggesting programs, writing letters and asking politicians during elections if they support library funding at the top of their lists—and what they have read lately.

Oh, and try to avoid electing illiterate politicians. Ask them who wrote *The Sound and the Fury*, and if they say either Shakespeare or William Faulkner, don't vote for them. I think this is about all we can do.

Appendices

Bibliotherapy: Another Conclusion But Not an End in Itself

Question: If reading fiction and poetry can have all these beneficial results for readers, how come it isn't used in psychotherapy, in helping people deal with specific problems?

Answer: It is!

Biblio comes from the Greek word for book, and is used as a prefix for other words that name things having to do with books. A *bibliography*, for instance, is a list of books. The French word for library is *bibliothèque*, and the *Bible* is a collection of separate books squeezed together to make one. A *bibliomaniac* is someone crazy about books, and a *bibliophile* likes books a lot but has not yet been driven mad by not being able to read all of them.

As for therapy, there are many kinds familiar to most readers of this book. There is music therapy, dance therapy, hydrotherapy, drama therapy, art therapy, pet therapy, play therapy and primal therapy. There is no TV therapy All these normal human activities become therapies when they are applied in a controlled, formal and focused way by professionals who have made a special study of the approach. Such professionals are usually accredited in some way as psychotherapists—that is, they are trained to deal with people's emotional and mental well-being. Most of these therapies are used as part of a program, not as exclusive treatments. For instance, in several institutions for assisting those with severe handicaps, or in geriatric nursing centres that care for the disabled elderly, music therapy is very successfully used to provide pleasure, stimulation, and even communication in groups.

I have all through this book been discussing the value of reading, its therapeutic value, but I have not discussed its formal application by professionals in a clinical setting. Over the library at Thebes was inscribed, "Healing Place of the Soul." People have long attested to the soothing and healing power of literature. Modern uses began about the same time as widespread literacy and followed the same pattern. Reading as therapy in North America began with the Bible and other religious material—for instance, in the Massachusetts General Hospital in 1811. With the great blossoming of public libraries in the first decades of the twentieth century, books were being used by physicians in clinics and hospitals. One Dr. Bagster ran a "Bibliopathic Institute." Dr. Karl Menninger, founder of the Menninger Clinic, was an enthusiastic advocate of reading as therapy. Today, programs of therapy at many hospitals and clinics include reading groups, led by professionals, and the use of hospital libraries. Programs for personal growth and self-exploration are in place in many community centres, libraries, correctional institutions, nursing homes and private group therapy sessions.

This book is not the place to write a guide for professional counsellors and therapists. I can, however, summarize the benefits of using reading, so that readers of this book and mental health professionals and educators can see how reading works to promote changes in perception that can heal and make whole, that can move people onto new and fertile ground for the growth of new life. There are benefits to using literature as the *ground* in psychotherapy, on which exchange and change between therapist and client take place. I have already said that fiction and poetry are the appropriate materials for therapy because 1) they are products of, and a key into, the storymaking faculty of human cognition, and 2) they evoke feeling, and feeling must be evoked if we are to work with human emotions. *Language is the human link between thought and feeling; story is the most memorable organization of language.*

As a device in a therapeutic setting, literature can render a painful or tiresome process more comfortable, efficient and time-saving, and so incidentally reduce the cost of treatment. To understand why that should be so, it is necessary to look at some of the typical procedures of psychotherapy without the bibliotherapy component.

People who find their way into psychotherapy treatment are usually in enough discomfort that they no longer feel able to control or suppress signs, symptoms, feelings, or behaviour. These symptoms can cover an infinite variety of signals that something is not right. The signs might be behavioural/social—inability to keep a job, fighting with colleagues, friends, or family, falling in and out of love, or making a number of bad decisions at work, home, or with finances. Or the signs might be physical—inexplicable aches and pains, especially backache and neck pain, nausea, dizziness, headaches, overeating or loss of appetite—problems for which the attending physician can find no organic source or reason—no ulcer, no cancer, no injury, no infection—but the discomfort of which persists. Or maybe the signs are phobic—fear of going out, of staying in, of heights, of public speaking, of taking exams, of meeting people, of being alone and so on. There are varying grades and kinds of depression. There is a feeling of failure, of helplessness, or of being overwhelmed with tasks. There might be compulsive gambling or drinking. Alcohol abuse is a very common sign of a problem. The case might involve violence in the family, the abuse of a child, a criminal act outside the family. There is really no limit to the possibilities of human response to what is vaguely called "stress," by which we mean the experience of conditions that are out of our control, that make us feel weak, helpless, unhappy, unable to cope, angry and miserable.

At the point, then, when the sufferer feels ready to seek help, maybe with encouragement from a physician, friend, family member, or minister, she presents herself at the therapist's office. A typical course of treatment might take the following pattern. Let us assume the client will need ten one-hour weekly sessions to sort out and change the response. Here is a summary of the first six sessions:

Session 1. The client explains that she has begun to have serious conflicts with her daughter, who gets along well with her father—the daughter will not come in to the sessions.

Session 2. The client talks about her marriage and her history and begins to talk about her own mother.

Session 3. The therapist becomes more active and tries to get the client to describe her feelings about her own parents. The client deflects the conversation elsewhere.

Session 4. The therapist persists. He wants to know what the client wants from her mother, her daughter, herself and him. She is not sure and has a hard time expressing feelings.

Session 5. The client has had a big blowup with her daughter. Her husband is staying out of it—doing his carpentry in the basement or watching TV. The mother says she is fed up being a mother. The therapist wants to know about the fight, how she felt and so on.

Session 6. The therapist says the client is angry, and she angrily denies it. She is concerned about her daughter staying out late, catching AIDS, getting pregnant, missing school, having "bad" friends. She says she was never like that. The therapist asks for more information about her mother.

This outline is typical, and every therapist will recognize it. The client is not a language expert, not comfortable talking about feelings, is keeping some secrets about the past, is not willing to express anger at her mother because that would be disloyal and she was taught to respect her parents. The client holds all the cards here, has to learn to trust the therapist, has to find a way of expressing herself and might very well find the process confusing. She might say, as Alice says of herself, "How puzzling all these changes are! I'm never sure what I'm going to be, from one minute to another!" And to the therapist she might say, like the Duchess in *Alice in Wonderland*, "You don't know much, and that's a fact!" The therapist is working in the dark. The daughter won't help, and the woman's parents have implanted their self-protective messages and behaviours in her memory so that she censors herself.

So there they are alone, pursuing the talking cure and doing their best to overcome gaps, time, strangeness and many other barriers. It does work, and many skilled therapists are able to help many clients to see their problems differently and make changes in behaviour that improve situations and give more control of their lives to people who are floundering. The process can, however, be greatly assisted, paths smoothed out and information called forth, by literature.

Let us for the sake of argument say that the therapist wants to focus on the mother's relationship with her own mother, and so explore the whole question of mothering, roles, frustrations and fears. He has tentatively reached the conclusion that the mother wants to control the daughter; that the mother is angry at her own mother because of the tight control under which she grew up; that she is also genuinely afraid for her daughter; and that she is angry at her husband for not understanding any of this. She thinks men don't care! In order to open up a number of possibilities, the therapist asks the client to read a short story about a mother and daughter in conflict. He chooses, for instance, one of the stories in Geri Giebel Chavis' *Family: Stories from the Interior*—"Mother and Daughter" by Phyllis Bentley. Without explaining his theory or telling his client what to look for, he makes it possible for her to talk about herself without talking about herself. She can deal with a concrete, detached story. She may relate to it or not, and either way she provides valuable information. She feels less alone in the conflict. She sees that others can find life complicated. She can speculate about the characters. She can reveal an area that tells the therapist what the next reading should be. The story is a neutral ally to both parties in the exploration. The story has no stake in the outcome. The story has no feelings that can be hurt. The story is a link between therapist and client, a respectful link. It is inexpensive, portable, in the control of the reader to put down or pick up or reread or ponder at will. I get my clients to make notes, underline, quote and report. The readings link the sessions and overcome the time gap between them. Then there are a great many spinoff benefits. Here are the ten psychological consequences that I have ascertained arise from the use of story and poetry in therapy:

1.   Language Growth. We have seen how language is an organizing and ordering tool for human beings. It is the code by which the material of the outside world and the feelings inside are described and made communicable. Those who are illiterate (can't read or write) or inarticulate (can't talk) have less control over environment, relations, or their own destiny because they cannot manage through language the bits and pieces of their experience.

In order to make sense of reading, the reader must use and practice the language he already has. By using the words and syntax he already knows, but in a great variety of new contexts, the reader learns more ways to use language. By having to make sense, he learns new words, new meanings for known words and new organizations for words.

2.   Life Information. Information absorbed as fiction is acquired in huge quantities and is well remembered. A number of research tests show that people from very early ages remember lots of information from stories that interest them. This means that story is a very good vehicle, maybe the best vehicle, for conveying large amounts of data painlessly, even pleasurably, without any rote learning or memorization exercises on the part of the reader.

The information that may be acquired from reading fiction covers the whole range of human experience. When we read we see through the mind of the writer. The writer is especially skilled in language, is a close observer of life and the world and has researched a huge amount of material for one or more pieces of fiction. Readers pick up information about human relations, food and drink, foreign customs and practices, weather, sports, animals, schools in other places, sex, clothing, lifestyles in places like New York, Tokyo, and Prince Albert, Saskatchewan. There is obviously no limit to the range and quantity of learning from reading. As avid readers have always known, literature is the surest route to a liberal education, and well-read people stand out as well informed.

3.   Identification. Pleasure in reading fiction is often regarded as depending on the reader's being able to see herself as somehow *represented* in some central figure in the story. This is often the case, and no doubt it is very satisfying to *recognize* oneself and so learn more about one's own feelings as they are called forth.

Two things should be noted about this:
a) The pleasure consists of being able to identify while still being safe and not in the book. In reading fiction you can be someone

else and yourself at the same time. This is like role-playing, and I call it having a pseudo-self. It makes me think of "trying on" in a clothing store—do I like this? or do I like that? I don't have to choose to make the clothes mine, me, unless they fit and I feel good in them.

If you do identify fully with the hero of fiction you may experience what the Greeks called catharsis. This is a strong emotion, often resulting in weeping, that comes from empathy, from feeling at one with the suffering or sadness of the fictional character. From this release of emotion sometimes comes insight, understanding of some important or deeply disguised aspect of the self, discovered by realizing the source, the trigger, of this powerful emotional response. In this sense, the sense of *recognition*, people are always reading about themselves.

b) It should be remembered, however, that catharsis traditionally applied to tragedy. The emotion that tragedy was supposed to "purge" or uncover was a negative emotion that was hurtful to the reader by being suppressed. This was ancient Greek psychology. I admire the Greeks and their great critic Aristotle for recognizing that drama was useful, healthful and practical to audiences, something we seem to have forgotten along with a lot of other ancient truths.

But not all literature is tragic, and to confine the mental health value of reading to catharsis is a mistake. All the emotional responses are important—for instance, anger at reading of injustice and cruelty. To recognize our own fears, vulnerability, sense of fairness is to sensitize ourselves to the suffering of others, improve our personal relations and help ourselves to humanize our society.

Laughter and joy improve our immune systems and keep us healthy, happy and distanced from being too caught up in trivia and anxiety. Reaction against what happens in fiction, or dislike of a character, helps us to sort out what we want to be and what we want to avoid. This is called abreaction. All this is part of the range of response that is basic to the value of fiction.

4.   Modelling. Developmental psychology, studying how we grow, change and develop, has had much to say about modelling. This is like copying, except that our goal is not, cannot be, to reproduce exactly what we copy so much as to use the model to guide our own behaviour. Remember that we can learn and copy only with the equipment we have. When I was a teenager, I took up smoking a pipe because my dad smoked a pipe. If my father had been a lawyer and I had wanted to be a lawyer like him, I could maybe have been somewhat like him, but because I am a different person, I would have had to be me trying to be like him.

Modelling can apply to behaviour, appearance, speech, conversation, housing and lifestyle. Modelling can be good or bad. A good deal of alcohol abuse and physical abuse seems to come from modelling. The normalizing of violence on U.S. television is held by many to model an acceptance of violence for viewers. It is very doubtful that the majority of those who commit crimes in the U.S. are avid readers, judging from normal literacy figures and especially from the statistics of prison populations. It is certain that they have watched a lot of TV and continue to do so in prison. Suicide can be modelled. Laughter and confidence can be modelled.

Literature is particularly useful in modelling because it permits safe, experimental risk-taking. The reader can participate in a drama, war, adventure, relationship by means of a pseudo-self—a trial self that sees what it feels like. By admiring others, learning how it feels to dress or talk in a different way, the reader escapes the trap of being in an unalterable role or behaviour. People who feel that they are stuck in a situation or pattern of behaviour that is inescapable, do escape it if they can be encouraged to read and pay attention to their own feelings and the experience of reading. Modelling is learning to expand the repertoire of roles.

5.   Cognitive Shift. Related to identification and modelling is the ability to see things differently. Literature can help readers to see their own situations from other angles. For instance, if a husband regards his wife as a nag, demanding and critical, he may arrive at a different version by reading about a wife who is regarded by her husband as a nag, but who is shown by the writer to be worried, anxious and afraid of her husband. The reader of such a portrait can now wonder if his own wife has feelings that he does not know about or thoughts different from what he had assumed.

The "reframing" power of literature comes from the story's not being exactly the same as the reader's story. In fitting the two together, the reader has to shift his point of view and so moves out of what seemed like an immovable and rigid framework. In this way, reading breeds tolerance and sympathy for people and attitudes not seen like this before. Readers revise their view of their own problem by reading of those worse off than themselves. Readers learn to understand the other gender, other sexual orientations, the elderly and the poor. Only a slight shift in perspective is required to make a lot of things seem different.

6.   Problem Solving. Another result of this frame-shift technique is the ability to solve problems by following through a simulated problem-resolution in literature. A famous example of this result is the psychologist Erik H. Erikson's report of a case of a sexual problem. A man suffering from premature ejaculation was hypnotized and asked to solve a problem in a story apparently unrelated to his own problem. When he returned to his own normal life, his problem was solved. This was not a case of reading, but it was a case of storytelling. It suggests that problem-solving imagined situations in literature can lead a reader to a sense of control and success in solving his own problems.

A woman who described her situation as lonely, middle-class and prosperous but sterile was asked to read Doris Lessing's story "To Room Nineteen," and then invited to solve the problem of the character's loneliness and lack of identity. The reader suggested that a lack of communication about feeling and a lack of assertiveness led to the character's despair. Without any instruction from me, she was able successfully to apply her own conclusions to her own marriage.

Detective fiction serves effectively to provide readers with problem-solving practice. Readers are thus enabled to figure out strategies that *carry over* to their own lives and so gain some control and influence in problem areas where they otherwise seem helpless and out of control. The writings of Ian Fleming and Len Deighton—spy stories— have helped me to see how to avoid dangerous situations. Not the same dangers, of course, but the dangers of abusive and destructive relationships, which are, in their own way, as crippling as the traps into which spy-heroes can fall. Where the reader recognizes the *design* of the story as relevant, we may call this "template recognition."

Reading of those who overcome hardship and who survive, whether in the wilderness or in a prisoner-of-war camp, can help readers to resolve difficulties that threaten comfort and peace of mind.

7.   Immunization. We all know that you become immunized by being inoculated against something. The principle is that if you get a little bit of measles, for example, you stimulate your immune system to produce antimeasles antibodies, and these protect you from a lot of measles. In psychology, the theory is that a little simulated stress ahead of time produces coping strategies for much stress later. The loss of and grief for a pet in childhood, for instance, is partial preparation for more serious losses later. You can practice grief. You can practice going to the dentist or skiing by imagining doing these things. If you can imagine your way through a stressful experience to a successful and comfortable emergence on the other side, then you will be prepared to go through the real thing with the positive survival experience under your belt.

Reading is extremely effective in *safely* eliciting and arousing powerful feelings, which thus become part of a positive experience and so can be used later in real-life situations. I am finding this to be the case in working with students and the literature of aging. There is among many people in our culture a great fear of aging, involving a fear of economic dependency, of physical and mental helplessness and loss of power, and of death. Whether repressed or not, these fears produce some chronic anxiety in the present, anxiety that not only stresses the anxious one, but makes it very difficult for her to deal with the elderly. The elderly become mirrors of the repressed fear and so are avoided. Students working with literature that presents images of aging, experience a number of feelings they then express in conversation and writing. They are able to confront their fears. They can make plans for their future. They can see that the real situation is more complicated than their fears, that things are not just black and white. Reading prepares for the future.

8.   **Feelings.** Readers survive their reading and so discover that the experience of negative emotions is not final. For some set of reasons that are characteristically American in their progressive, upbeat, Pollyanna way, we have been led to believe that negative emotion is a bad thing. Sadness, depression, anxiety, disappointment, grief are all bad. This is obviously nonsensical and extremely

dangerous. Negative emotion is natural, necessary and adaptive. Denial of some feelings is not only unhealthy because false and difficult, but destructive to relationships and extremely stressful. Such denial makes coping with life situations very difficult.

Fiction articulates feelings. We are shown the context in which certain feelings are experienced and are appropriate. If the world around us says don't be angry, don't be sad, don't be depressed or frustrated, literature shows us that our feelings are recognized by the writer. We gain strength, permission, justification for inner feelings by witnessing and empathizing with the feelings of characters in books.

Literature shows us the inner life, the emotional, reflective life, of people we grow to know, even to love and care about. Then we can bring this experience back into our own lives to help us penetrate and understand the feelings of others and ourselves. Good, careful, honest literature raises feeling into consciousness and so helps us to develop an assertiveness about our own feelings—we can learn to own our feelings.

In this way, through the courage of writers, who give us the gift of their knowledge and understanding of fully human characters and situations, we are helped to become responsible.

9.   Normalization. The trauma or wound of private suffering produces in the sufferer a kind of exile and loneliness. Grief, separation and divorce, accident and disability, job loss, home loss, rape and other experiences of violent assault are all liable to produce a sense of isolation. Who can know what it feels like, especially in the kind of upbeat, falsely jolly cartoon world we live in? Hardship is not popular. So we need stories that normalize our suffering and show us we are part of a community of pain, sin and suffering. We need to be known, to be understood. Fellow sufferers who can empathize contribute to the process of normalization. For this reason, group therapy and self-help groups of fellow sufferers are important and useful. A client of mine helped start such a group for breast cancer victims at a local hospital. People in our world have a hard time exposing their feelings, especially deeply wounded or angry personal feelings. They are, in any case, usually limited by their language and by a lifetime of being trained not to converse about personal matters. Many of us have been trained to suffer in silence. Daily I meet people who have learned to bottle up feelings. For this reason, literature can be extremely useful in expressing for us the sympathy and understanding that normalizes trauma. Literature should be part of group treatment.

10.   **Sharing.** By means of reading, which gives us the images, stories and characters for expressing our own feelings and situations, we are provided with a powerful tool for sharing and bonding with other readers. Because we can respond intimately to literature, the gift of a loved or valued book is an intimate exchange, and people who cannot otherwise express their feelings for or knowledge of another person can do so by means of a book. Reading together or sharing a book in turn gives couples and families a precisely shared experience. Fiction can bring parents and children together. It can bond spouses and friends. A body of shared reading can be a reference map or guide to call upon in exploring life experiences between people. Spouses who lived separate and different lives before they met, lives that can never be properly explained or actually shared, can achieve some sharing with material that explains what it felt like, what it was like. Reading can be like calling someone to the window to share a scene that is important to the viewer. Through the window of story we can look out together on a world of experience that would otherwise be invisible to the other, retained in a private past.

Literature in Professional Training

T raining in the helping and service professions could be significantly enhanced by the use of appropriate literature as a
source of models of patient and client experience. These professionals especially would benefit from fiction and poetry: doctors,
nurses and medical service workers; psychiatrists and social workers;
marriage and family therapists; physiotherapists and occupational
therapists; recreation leaders; elder care workers and administrators;
child care workers; police and corrections workers; counsellors and
pastoral workers, of all kinds; government welfare, immigration and
legal service workers.

The training of many professionals consists at present of the
transmission of theory, of information including statistics and social
surveys, and of textbook-style practical instruction; it can also
include some supervised practical experience. Literature, because it
is narrative/affective and invokes multiple viewpoints, is able to put
the practitioner into the mind and circumstances of others, both
receivers and givers of care/service. In some instances this is superi-
or to practical experience, or at least an important addition to and
expansion of experience.

In practice, the caregiver in actual situations cannot escape
the role of "outsider" in dealing with the patient. The nurse or coun-
sellor, however caring, sensitive and empathetic (and many professionals are not), cannot leave the separateness of being the care

provider. The patient more often than not is intimidated, not assertive, relatively powerless, inarticulate and dependent. The professional has status, knowledge, control of the setting, access to a hierarchy of authority; often is in the disguise of a uniform; often has more education than the patient and maybe more money; and usually has more health and good luck—which is why the client is there getting help.

The skill of the teachers of professionals depends to some extent on their language skills and their ability to explain to professional students what it feels like to be a patient. This is usually abstract and theoretical; patients are reduced to cases and precedents. Lecturing is the method of teaching most favoured in our culture; personal, subjective, emotional story material or format is avoided.

Since the professional cannot, either by listening to lectures or by playing the role of helper, get into the shoes of the patient, we must look around for some other method of enabling the caregiver to feel the experiences and needs of the patient. The best professional will have some idea of what it feels like to be on the other side of the stethoscope or desk.

In recent years we have been deluged with cases of elder abuse in both the press and various government reports. The concern I have here is with the abuse practiced by professionals. It is at least strange, at best unacceptable, that those placed in positions of caregiving and support to the elderly should be able to experience dislike of, indifference to, hardness of heart towards, anger at, or hatred for their wards. In some ways it is far less bizarre that parents abuse, hurt, or kill their own children, because they have no training at all—none is required for parenting. Parents have no salary, no performance review, no exam, no time off with pay, no malpractice insurance and no staff supervisor, unlike elder care professionals. But ours is a youth-worshipping culture, and caring for the elderly is not glamorous. The tasks are often disagreeable. The needs of the disabled elderly are often many and continuous. Fear of growing old and being like one's patients is not just a matter of, "There but for the grace of God go I," but of, "There is the mirror image of my future state." The hatred and rejection of the image of what one is afraid of becoming would be enough to generate behaviour that is often cruel and indifferent.

This raises the question of "countertransference" in practice, about which explanation is required in order that we may see the force of literature in its role in training. In psychotherapy of all kinds, there is a phenomenon of relationship that has come to be known as "transference," a perception or view on the part of the client projected onto the therapist. The most common experience of transference is the client's perception of the therapist as a parent figure, either a parent that he had or a parent that he wants. The transference might also be a perception of the therapist as lover, spouse, or teacher—but not as a child, since the therapist is an authority figure and if viewed as a child is rendered ineffective. Transference in good therapy is a phase and is used by the therapist as a benign opportunity to play an influential role and give power to the client so as to free him from dependence.

Countertransference is the reverse of this process. The therapist recognizes and is "hooked" by some aspect of the client that removes distance, control and helpfulness. For instance, the client reminds the therapist of his ex-wife and so evokes anger and frustration, which, if unrecognized and uncontrolled, render the therapist worse than useless. The therapist may be intimidated by the client, who becomes some other haunting figure from the past, teacher, father, tax collector, judge. For the therapist, the only antidote to this is self-knowledge. In actual practice, psychotherapy, especially marriage and family therapy, and psychoanalysis, is the only profession the training for which has self-knowledge at the heart of the process. It takes a great deal of time, courage, dedication and good supervision. In the health professions, time is a critical factor. Nurses, for instance, have much else to learn, and the constraints of economic cost limit the time available for self-exploration as part of the training program.

It is in the face of these constraints, time, cost and need, that literature emerges as an extremely efficient unit in the training program. Literature is very effective as a device for eliciting countertransference, and this emotional response can be effectively used as a self-exploration opportunity. Reference to Questionnaire II in this book will illustrate. A list of even a half-dozen relevant novels and stories and as many poems, assigned to student professionals and treated as the basis for class or group discussion, will produce results that would otherwise take a long and painful time to achieve. My experience with students of gerontology studying literary models clearly reveals the power of literature to generate self-knowledge and personal growth. Stories about the elderly, about fears and joys, relationships and dependencies produce empathy and conscious awareness. Without practicing on cases, the student can explore feelings evoked by characters and events that uncover past events and future fears. The stories read join with the reader's story to realign and rearrange attitudes and values. The student discovers links with the feelings and experiences of others; the springs of her own responses; the differences and complex life experiences of people unlike herself; and the ways in which situations can be improved. No other source of material is as efficient, in terms of cost, time and result, in bringing about self-knowledge and empathy and in providing case experience, when carefully managed in a training situation.

Real-life crises proceed on their own timetable, with very little control over events possible for the therapist. Life will not stand still—the case cannot be frozen for examination. By the time the next therapy session rolls around anything may have happened—the patient's dog may have got run over, the patient's spouse may have lost a job, or the patient may have found another therapist. You can't examine a moving target. Story stays still long enough to be helpful and to illuminate the changes in the reader in relation to the story. This is the theory of reading relativity.

There is no reason that a literature-reading component cannot be incorporated into the programs of caregiving professionals. Since telling stories is part of the history of human experience, the principal strategy for managing life events, there is no end to the supply of material. There are books on aging, imprisonment, disability, divorce, grief, immigration, poverty and racial prejudice. Literary material is not memorized but experienced, which means it can be a real and pleasant, an interesting—even when uncomfortable—part of the learning experience. The student can experience language and its power to reveal the inner person, the nuances of relations and the organizing and structuring of otherwise chaotic and incomprehensible happenings.

Awareness, of self and others, of bonds and differences, of complexity and complication, of feeling and thought, is the heart of successful training. To omit the use of imaginative literature as a component in raising such awareness is to miss a natural opportunity that lies at hand. The literary resource is given to us for just such purposes. Only educational confusion, prejudice, naiveté, or fear could have helped us to ignore the potential of literature as a primary social bonding force. We can greatly improve our mutual caring by reading literature as part of professional life.

Questionnaire 1: Reader Response

After reading a story, novel, or poem you can explore your responses to it by using this section. This questionnaire is designed as a training exercise to maximize the usefulness of your reading to you. It will repay you to take some time to think about and answer these questions. Take a pencil and paper and find a quiet time and place. Think of doing this as a gift to yourself—if you like, think of it as a spiritual, mental, or psychological training session, a bit like using your exercise bike for your body. Look inside yourself and carefully scan your reactions for answers. All answers are valid—even irritation at the questions.

If you find that the story does not lend itself to these questions, that you just did not care enough about it to bother answering the questions, put aside the questionnaire until you read another story and then try again.

If you can, share a story with someone very close to you, whom you trust, and then share some of the answers. This is a particularly valuable marital exercise. It can help clarify similarities and differences. Since it focuses on a concrete subject (the story) outside of yourselves, it is a safer and easier way to talk about who you are and what concerns you than plunging into self-revelations and complaints.

The exercise will help you to learn to think and talk about "I" in relations, your role in relations, rather than "you" and what the you, the other, does that is "wrong" or annoying.

If the exercise ends up being very disturbing or uncovers some chronic discomforts, emotional pain, or significant unresolved issues from your past, then you may want to seek professional counselling around what you have uncovered.

1. List some of the things you like/dislike about the story, in two lists.

2. Are there features in common among the items on the two lists from question 1? For instance, do you always like or dislike the same character, the same gender of character, the same type of behaviour, the same setting and so on?

3. What are the incidents, scenes, or moments in the story that you remember most vividly?

4. Does anyone in the story remind you of anyone you know, including yourself, in any way?

5. Does any event or occasion in the story remind you of any time in your own life?

6. What do you think are the three "things" that this book/story is "about"? List them in order of their importance to you.

7. What are the three concerns that are foremost in your life right now?

8. Do you see any connection between your answers to 6 and 7?

9. Can you list any problem the story points to, explores, or deals with?

10. Does the problem(s) get resolved, or is it simply presented?

11. How would *you* handle the problem, if differently?

12. Is there something you would have liked from the story that you did not get?

13. Did you learn anything from the story that you did not know before?

14. If yes, then in what ways is that useful to you?

15. Does the story puzzle or irritate you in any way?

16. Does the answer to 15 tell you anything about yourself?

17. Can you identify any feelings you experienced, however fleeting, while reading the story? For instance:

Empathy (Fellow-feeling)	❏	Joy	❏
Anticipation	❏	Sadness	❏
Boredom	❏	Anger	❏
Sexual Arousal	❏	Frustration	❏
Calm	❏	Fear	❏
Relief	❏	Anxiety	❏
Hope	❏	Nostalgia	❏
Revulsion	❏	Affection	❏
Embarrassment/Shame	❏	Sympathy	❏
Surprise	❏	Curiosity	❏
Gloom	❏	Humour/Gladness	❏

18. What is it in the story that produced these feelings? Choose up to three of the feelings identified in 17.

19. What three people or events in your own life are most likely to produce these same feelings?

20. What, if you could, would you change in the story to make it happier?

21. Does the answer to 20 tell you anything about what you care most about?

22. Is the story relevant to any of these issues or experiences in your life?

Spousal Relations	❏	Grief	❏
Parenting	❏	Childbearing	❏
Growing Up	❏	Menopause	❏

Sexual Experience	❑	Loss of a Friend	❑
School	❑	Success	❑
Career	❑	Survival	❑
Separation or Divorce	❑	Homebuying	❑
Grief	❑	Falling in Love	❑
Relocation/Moving	❑	Loneliness	❑
Job Loss	❑	Retirement	❑
Financial Hardship	❑	Frustrated Ambition	❑
Your Appearance	❑	Your Next Holiday	❑
Aging	❑	Sickness	❑
Leaving Home	❑	Romantic Love	❑

23. Can the story tell you anything about your response to any of the list in 22?

24. Is your response to any of 22 satisfactorily over, as far as you are concerned, or is it unfinished business?

25. Can the story help you to control any difficult events or situations?

26. What would you like to read more about after reading this story?

27. Does the story help you to feel more like other people?

28. Does the story help you to know what characteristics you like or dislike in other people?

29. Does the story help you to clarify what you need to know about yourself?

30. Are there any thoughts or feelings you need to express that are not covered in this questionnaire?

Questionnaire 2: Reading Selection Self Guide

This questionnaire is designed to help you to select reading material relevant to your current interests and needs, those that are personally, socially, generally important at this stage of your life. By focusing your attention on your present concerns, your answers will help to direct you to some material that can be used for better understanding what is happening to you. Your goal is to gain control of your life and to feel and do what you want to feel and do. Many obstacles stand in the way of these objectives. Some of these are external, like lack of money, an ailing relative to care for, a physical disability, and some are internal—attitudes and beliefs that can hinder your freedom to choose or even think about what you can do. Some of these beliefs come from the past, from previous experiences, from religion, or from family influence; some come from your genetic makeup, whether you are musical, athletic, or a slow learner, for example. Answer all of these questions as fully as you wish.

1. What are the three areas of greatest concern to you right now? Rank them in order of their problem making.

2. Do you know what kind of life you would like to lead?

3. If you solved the problems from 1, would you be able to lead the life you want?

4. Check off the characteristics of your reading tastes:

   I like stories that have:

a.	a female hero	❑
b.	a male hero	❑
c.	foreign places and travel	❑
d.	familiar places	❑
e.	adventure and violence	❑
f.	erotic content	❑
g.	crime detection	❑
h.	marriage exploration	❑
i.	parent-child interaction	❑
j.	career pursuit	❑
k.	romantic love theme	❑
l.	fantasy content	❑
m.	poor people	❑
n.	rich people	❑
o.	happy endings	❑
p.	realistic endings	❑
q.	people coping with hardship	❑
r.	courage in survival	❑
s.	historical content	❑
t.	elderly people	❑
u.	children	❑
v.	adolescents	❑
w.	internal reflection and feeling	❑
x.	animals	❑
y.	sports	❑
z.	the sea or boats	❑

aa.	war	❑
bb.	space and science fiction	❑
cc.	espionage	❑
dd	strong victorious heroes	❑
ee.	ordinary people	❑
ff.	life in the country	❑
gg.	city life	❑
hh.	an ethnic group	❑
ii.	horror, scary content	❑
jj.	long novel	❑
	short novel	❑
	short story	❑
kk.	the law	❑
ll.	medicine/nursing	❑
mm.	high finance	❑
nn.	politics	❑
oo.	mystery	❑
pp.	biography	❑
qq.	pioneering	❑
rr.	school	❑
ss.	theatre	❑
tt.	wilderness and nature	❑
uu.	death and dying	❑
vv.	religion	❑
ww	humour	❑
xx.	ancient times	❑
yy.	family life	❑
zz.	folklore	❑

5. Choose five items you have checked in 4 and rank them in order of their importance to you.

6. What one characteristic of your way of thinking, or what habit, or what behaviour would you like most to change now?

7. What have you ever done that you would do differently if you could do it again?

8. What would you change about your present lifestyle if you could?

9. Where do you want to live?

10. Name three of the stories you have enjoyed most in your life.

When you have answered these questions as honestly as you can, describe five elements of a book you would like to read now, under these headings:

 a. the mood
 b. the setting
 c. the kind of action
 d. the kind of character
 e. the problems dealt with

The information you have gathered from this exercise should help you in selecting reading material that will be useful to you at this time. You can share your conclusions with a librarian or bookseller, who will assist you.

Behind This Book—
An Afterword

This book has been a long time in the making. I want to outline the provenance of the ideas presented in these pages and acknowledge those who supported my research in the last fifteen years.

In 1973, when I was chairman of the organization of heads of English departments in Ontario, Canada, I proposed and convened the Glendon Conference, "The Survival of Literacy." In 1975 I edited a version of the proceedings of that conference entitled *In the Name of Language*. Margaret Fulton, who later became President of Mount Saint Vincent University, played a large part in making that conference possible and helped me then and later with practical and moral support. I want to pay tribute also to the late esteemed George Whalley, whom I was proud to call a friend and colleague in the struggle for literature in education.

In 1975 also I had turned my attention to the origins of story and human perceptual processes. I decided to study preliterate art and cult objects and pre-Biblical ceramic decoration. The Social Sciences and Humanities Research Council of Canada gave me a grant that included a magical airline ticket to Israel, magical in that it enabled me to stop anywhere en route. I visited many of the world's great Musea—in Amsterdam, Rome, Athens, Budapest, Istanbul, Crete and all across Israel—and spent a long and educative study period at the State Museum in Jerusalem. I was already familiar with the British Museum and the Met in New York. In hindsight, it is clear to me that this book had its origins in the thinking I did then. Somewhat belatedly, though they are not less sincere for that, I publish here my thanks to the SSHRC.

In 1976 I read a paper to the University of Alberta Conference on Literacy, published as *Literature, Language and Culture* in 1977. In that paper I discussed the application of research findings about neocortical processing of language to the study of literature and reading. It was, I believe, the first essay in the field of English studies to bring the work of the neurosciences into a consideration of the value and importance of literature in education.

It was in preparing for this presentation that I began a long-term study of neuro-anatomy and cognitive psychology, looking for the elusive processes by which the brain reads and understands what it reads. I discovered that in this area as in so many others we know very little of the unimaginably complex procedures of human knowing. I was searching for the biological and physiological foundations of literature as a human perceptual strategy, though I had not at that time formulated my concept of literature as an adaptive behaviour. I began by reading everything in print by Wilder Penfield, and have been puzzled ever since that he did not win a Nobel Prize. To pursue current research on brain function seemed at the time an awesome undertaking, but an exciting one also. I read hungrily among the works of David Premack, the Bogens, Karl Pribram, Jerre Levy and Fernando Nottebohm and countless others in the journals that I pored over for a year in the library of the Kitchener-Waterloo General Hospital. All of this seemed to me somehow so connected to language and reading that I began to marvel that those of us who had done and were doing PhDs in literature had been given no introduction to the science of reading and learning.

At that time the split brain work of Sperry and others was at the forefront of new explorations into brain function and many researchers were pursuing lateralization studies. I contacted Sandra Wittelson at McMaster University, where she was making comparisons of male and female brains. She was always patient and helpful to me and permitted me to attend her case-conference on hearing disability and behaviour. Following this I was able to participate in some research at the

Technion in Haifa with Dr. Hal Gordon, who taught me a great deal, entertained me in his home and gave me the benefit and pleasure of many hours of wonderful conversation with him and his wife.

I want to acknowledge here the privilege of long and intriguing discussions at Princeton University with Julian Jaynes, Stephen Harnad and Earl Miner. I will always remember with gratitude the time provided for me by Alexander Marshack, who shared some of his exciting ideas on the history of human intelligence in his apartment in Manhattan, where we looked over the lights of the city, so strangely reminiscent of Sherrington's famous image of the brain.

All of this preparation led to my paper "Recombinant Language: The Biological Imperative," published in *English Studies in Canada* in 1981. I want to thank Lauriat Lane, Jr., who was editor at that time and who believed in the importance of what I was doing. In that paper I began the discussion of feedback that I have continued in this volume. I relied heavily then on the elegant work of two great scientists, Ulrich Neisser for his discussions of cognitive psychology and J. Z. Young for his presentation of the concept of the brain as having "programs," a concept that linked for me the fields of cybernetics and neurology. My paper was, I believe, the first to propose a neurological, cognitive and cybernetic model for the responses of readers to literature.

It seems to me that a crucial component in the development of the ideas that lie behind this book was General Systems Theory. I could not have grasped the full impact of this without my training as a marriage and family therapist. This discipline rests heavily on the work of Gregory Bateson and Ludwig Von Bertalanffy. It was in family systems and working with the networks of family relations, information theory, double binds, and the story exchanges of family members that I began to see the implications of systems in the feedback analogues of reading. Only by crossing fields and blending concepts from different disciplines has the work progressed. This is the great virtue of systems theory, which is a new epistemology, not just another path into another field. For helping me grasp the scale of this second order shift in thinking, I am grateful to two colleagues, Keith Hipel of the Faculty of Engineering and James Kay of Environmental Studies, both at the University of Waterloo. They always cheerfully made time for me and supported my interest, and often directed me to lists of relevant material, including Fuzzy Set theory, which seems peculiarly appropriate to literary criticism. I hope to explore this connection and the synergistics of story as a response-control of humans with parallels in other organisms in a forthcoming book.

In 1985 SSHRC again came to my assistance with a grant to research a cognitive approach to the uses of story, and this work led to the publication of "Affective Reading and its Life Applications" (with Fred Gloade) in *The Arts in Psychotherapy* in 1988. Our goal was to find out if and how people actually made use of fiction (reading) in their life situations.

In April of 1987 I was invited to Brown University to give a paper to the anniversary conference of *Novel* on "Why the Novel Matters." My essay, "The Function of Fiction: A Biological Model," was published in the proceedings of the conference in the spring of 1988. Here I attempted to outline the directions in which I thought literary criticism could usefully develop.

Along the way I was privileged to share some of these ideas with a number of groups whose questions and comments helped me to clarify many issues. There are too many to list here, but they include the Ontario Library Association, the Voyageur Library Association, the Foothills Library Association of Alberta, McMaster Medical School (Education Rounds), the Department of English at Hebrew University, Jerusalem, the Modern Literature Conference of Michigan State University, the Canadian Literature Symposium at Ottawa University and the Institute for the Humanities at the University of Calgary.

To these and all the other institutions who have given me a hearing over the last fifteen years, I am deeply grateful.

Credits

Index

JOSEPH GOLD was born in London, England. He attended the University of Birmingham and received his Ph.D. from the University of Wisconsin. He was a university instructor for over 39 years, spending 10 years at the University of Manitoba and 24 as professor of English at the University of Waterloo. Dr. Gold is a clinical member of the American Association for Marriage and Family Practice and currently runs a private practice in Northern Ontario. He is the author of books on Charles Dickens and William Faulkner. Joseph Gold is a veteran leader in the fight to preserve a central place for literature in education.